The

Rise of the Revolutionary Party

in the

English House of Commons

1603 - 1629

By Williams M. Mitchell

PROFESSOR OF HISTORY

WASHINGTON AND JEFFERSON COLLEGE

Columbia University Press, New York, 1957

THE
RISE OF THE REVOLUTIONARY PARTY
IN THE
ENGLISH HOUSE OF COMMONS
1603-1629

C

LC 57013029

TO MY WIFE

Katharine Brodie Mitchell

PREFACE

THIS study of the rise of the revolutionary party in the English house of commons is the outgrowth of a dissertation for the degree of Doctor of Philosophy at Yale University. The original study was a comparison of the English and Irish houses of commons from 1558 to 1615. It revealed a lack of similarity between the two bodies in the period under consideration, since the Irish house, under the restrictions of Poynings' Law, was unable to develop the initiative which the English house achieved in the latter part of the reign of Elizabeth and in that of James I. Beyond a somewhat superficial and ineffective bumptiousness in the Irish house of 1613 there was little to disturb the English officials in Dublin, and Strafford had no difficulty in bending the house to his will a little later.

The research in the records of the English house, however, opened the intriguing possibilities of a study of the relation between two phenomena, the emergence of a real opposition and the development of procedural forms. The present study is an investigation of this relation, carried into the latter part of the reign of James I and on into the first four years of Charles I.

The contribution of this volume to knowledge concerning the house of commons is statistical. All speeches, committee memberships, committee reports and readings which appear in the various records of the house have been noted. From the tabulated information the trends in procedure and in the influence of members have been traced, with as much accuracy as the nature of the records would permit. The sentiments of members and the bearing of their activities upon politics have been searched out, both from records of the house and from other sources. Political fortunes have been examined to discover how they disposed members for or against the government. The attempt has been made, by means of a synthesis of these various kinds of information, to tell the story of the slow, faltering emergence of an opposition which by 1629 can be called a party and to show how the newly developed procedure was exploited by the men who made themselves this opposition group.

I am in the debt of many people. Professor George Matthew Dutcher of Wesleyan University first interested me in the study of history. His concern for accuracy and his great kindness as a teacher made an abiding impression on me. Professor Wallace Notestein of Yale University introduced me to the fascinating field of the English parliament. His criticisms and guidance in the first part of the work and the inspiration of his vast knowledge of the whole subject provided the motive for continuing it. For the conclusions reached, however, and for any errors made, I am entirely responsible. The staff of the Sterling Memorial Library of Yale University were helpful and cooperative. To William Bridgwater, Evelyn Boyce, and Gwendolyn Jones, of the Columbia University Press, I am indebted for meticulous editing and many helpful suggestions. Finally it is a happy duty to acknowledge not only the sturdy encouragement of my wife, but also the hours of patient toil that she gave to the laborious compiling of lists and data.

W. M. M.

Washington, Pennsylvania
August, 1957

CONTENTS

INTRODUCTION

IT is common knowledge, wherever English history is studied, that the house of commons, in the period between 1603 and the beginning of the civil war, underwent a great change. At the death of Elizabeth it was still a tool, albeit a somewhat less ready one than formerly, in the hands of the prince. By 1629 it had become exceeding powerful. In fact, it had become the focal point, and the arena, and the potential instrument of those who opposed Charles I. By 1629 these men, later to be commonly and somewhat inaccurately called the Puritan Party, had become a group which could already claim the name of "party," in the sense that they had combined their efforts to achieve certain political ends. Largely academic is the speculation as to the exact time when opposition men came to act in this manner. Let us say that there was a party, as I have defined it, in the 1620's—from 1626 onward.

Use of the word "Puritan" to describe this group of men is justifiable only because it serves better than any other adjective. Even in the midst of the civil war it was not entirely Puritan, for constitutional objects, and even other motives, brought under the "Puritan" banner many who were not Puritans in religion at all. Yet after 1640 religion came more and more to serve as a symbol. In the years preceding 1629, questions of political power and of constitutional right, or of specific points of policy not primarily religious in nature, had more often been the objects of the opposition men than had matters of religion.

Union with Scotland, naturalization, subsidies, impositions, foreign policy (though here religion comes importantly if indirectly into play), the hatred of Buckingham, the rights of the subject at law—these were the chief bones of contention.

Nevertheless, although it was hardly at first Puritan in its outward aspect, the opposition to the crown was yet becoming a party. It was moving constantly in that direction all through the early reign of James I. The trend seems to have been arrested in 1621 and 1624.

To explain the cause of this development is difficult. Any single explanation is, by itself, naive. Was James an inept ruler with respect to parliamentary maneuver? Undoubtedly. Professor David H. Willson's *The Privy Councillors in the House of Commons, 1604–1629* has told that story well. Was the house of commons changing its position in government from the sham of Tudor days to the power it had long theoretically possessed? Professor Wallace Notestein's *The Winning of the Initiative by the House of Commons* has long since secured that point. Was all this a constitutional manifestation of the rise of the English middle class and a phase of renaissance and reformation thought? It is incontestable. With these things this book is concerned, but not primarily, for these things have been dealt with, and sufficiently, by others.

The purpose of this book is to trace the coming together of the opposition party. It was a halting growth, and the "turnover" was considerable. It was facilitated by the blunders of the king, and particularly by the introduction of new modes of procedure in the house, of which the opposition members were quick to take full advantage. I refer particularly to the expansion of the committee system, the use of the committee of the whole house, and curtailment of the power of the speaker. The growth was temporarily impeded by the strategy of the crown—in detaching members from the opposition through fear or favor or preventing their reelection and even (for a time, in 1624) in adopting a conciliatory policy toward the house.

For these reasons it has been necessary, in following the vicissitudes of the growing opposition, to construct a rather general political and procedural picture of parliament over a generation. Procedure and patronage have constantly to be considered, parliament by parliament. So also has the matter of the rise of *esprit de corps* in the house. Since these aspects of the study must be presented at some length and with the support of evidence drawn from tedious counts and tabulations of the journal and other records and from analyses of patronage data from the *Calendars of State Papers* and other sources, there is some danger that the main theme may be obscured. This is inevitable, but I have tried to employ only such tables and charts as are necessary to justify the conclusions.

No thoughtful student ever expects to find in the history of an institution such as the house of commons a "magic year," an abrupt change without antecedents, a change entirely attributable to so artificial a cause as the change of sovereigns. It is not surprising, therefore, to discover that the tendencies so marked in the reigns of James I and Charles I had their origins in that of Elizabeth.

The power gained by the commons as a result of the interesting dawn of consciousness and deliberate perfection of organization reached a high point during the first sessions of the Long Parliament, but was temporarily submerged in the political excesses of the dictatorship. It reasserted itself under Charles II. Formally recognized in 1689, it headed England in the direction of that political democracy which has been ultimately attained through the reforms of the eighteenth, nineteenth, and twentieth centuries. Viewed from this angle, the changes in usages and personnel of the house, between 1558 and 1629, become interesting and highly significant. They constitute a dramatic episode in a long, steady institutional evolution which had its roots in the middle ages and its culmination in the Parliament Act of 1911.

What actually happened between 1558 and 1629 I have attempted to summarize in the ensuing paragraphs.

Elizabeth's reign opened with parliament well under the control of the privy council, after the manner of Henry VIII and the Edwardian protectors. Committees were few and were dominated by courtiers. But it was a long reign, and it was a time notable for the rise in power and wealth and spirit of the gentry and the townsmen—lawyers and merchants. It is not surprising that we find, beginning about 1592, a restiveness in the house and outbursts of daring individuals. Yet there was no party, and there was little in the way of procedure that the restive element could exploit save an increase in committees. That the position of the young "opposition" in committees became more prominent was due in part to a decline in the number of privy councilors and other great men in the house. A few of the later opposition men were growing in spirit and sagacity, but the reign was very definitely a "background" period. The queen's influence was a restraining one still.

In the parliament of 1604–10 things moved rapidly. The leadership of courtiers declined, while the leadership of opposition men increased. This was the time, perhaps, in the whole long life of parliament when procedure developed most quickly. Those who took advantage of the innovations were the opposition men. Whether a "party" or not, they had real leaders—Sir Edwin Sandys, Nicholas Fuller, Henry Marten. There were fifty or sixty of them, and they got results, both in obstructing the king's business and in tearing down the prestige of speaker and court party. In fact, their success was so galling that James I attempted, with some success, to break them up before the time of the Addled Parliament. He was only partially successful, however, and the old leaders of 1604–10 became the new leaders of 1614. So began a continuity of membership, from parliament to parliament, of the little core of opposition.

The Addled Parliament of 1614 contained a much smaller opposition group, but, as in 1604, it was well organized, while the courtiers had practically no organization or inspiration of leadership. For the score that had fallen off, a dozen or so of new recruits appeared. Chief among these was Sir Robert Phelips. There was venom in the tactics that made the parliament of 1614 "Addled"; there was finesse. It was punished too; for the king tried again to break up "the party." This parliament is not very important for development of usages, but is very important in the battle of court and patriot, in the *tradition* of opposition. The continuity of firebrands was established.

The opposition came the nearest to dying out in 1621 and 1624, because James was more skillful than formerly in the matter of elections and in his other dealings with parliament. In 1621 less than thirty "patriots" can be discovered, and their leaders shared with the courtiers the leadership of the house. James's old policy of placating the troublesome and enticing the neutral, by petty bribery and offices, was working well. The "party" languished. The extent to which this was the work of Prince Charles and Buckingham—and Professor Willson shows that it was largely theirs—does not bear on my thesis. Whoever initiated it, it worked well. In 1624 it went even better. There was lawmaking in place of feuding. The patriots were shrunk to about thirty still. Yet several of the most violent of the later Puritans were there, including John Pym. This strange state of affairs has an obvious bearing upon the question of the inevitability of the civil war.

In 1625 the opposition was lively again, though the number of its members was small. Those who were its leaders were the men who had been active before—about twenty of them. The significant thing about the opposition in 1625, however, is this. The old leaders were nearing the end of their activity, while most of the great leaders of the Long Parliament were present but not yet heard from. The core of the party was shifting.

In 1626 the government tried to break up the opposition and to build a following by patronage. The results are obscure. The opposition was not clearly partisan in the sense that it was against everything the government sought. It was aimed at Buckingham primarily. Two very important men, Pym and Sir John Eliot, became articulate leaders. There was a strong opposition but not a real party. Most of the men were there, but they were not organized.

A truly climactic result in the parliament of 1628 follows the rather baffling story of the earlier parliaments, and ends this study. The house of 1628, stung by Charles's bungling return to open electioneering and tense with fear and anger, showed at last a true opposition organization. Opposition worked through committees, and opposition members, clearly organized, dominated the committees. Nearly all the important "Puritan" leaders of the Long Parliament were present, and over a hundred of the party members of 1642–43. Most of them were old parliament men. "The party," or at least its powerful nucleus, had come into being.

THE
RISE OF THE REVOLUTIONARY PARTY
IN THE
ENGLISH HOUSE OF COMMONS
1603-1629

I

FIRST STIRRINGS

IN THE HOUSE OF COMMONS

THE long reign of Queen Elizabeth saw a mighty transformation in parliament. This change was the political manifestation of a vast reorganization in the life of England. Call it what you will—English renaissance, commercial revolution, or birth of modern nationalism. The young queen in 1558 ascended the throne of a nation bewildered and frightened by religious changes and proscriptions, a nation whose great trading companies were yet to be, or at least were yet to bring back in volume the riches of the East, and whose middle class of townsmen and prosperous farmers was still too young to resent the political domination of the great. Elizabeth's death in 1603 was mourned by a people who had withstood the might of Spain, a people whose newly got material wealth had brought a proud, confident flood of song and verse without precedent, whose burghers and gentry had outgrown their amenability to noble tutelage. In no reign have the feelings of Englishmen changed so fast. In none has social change been so clearly reflected in the organs of government.

The analysis of institutional development in the house of commons makes little sense unless this fact is borne in mind. He who would understand it fully must exercise his historic imagination. He must dissociate the word "parliament" from the familiar picture of modern power and return in fancy to the little Chapel of St. Stephen in the city of Westminster, not yet a part of London. He must think, for the year 1558, of curled and perfumed gentlemen in fine hose, with rapiers and retainers, and again of many other gentlemen, somewhat rustic, whose servants got drunk in London taverns and whose feeling for the great courtiers was one of awe. As the reign progresses, the picture changes. The little Sir John's and simple Mr.'s are richer and more sophisticated. Their doublets are finer and their servants more numerous. Now and again members become individuals who appeal to the imagination.

Such was Peter Wentworth, a pioneer of the opposition, sent to the Tower in 1575/6 for protesting the queen's prohibition of debate on religion and again in 1586/7 for his refusal to take "no" from the speaker. In 1571 he had accused the courtier Sir Humphrey Gilbert of flattering and fawning upon the queen and in very elegant language upon the floor of the house had called him a liar and hypocrite. Sir John Puckering, speaker in the parliaments of 1584–86 and 1586–87, is a sychophant easy to picture. Suave and self-seeking, he had a member imprisoned for opposing a bill favored by the government, and for his various loyal acts he received the lord-keepership in 1592. William Strickland in 1571 took his life—or at any rate his liberty—in his hands when he introduced without permission of the queen a bill to reform the prayer book. A fearless man, "grave and antient" according to Froude, we know little about him; yet the hot scene and temporary sequestration that followed his audacious act lifted him from obscurity and made him a person. No great imagination is required to see Sir Edward Coke, speaker in 1592, calmly ignoring those who would claim the floor, terminating debate, and hunching his shoulders to the angry protests of the more daring members. Him we encounter later as the "oracle of the law," successively solicitor general, recorder of London, attorney general, chief justice of common pleas and later of king's bench, and finally the parliamentary gadfly of both James I and Charles I. In the early parliaments of the reign sat Sir William Cecil, later Lord Burghley, the most powerful man in England at one time, lifetime politician who served Edward VI, Mary, and Elizabeth. Master of the court of requests and secretary of state, he was the spirit of conservatism, wise but not vindicative, a presence restraining and dignified. No history is all institutions, and the Elizabethan house is no exception. Love affairs and pride and personal ambition moved men as they always have. In the dreary waste of statistics by which in part the changes in parliament are measured, one must, to get the true picture, attempt to see Speaker John Crooke squirming and coloring as disorderly members clanked noisily in forbidden spurs and to hear the dry nervous passion in Peter Wentworth's voice as he reprimanded the speaker for being the crown's stool pigeon. It requires good imagination, for the record is scant.[1]

It must be said at the outset that this study of the rise of a party depends for its evidence upon a close examination of procedure and personnel and of the interaction of the two. The reader must bear this in mind as he follows the frequent descriptions of successive parliaments in their general and particular aspects. These descriptions, necessary to the support of the central theme of *party*, are the result of considerable tabulation. Tedious in the compiling, they are far from lively even in summary. But they are related to the main story.

How big was the English house of commons in Elizabeth's day, and what manner of house was it? It had in 1601 a potential membership of 461. During most of the reign, at least after the enfranchisement of a number of new boroughs before the elections of 1562, the official list shows approximately the same number. Probably no such multitude ever assembled for the actual transaction of business at any one time in St. Stephen's Chapel. In fact, the largest division on record during the reign, one taken in 1593, shows an attendance of only 345.[2] This simple fact is in itself an important commentary on the Tudor parliament. It means, apparently, that the average member was not very stable in his interest in parliament. Attendance has always been, in theory, at the command of the sovereign—a survival of the old idea of feudal court service. A point came, to be sure—I believe it was in James I's reign—when attendance was regarded as an opportunity and not as a burden, but that point was not yet. Membership in the house was an honor—and a chance to see London and to turn an honest penny there. Yet it was distasteful to spend weary hours listening to Coke's stuffy precedents of Edward I or to Cecil's mealy-mouthed harangues, when everybody knew that the big men were running the show anyway.

That this attitude prevailed can be shown by statistics. Of fifty-three divisions noted for all the parliaments of Elizabeth, only thirteen record more than 250 members, while twenty-five fall below 200, and four below 100. At the time of the lowest recorded number, in 1601, when only 80 men took part in the division, the potential membership was 461. In a division, all who remained in the house were counted, as were their opponents, who filed out into the lobby. We must conclude that members just did not come to the sessions with much diligence. The small divisions do not mean that the men had left London. Two divisions on the same day might vary by as much as 52 or even 87 members. Lawyers of the house were busy at their practice and neglected their attendance. One day in 1585 the sergeant at arms was sent to make the rounds of the courts, to bring the lawyer members back. Interesting picture that—the agent of the Mother of Parliaments trudging the cobblestones of London to drum up a quorum! But it did not work. Nothing worked. Under Elizabeth, as later under James, various expedients, in the form of fines and loss of wages, were attempted to force attendance, but without success.[3]

The number of men given "license to depart" in any session

was negligible and does not go far to explain the large discrepancies between the total membership of the house and the number actually present and voting at divisions. The largest number recorded as being allowed to go home was 32, in the lengthy parliament of 1562–66. This parliament had a membership of 421. One division of only 87 is recorded. But this habit of running off home tells a story too. With the exception of a few distinguished lawyers allowed to absent themselves on the queen's business, those who left before the end of the session were mostly obscure men—men who spoke little and who must have felt that their influence upon legislation was slight. Their wives continually got sick, or "necessary occasions" called them home. The season of the year seems to have had little to do with it. More left in March (53) than in any other month. No doubt spring plowing played its part. What country man would not tire of London when the smells of an English spring were in the air? Yet 20 left in February, and 16 in December. Sheer boredom and a realization of the futility of their efforts detracted from the glamor of sitting in the house after the first interest had worn off or the little axes of their private bills had been successfully ground and laid by for the royal assent at the end of the session. Even allowing for the increased influence in the last three Elizabethan parliaments of members who were not courtiers, the work of the house was still carried on by a relatively small group of men. The courtiers were still most influential. So why should Mr. George Lee of Rippon in Yorkshire stay in London after he had tired of it? He had probably done his business for the folks that sent him, or he had discovered that it could not be done. He had made no recorded speeches and had served on no committees. Accordingly, "for his affairs" he departed March 13, 1562/3.

For these considerations, since it was the privy councilors and other courtiers who rendered Mr. George Lee's presence somewhat superfluous, we pass logically to the question, "What did

the privy councilors do in the house and how did they get there?"
The starting point for an answer lies in the elections. It has been
commonly assumed, from scattering but cogent evidence, that the
privy council of the Tudors was careful to influence elections and
returning officers in favor of the crown. There is little doubt
that such was the case in Elizabeth's time. Sheriffs, who were
royal officers, often sat in the house. Their presence greatly
interested our antiquarian friend, Sir Simonds D'Ewes, for it
was contrary to law.[4] Evidently it was regarded as legal if the
election preceded the formality of pricking as sheriff. At any rate,
there were many sheriffs in the house, and they were naturally
queen's pawns. The old requirement that a member must reside
in his constituency was also disregarded,[5] in part, perhaps, to
make more convenient the election of courtiers. There are some,
but very few, tales of violence practiced at elections by agents of
the crown.[6] The best evidence of parliament packing is in letters
of the privy council to sheriffs.[7] They contain definite instructions
for the return of particular representatives.[8] It is clear from
scraps of information, from what is known of the same sort of
thing all through Tudor times, and from the clumsy attempts of
James I to imitate the custom in 1614 that such was a common
practice of the Elizabethan council. An incident of the parliament of 1586 fairly clinches the matter. In a contested election
of that year the queen insisted upon the competency of the court
of chancery as against the jurisdiction of the commons themselves.[9]

Elizabeth's parliamentary tactics were as a rule subtle. Though
she might curse and fume and browbeat intimate courtiers and
attendants even to the point of physical violence, she shrewdly
played toward parliament the role of a goddess behind a cloud
of mystery—awful in her wrath, but gracious and patient with
her beloved lords and commonalty. She wrangled with the house
only to maintain points of principle to which she attached peculiar importance. We must therefore conclude from this show

of force in 1586 that the control of elections was of more than casual interest to the crown. To lay down the general rule that Elizabethan elections were manipulated would be preposterous. They often involved large numbers of voters,[10] and under such conditions bribery and intimidation are difficult. Various signs of independent elements in the house show that by no means all members were in sympathy with the crown. One can say only that the sheriffs very often had instructions from the privy council and that they sometimes made false returns to satisfy the demands of the queen's officers. Sir Edward Hobby, the diplomat, then member for Berks, complained of this last practice in introducing a bill in February, 1588/9.[11] Evidence to support this hypothesis continues to the end of the reign, but is so scattering that it is impossible to show any progression either toward or away from free elections.

It is very clear that the courtiers within the house ran its affairs and that their presence there was one of the major techniques of Elizabethan statecraft. Certain it is that toward the end of the reign the power of the courtiers declined. Yet if all the parliaments of Elizabeth are compared with all the parliaments of James, it is equally certain that court influence, in the activities of the speaker and of other members, was, under Elizabeth, great indeed. As one considers this fascinating angle of the drama of sixteenth-century legislation, let him bear in mind that, for the great men who acted in it, it was but a part of that "climbing of the greasy pole"; at its foot might stand the scaffold, or at least might lie financial and political ruin, and at its top was a precarious perch, well greased, too, and shaken by ruthless rivals. Advancement in that day was often at the cost of unscrupulous intrigue. As Sir Francis Bacon compassed the dismissal of his lifelong rival Sir Edward Coke, chief justice of king's bench, in 1616, so Coke himself was the chief agent in securing the impeachment of Bacon, lord chancellor in 1621. In each case the charges of malfeasance veiled with almost indecent thinness bitter personal hatreds. When Sir Walter Raleigh helped the earl of Essex along the road to execution, after the earl's foolish threat to the queen's person in 1601, he but showed the persistence of his jealousy for Elizabeth's favor. His letter to Sir Robert Cecil concerning his rival was treacherous and damaging. Yet Raleigh himself soon faced a hard prosecutor when Coke as attorney general secured his conviction of conspiracy in behalf of Lady Arabella Stuart in 1603. Coke's venom against the prisoner was unnecessary. Personal politics was grim business. In this treacherous and glittering game of all or nothing, the doings of the house of commons were a part. The house was one of the places to serve the queen and to gain advancement.

The steering by the privy council and by such courtiers as Sir Francis Bacon was as a rule subtle. Peter Wentworth, in his afore-mentioned memorable speech of February 8, 1575/6, spoke of "a rumor which runneth about the House and this is it, take heed what you do, the Queen's Majesty liketh not of such a matter, whosoever preferreth it, she will be offended with him; on the contrary, her Majesty liketh of such a matter, whosoever speaketh against it she will be such offended with him." [12] Jaws must have dropped and angry veins must have swelled on necks and foreheads as Wentworth's bold words fell on a hushed, astonished house. There must have been a great deal of whispering guidance by courtiers of which the record bears no trace. But their influence was not always subtle. A direct command was sometimes delivered from the queen by a privy councilor, as when Sir Francis Knollys, treasurer of the household, forced the house to desist from debating the execution of Thomas Howard, duke of Norfolk, then under sentence of death for his complicity in a plot to free Mary Queen of Scots.[13] It was Sir John Fortescue, chancellor of the exchequer, who, on February 7, 1597/8, informed the house that a bill for draining in Norfolk was forbidden to be read.[14] Sir Christopher Hatton, vice chamberlain of the household, opened debate on the "Great Cause" (the disposition of Mary Queen of Scots) in the parliament of 1586.[15] It is not surprising to find that on repeated occasions members of the privy council were the lively promoters of the bills for subsidy or that on March 26, 1589, Sir James Perrott, son of the lord deputy of Ireland, was the mover of the government bill against "imbezelling" of munitions, which, in disregard of the usual custom, was pushed through in three immediately consecutive readings.[16] Sometimes speeches of members were interrupted by courtiers, in violation of the rules of the house, in order that government business might be introduced.[17] Members of the court group stood together to uphold their own dignity. In 1592 Sir Robert Cecil, then a privy councilor, and Secretary Sir John Wooley fairly flew at the throat of Sir Oliver St. John for presuming to criticize the conduct of the vice chamberlain, Sir Thomas Heneage. Cecil again in 1601 indignantly replied to the the suggestion that Sir Walter Raleigh be called to the bar.[18] Courtiers had no diffidence in asserting their leadership, as Knollys and Hatton demonstrated in 1584 when they resisted the reading of Dr. Turner's bill.[19] Cecil was very frank indeed when he threatened the whole house with the queen's displeasure in connection with a bill which he agreed was reasonable, but which they had been forbidden to discuss.[20] Courtiers urged cooperation with the lords.[21] They spoke against parliamentary privilege when the prerogative was involved.[22] They recommended adjournment at times when the strategy of the crown demanded it.[23] It is very interesting, however, to observe that, with few exceptions,[24] such actions are all before 1597. This fact does not support the theory of Professor Roland Usher that the crown, losing power in the speaker's office after 1597, was asserting itself more forcefully through the members of the privy council.[25]

The speaker was always a queen's man. The engineering of his election was the special and exclusive responsibility of the members of the privy council in the house, even at the end of the reign. Without exception the speeches in which his nomination was made and seconded were the speeches of great courtiers. In every case the crown nominee was elected.[26] In fact, this election was one of the choicest bits of comedy in the whole drama of parliament. Nominated, let us say, by the fulsome oratory of Mr. Treasurer of the Household and seconded by the equally tawdry effort of Mr. Vice Chamberlain, the nominee, who had known for months that he was to be thus foisted upon the house, "disabled" himself with mock humility, praying the house to choose one more able than himself.[27] Then he was pressed and coaxed by some of the courtiers and, accepting with feigned reluctance, delivered himself of a long prepared speech, creaking with labored figures. Sir Thomas Smith describes the affair thus: "The Speaker is he that doth commend and preferre the Bils exhibited into the Parliament, and is the mouth of the Parliament. Hee is commonly appointed by the King or Queen, though accepted by the assent of the House." [28] Except for the election of Richard Onslow,[29] whose case was somewhat unusual, the choice of speaker was, in this part of parliament's history, always unanimous. Onslow, nominated suddenly to fill the office at the death of Speaker Thomas Williams, had a seat in the house of lords, as solicitor general. For this reason the house divided, 82 to 60, on his election. The office was to such an extent the property of the crown that it was regarded as a regular step in a sort of Elizabethan *cursus honorum*. Ex-speakers were usually advanced to high legal positions under the crown. Six out of the eleven Elizabethan speakers were so rewarded. Sir Christopher Wray, speaker in 1571, became chief justice of queen's bench; Sir Robert Bell, 1572, chief baron of the exchequer; Sir John Popham, 1580–81, attorney general and later chief justice; Sir John Puckering, 1584, queen's sergeant and later lord keeper; Sir Edward Coke, 1592, attorney general and, under James, chief justice of king's bench and common pleas; and Sir John Crooke, 1601, king's sergeant. Sir Thomas Williams,

1562–63, died in office; Sir Thomas Gargrave, 1558–59, was returned to his useful work on the council of the north; and only Onslow, Thomas Snagg, 1588–89, and Sir Christopher Yelverton, 1597, seem not to have been given preferment. The speaker was always a lawyer and usually an old parliament man, though not necessarily one who had taken an active part in the work of previous sessions. He need not always have a perfect record of servility, for both Bell and Popham had, before their speakerships, offended the queen by their too independent utterances in the house.[30] Bell had criticized, in 1566, the queen's answer to a petition concerning her marriage, and Popham, in 1571, boldly criticized the treasurers of the crown. Yet the man put forward as a speaker was one whom the crown could trust and whose career it was, so to speak, willing to guarantee.

The speaker's power was tremendous. Without him the house could not proceed to business. He was the mouthpiece of the commons to all the outside world, including lords and queen. His was the right to grant permission to speak. The order of reading bills was determined by him, and he could kill bills with this power. On occasions, he even appointed committees [31] and deputations [32] although this practice was unusual.

Mr. Speaker was very often guilty of partiality. He was constantly on the queen's side in controlling debate and readings. In 1580/1, Popham was openly accused of influencing debate by speaking without permission and by prejudicing the speeches of members.[33] In 1586/7 Peter Wentworth inferred that Speaker Puckering had interrupted members, broken off debate, overruled the house (presumably in the matter of reading bills and putting the question), and reported the contents of bills to the queen, contrary to the privilege of the house.[34] For his pains, incidentally, Wentworth spent a short time in the Tower. There is clear evidence that the same speaker, Puckering, took upon himself the pushing of the "Great Cause," to the exclusion of other business. Both Puckering and Coke ran to the queen with unauthorized information. Coke freely admitted it—tough and defiant even as a young man. He calmly informed the members that Her Majesty had forbidden him to read a certain bill. Wray in 1571 obviously took his cue from the privy council in guiding debate on the famous Strickland case, for the clerk indiscreetly put it down that "during which speech the Council whispered together, and therefore the Speaker moved, that the House should make stay of any further consultation thereupon." (The issue in this case was the right of the house to deal with ecclesiastical matters without the queen's consent.) How clear a picture! And how piquant a tidbit the clerk sometimes dropped quite without intent! Nowhere else do we have any hint as to how the members sat. In this short entry the clerk casually let it fall that at least some of the privy councilors sat together. This information sharpens the impression of how the house was run. By all sorts of devices the speaker could, and did, check offensive procedure. He might introduce other business. He might pocket a bill. One bill he turned back, unread, to the author. He silenced members simply by declaring them out of order. He promised to present matters to the queen and then forgot to do so. Or he just stayed away from the house altogether. On February 24, 1592/3, Peter Wentworth submitted a petition concerning that delicate and forbidden matter, the succession to the throne. It is passing extraordinary that Speaker Coke, durable fighter of iron nerves and physique, was sick only one day of his speakership— and that day when Wentworth's ill-starred petition would have been discussed. This convenient illness gave time to arrange the handling of a very ticklish business. Speaker Bell tried to force the house into harmony with the lords against its will. And again, Coke "did over-reach the House in the subtile putting of the Question."

This fairly obvious sort of court leadership or chicanery is easy enough to discover. It suffices to show how the wind blew. But it took more than a little browbeating and heading-off of malcontents actually to get the queen's business done. It took speeches and committee work too. This is a matter a little harder to unearth and a little harder to appraise, but the record tells the same story. By examining every speech noted in D'Ewes and the journal, we find that roughly half, in each parliament, were made by courtiers.[35] There was always a little band who carried the burden of debate. In 1571 it was Sir James Croftes, comptroller of the household, and Sir Francis Knollys, treasurer of the household. In the parliament of 1572 the chief speakers were Croftes and Knollys again, together with Sergeant Flowerdewe, Sir Christopher Hatton, captain of the guard and vice chamberlain of the household, and Sir Walter Mildmay, chancellor of the exchequer. In the 1584–86 sessions Hatton, Knollys, and Mildmay did most of the speaking, and the same three again in 1586–87. In 1588–89 Knollys and Sir Thomas Heneage, vice chamberlain of the household, made the most speeches. In 1592–93 it was Sir Robert Cecil, a privy councilor and unofficial secretary of state, Heneage, Sir Walter Raleigh, and Sir John Wooley, secretary of state. In 1597 Cecil again had a big record, along with Sir Francis Bacon, at that time a new but aspiring member, Sir John Fortescue, chancellor of the exchequer, and Thomas Snagg, the former speaker of the house. In 1601 Cecil was by far the most articulate member of the house. Among the courtiers, Raleigh was his closest rival. It is interesting from this list to see how few men served the queen thus, and for how long a time. The most interesting aspect of the debate is not the courtiers who spoke all the time, but rather the noncourtiers who spoke in 1601. More of that presently.

In the matter of committee service, exactly the same thing is found. A careful tabulation of every name recorded in committee lists shows that in all the parliaments there was again a little knot of courtiers who faithfully attended committee business. They were in part the same men who bore the brunt of debate: Knollys, Mildmay, Cecil, Bacon, Croftes, Hatton, Heneage, Fortescue, Wooley, Raleigh. In part they were members less active in debate: Sir Henry Sidney, former lord deputy of Ireland and later lord president of Wales; Sir Thomas Smith, Dr. Thomas Wilson, and Sir Francis Walsingham, all secretaries of state; Sir Thomas Brograve, attorney of the duchy; Sir Ralph Sadler, chancellor of the duchy; Sir James Perrott, former lord deputy of Ireland; Sergeant Harris; Sir Francis Drake, the well-known favorite and adventurer; Jerome Horsey; Sir Robert Wroth; Sir Thomas Fleming, queen's solicitor. All of them were courtiers. Again, as in looking at the debate, the surprising thing is not that these men served, but rather that an increasing number of other men encroached upon them in committees toward the end of the reign.

The first parliament of James thus inherited a tradition of courtier leadership, but it inherited something else—a spirit which was the same as the spirit that locked Black Rod out in 1629 and attainted Strafford in 1641. Was it a political reflection of the commercial revolution? Surely it was. This spirit was the greatest thing, politically, that grew on English soil in the sixteenth century. It doomed James I to political failure and Charles I to the block. It is seen in words and gestures. It is seen even in the bleak statistics of speeches and committees. In fact, its growing effectiveness at the end of the century and of the reign can hardly be understood without examining speeches and committees. Changing procedure and changing spirit went hand in hand.

In the early days the spirit of heckling was rather cautious. Yet it was probably there. The ordinary member did not venture to test issues with the speaker or with courtiers. Instead, he puffed up his ego by talking about parliamentary privilege, clinging to the idea that he belonged to a very important body. The clerk tells us that the members debated privilege often and with enthusiasm, for he records the details of their arguments, while he often omits entirely the arguments on bills. The cases sometimes approached comedy. Officers of the law were brought to the bar, solemnly lectured, and sometimes imprisoned for having arrested the drunken servant of some member. Members often escaped, at least temporarily, the consequences of failure to pay their just debts. The incidents were usually rather picayunish, except for the few occasions when freedom of speech in parliament was involved. How much all this amounts to is doubtful. It seems to show that the house was suffering under a sort of group inferiority complex. Afraid to oppose the queen, it asserted itself in a safe and harmless way. There was much more talk of privilege in 1601 than before.[36] That was natural. The house of 1601 was bolder in all respects.

The earliest recorded defiance of majesty was in 1576, when Peter Wentworth alluded to the unwholesome condition which enabled courtiers to influence legislation by whispering about the queen's favor and disfavor.[37] Wentworth "got by" with this speech, though he was cut short by the speaker and was "sequestered the House." Examined at length by a special committee, he protested his loyalty to the queen and was graciously restored to the house by the queen's order.[38] He was bolder in 1587, and he landed in jail. This time he had been taxing the speaker with partial conduct. He accused him of interrupting members, breaking off debate, overruling the house in the matter of reading bills and putting the question, and bearing tales to the queen of what went on in parliament. Feeling was running high in 1587, because of excitement over the Mary Stuart affair, and Elizabeth decided to curb this bumptiousness. Wentworth went to the Tower. In 1597 Fortescue, chancellor of the exchequer, asked the house to change the time of a committee meeting, on the grounds that it conflicted with another committee meeting and that he and Secretary Cecil had an important conference with the queen that afternoon. The house refused to change.[39] It would not have refused at an earlier date. Coke had been even more highhanded as speaker in 1592 than Puckering in 1597.

The clerk mentions it casually, but members dared not complain. But then, that was Coke—a bad personality to meddle with, at any time, and especially when he was that sacred cow, Her Majesty's Speaker.

The year 1601 saw the climax of spirit. "And Mr. Brown the lawyer stood up and said, Mr. Speaker, Par in Parem non habet Imperium, we are all Members of one Body, and one cannot Judge of another." [40] It was a question of whether Mr. Martin should be haled to the bar for a speech which had displeased the great Cecil. "Mr. Brown the lawyer" was speaking the mind of many members. They gave poor Speaker Crooke a lively time of it. Even if allowances are made for the clerk's fuller reporting in 1601 and for the interesting sidelights on the presiding officer which had never been included in the record before, there can be no doubt that members were riotous and disrespectful. We have knowledge of marks of reverence for former speakers, but of disregard and rebuff for John Crooke. Both Yelverton, speaker in 1597, and Crooke, speaker in 1601, were weak presiding officers. Yelverton is hardly mentioned in the record, and Crooke always in a negative fashion. The house was a veritable roughhouse—much like the Irish house of 1613. There was disorder at the door and on the floor. Members were heckled in debate with "hemming" and spitting. They were pulled by the sleeve, "like a dog in a string," at divisions. They wrangled, they boisterously reversed their own decisions and shouted for bills. They attended booted and spurred and with arms. The speaker himself was called to order by a member.[41]

Elizabeth was growing old. She took less pains than formerly in supervising parliament.[42] The consciousness of its dignity as a body, of the importance of its records and of its privileges, and of the equality of its members was growing upon the house. It was less subservient. It laughed at Sergeant Heyle in 1601,[43] when he said that all that they had was the queen's. In fact, "all the House hemm'd and laughed and talked." Poor Sergeant

Heyle tried again after the speaker had scolded the house, but they hemmed him down again. They were in no mood for the old saws about the sun, moon, and stars and the rhetorical glories of the Tudor firmament. The house of 1601 was a body of able men and no longer an assortment of timid yokels. Bacon and Cecil had to cope with them as intellectual peers. The privy councilors and other royal satellites were being engulfed. The loss of the speaker's power and prestige was but a part of a great movement. The day when only Stricklands and Wentworths dared speak was forever gone. The whole house could not be imprisoned, and everyone knew it. The courtiers must rely more upon eloquence and less upon intimidation and position. Spirit there was now aplenty, but how did the ordinary member go about increasing his effectiveness?

The answer, in brief, is that from 1592 to the end of James I's reign the procedure of the house was undergoing a change of such nature as to make the average member stronger and to make control by a clique more difficult. By 1601, there still existed a procedure of some flexibility, but one that was showing increasing signs of rigidity.[44] This fact itself is of more than antiquarian interest. Like the development of a more complex system of committees, the growth of a body of usage, which could not lightly be disregarded and which could guard against shrewd procrastination or surprise, played into the hands of the house of commons itself, in its seventeenth-century warfare against the courtier element in its midst. This change resulted in part from an increase in business. In part it was the deliberate work of rebellious spirits. It affected principally (1) participation in debate, (2) committee work, (3) the powers of the speaker.

There is much guesswork in any statement about the volume of debate in Elizabethan parliaments. The record is so scant that some ingenuity in the use of internal evidence is called for.[45] What the record seems to show is that never before 1601 was there considerable speaking by the less important members, but that in 1601 there was much of it. The same clerk served the house in the last four parliaments, but obviously had a better assistant or was more alert or conscientious in 1601 than he had been before. Up to 1601 he used a uniform rule in selecting the speeches to record, but in 1601 he changed.[46] Why did he change? What did he sense? Was it a tense undercurrent among restless men who whispered, very guardedly, over their wine, "The old queen will soon be gone, and then we shall speak out loud"?

At any rate, and for whatever cause, the clerk gave a fuller record, and for that reason his record may not be reliable for statistical comparison with his earlier work. It shows that while only three "unimportant" men spoke four times or more in 1592, and only one in 1597, there were thirteen in 1601. It shows a greater spread of speakers. More men who spoke but once or twice are recorded than men who spoke often. Before this, debate had been monopolized by a few speakers, mainly important men. Now there were more speakers who spoke seldom than members who spoke often.

In this matter of the increasing participation in debate of less influential members, it is quite clear that the parliament of 1601 was the one in which the change came. The accompanying tabulations supply the evidence.

Important as is the trend in debate, the extension of committee service was even more important. It was here that the principal gains of the average member were being made.

As in the matter of debate, the sloth or indifference of either the clerk or Sir Simonds D'Ewes or both renders the task of examining the committees rather difficult. Throughout the reign the record of committee membership very often ends with the exasperating words "and others." Perhaps the original note-taker's hand was tied. Perhaps Sir Simonds was not interested. In the later parliaments there was a tendency on the part of the house to nominate for committee service "all knights of the

RECORDED SPEECHES IN THE ELIZABETHAN PARLIAMENTS
(EXCLUSIVE OF COMMITTEE REPORTS)

	Speeches	Members Speaking	Members Making Four or More Speeches	Less Important Men Speaking Four Times or More
1558	3	3	0	0
1562	2	2	0	0
1571	94	39	7	3
1572	57	28	4	1
1584	39	22	3	0
1586	65	33	4	0
1588	47	34	2	0
1592	128	51	9	3
1597	64	34	6	1
1601	263	71	22	13

	Ratio of Frequent Speakers (Four Times or More) to Infrequent Speakers	Percent of Speeches by Frequent but Noninfluential Members
1558	1 to 1	0
1562	1 to 1	0
1571	1.3 to 1	8
1572	3 to 1	7
1584		0
1586		0
1588		0
1592	2 to 1	6
1597	5 to 1	7
1601	.7 to 1	18

shires," "all burgesses of port towns," "all citizens of cities," "all burgesses of clothing towns," "all those who have knowledge of the matter," "all Lawyers of the House," and the like. Some of these categories are impossible to run down. Judging from the importance that the notetakers evidently attached to the recording of committees, as compared with their interest in recording debate, it is likely that most of the committees were mentioned, although not all of their members were noted. Some general notion of size may be had, some interesting facts bearing on influence in the committees may be adduced, and a good deal of positive evidence on the general importance of committees is presented. There was more committee work toward the end of the reign than at the beginning. The size of committees increased sharply in 1597 and 1601. The number of members who served frequently on committees became greater in the same two parliaments, showing an extension of such work among the members in general. More noncourtiers served on committees after 1592.

Substitution of work in committee for debate on the floor was increasing year by year, especially in 1597 and 1601. This development is easily demonstrable. The number of committees in each parliament proves it: *1558*, 18; *1562–66*, 52; *1571*, 34; *1572–83*, 129; *1584–86*, 81; *1586–87*, 37; *1588–89*, 48; *1592–93*, 44; *1597*, 89; *1601*, 82. These figures require some explanation. The parliaments of 1562–66 and 1572–83 consisted of two and three sessions respectively, while all the others consisted of but one. In 1572–83 the largest number of committees in any one session was 56 (the second session). In the committees for the three sessions there was a great repetition of subject matter. The parliament of 1584–86 was a long single session interrupted by prorogations. The small number of committees in 1586–87 is explained by the fact that parliament was called for the express purpose of acting on the case of Mary Stuart, and the queen discouraged legislative activity. The parliament of 1597 lasted only from October 24 to December 19. When these facts are considered in connection with the number of recorded committees, it becomes apparent that committee activity in 1597 and 1601 was very much greater than at any previous time.

The size of committees was also increasing. Whereas only one committee before 1597 (the subsidy committee of 1592) numbered more than 100, in the last two parliaments of the reign whole groups of men (all knights of shires, all citizens of cities, all lawyers, and the like) were added to large select committees. It is certain that not all members listed as eligible to attend committees in 1597 and 1601 actually did attend. Yet the number of men who met in the committee chamber must have been larger than before. In many cases, anybody who wished could be of a committee. That meant that the courtiers who once controlled committees could do so no more, for they were overwhelmed by numbers. What did it signify as to initiative? It may have signified that the house was deliberately getting itself out of the speaker's control. When we recall how committees were named in those days, we are brought back to a question of personalities. Members stood up in their places and shouted the names of other members to serve on committees. The clerk took down "as many as he conveniently could," and the speaker evidently called a halt when there were enough. A strong speaker like Puckering or Coke might have prevented this random expansion into what was in some cases almost a committee of the whole house. But Yelverton and Crooke let it go on. It represented a sort of disorderly stage in procedure midway between the select committee system and the committee of the whole. The same thing started up again in the next reign. Whatever its cause, it threw opportunity into the hands of the common members, and it was yet another evidence of the disappearance of that awe for authority which had once kept the little men from naming other little men to serve on committees.

It was not simply a matter of noncourtiers serving on committees, but of all members increasing their activity. This is more easily proved than any other phenomenon involving a count of names from D'Ewes. The number of men serving on ten or more committees, from 1571 on, as far as the record of names shows, was: *1571*, 5; *1572–83*, 30; *1584–86*, 11; *1586–87*, 13; *1588–89*, 11; *1592–93*, 10; *1597*, 27; *1601*, 15. The high figure for 1572–83 is of course due to the three sessions of that parliament, in which there was a duplication of committees. It was not until 1597 and 1601 that the practice of appointing large groups of members not designated by name appeared. It is likely that if these groups could be tracked down the number of men found to be serving on ten or more committees in 1597 and 1601 would be doubled. The trend toward general participation is clear.

Naturally, since the courtiers were few and the politically unannointed many, this trend raised the proportion of noncourtiers in committee work. It is quite impossible to say from a record now three centuries old that such a man was a courtier and such a man was not. Yet this much one can say—and it suffices to prove the point. The list of ten-committee men for 1592 consists entirely of members with a known court connection,[47] while that for 1597 contains eight names of men of second rate politically.[48] In 1601 there were five.[49]

The curtailment of Mr. Speaker's power is possibly the clearest indication of the leveling process in the house. The greatest power lost was that of determining the order of reading bills. Usher explains it thus: So much complaint was made against Coke's arbitrary conduct in the reading of bills in 1592–93 that the queen and the council determined to reduce the speaker's power to a mere formality, to depend in future upon the eloquence and influence of courtiers in the house, and to admit the principle that Mr. Speaker must sanction the reading of whatever bills the house desired.[50] This is the obvious conclusion to be drawn from the debate of December 10, 1601, in which neither Speaker Crooke, Comptroller Knollys, nor Secretary Cecil, all of whom spoke upon it, denied the authority of the house to determine the order of reading or defended the arbitrary power of the speaker.

"Then the Questions upon the continuance of Statutes, were offered to be Read, but the House called for the Bill concerning Ordnance; yet the Clerk fell to read the Questions, but still the House cried upon the Bill for Ordnance.

"At length Mr. Cary stood up and said: In the Roman Senate, the Counsul always appointed what should be read, and what not; so may our Speaker, whose place is a Counsul's place: If he erre, or do not his duty fitting to his place, we may remove him, and there have been Precedents for it. But to appoint whose business should be handled, in my opinion we cannot. At which Speech some Hissed.

"Mr. Wiseman said: I reverence Mr. Speaker, in his place: But I make great difference between the old Roman Consuls and him. Ours is a municipal Government, and we know our own Grievances better than Mr. Speaker; and therefore 'tis fit, that every man Alternis vicibus should have those Acts to be called for, he conceives most fit: And all said, I, I, I.

"Mr. Hackwell said: I wish nothing may be done, but by Consent; that breeds the best Concorance. My desire is, The Bill for Ordnance should be Read; if you, Mr. Speaker, do not think so, I humbly pray it may be put to the Question.

"Mr. Comptroller stood up and said: I am sorry to see this confusion in this House. It were better we used more Silence and spake in order. Yesterday you ordered the Bill for Continuance of Statutes should be Read; now in a humor, you cry Ordnance, Ordnance. I pray you, that we first Decreed, let us stick to, and not do and undo upon every Idle motion.

"Mr. Secretary Cecil said: I will speak shortly, because it best becomes me; neither will I trouble your Patience long, because the time permits it not. It is a Maxim, Praestat otiosum esse, quam nihil agere, I wish the Bill for Continuance of Statutes, &c. may be Read, and that agrees with the Precedent Order of this House, and more with the Gravity thereof: yet, because the Spirit of Contradiction may no more trouble us, I beseech you let the Bill for Ordnance be Read: And that's the Houses Desire." [51]

The bill for ordnance was read. Now what does this signify? The loss of power of the speaker in controlling the reading of bills must be readily admitted.[52] That Elizabeth saw the commons displeased in 1592 and decided to humor them seems very unlikely. It would have been a weakening of her mainstay in the house. In fact, in the above-cited case, Speaker Crooke attempted at first to proceed in the old dictatorial manner of Coke, disregarding the will of the house, before he was overborne. As early as 1571 the house appointed a committee to determine the order of proceeding in bills,[53] but it apparently had little or no importance. The house made little complaint against Coke. Wentworth's accusation is the only one. Certainly there was no great popular indignation against him.

What probably happened is this. The precedent of the right of the house to determine reading was allowed to lie dormant, like other and even more ancient parliamentary rights, until the moment when circumstances favored it. Those circumstances presented themselves in 1601 when Crooke was speaker. Crooke tried to do as Coke had done. On November 18, 1601, he openly refused to read a bill.[54] His right to do so was still debatable. Moreover, there is nothing to support the other part of Usher's assumption—namely that the queen's interests were actually secured by the increased activity of courtiers, after the power of the speaker was voluntarily laid aside. There were fewer privy councilors returned into the house in 1597 than in any other Elizabethan parliament, and in only two others were there as few as in 1601.[55] The courtiers were, as has been shown, in a relatively weaker position in 1597 and 1601 than formerly, with regard to both debate and committee service. In fact, they showed less aggressiveness than ever.

The lengthy belaboring of the question of how the speaker's power came to be reduced may seem to be academic. It is not. Very clearly the commons made the change, and not the queen. The change is a part of a larger picture, and it fits the picture. The consciousness of its dignity as a body, of the importance of records and privileges, of the equality of members—this is all part of the psychological setting for the hissing and spitting that bedeviled poor John Crooke!

In the matter of the subject matter of legislation also, the Elizabethan house exhibited considerable independence. Numerous references are to be found to this or that reason for the calling of parliament.[56] Elizabeth made no attempt to deny that the session of 1586–87 was called to deal with Mary Stuart, and for no legislative purpose. Yet the fact stands that, of the 437 acts of parliament during the reign, 166 were private bills, and at least 21 of those classed in the statute book as public acts dealt with universities and town improvements, usually the matter of private bills. The house, too, initiated several matters distinctly hostile to the government's policy, such as the bills to regulate allowance for justices' diets, to curb monopolies and purveyors, and to bring about the execution of the duke of Norfolk.[57] There needs no elaborate analysis of the Statutes at Large to see that the house was legislating for the nation and not merely for the dynasty. The recognition of local interests in the mass appointment of committeemen in 1597 and 1601 was a forward step for a body with such a function.

There was no "party" in Elizabeth's time. There was not even "an opposition." But an idea had taken hold and a new procedure had begun to form. The idea concerned the possibility of the overturning of courtiers' control. It was not as yet antiroyal at all. The new procedure was moving, through new committee usages, toward arrangements favoring the participation of the many and militating against the management of the few. There was needed only an irritating and inept sovereign to bring together the idea and the forms and to make an effective opposition group.

II

DISCOVERY

OF SOME INTERESTING POSSIBILITIES

JAMES I's memory has been chiefly perpetuated by the Bible that his scholars translated and by his quarrels with parliament. But he assuredly was not "the wisest fool in Christendom." However shortsighted James's handling of the legislative branch may have been, it is clear that a major cause of his difficulties lay in a change that had taken place several years before his accession in the house of commons.

The house of commons of 1604–10 invites investigation and description along many lines. It was in rapid transition. The type of legislative body that historians knowingly style "Tudor" was growing into that house of 1621 which had acquired definite initiative and an organized opposition. The house of 1604–10 was more active and more self-assertive than its predecessors. So were its members. In its records may be traced a growing understanding of the large possibilities for power which could be achieved through a rigid, businesslike mode of procedure. From its ranks a definite group of opposition members was emerging. These men were not yet well organized, but they were becoming consistent and increasingly fearless. Conspicuous in the development of procedure were the extension and elaboration of committees. There was a halting but persistent inclination to secure the advantages of general discussion and informal flexibility by means of new devices. Fascinating in itself is the appearance during the four sessions of this first Stuart parliament of prominent leaders of a new type—the type of Nicholas Fuller, Henry Marten, Sir Edwin Sandys, Sir George Moore, and Sir Henry Poole. Their rise coincided, quite naturally, with the declining influence of such leaders as Sir John Herbert, Sir Francis Bacon, Sir Thomas Parry, and Sir Henry Montague.

Any one of these changes can be traced at length. The journal record for 1604–10 is better than for the earlier period and freer from baffling short cuts. Two things in the house of 1604 are of the greatest interest: the appearance of new legislative methods and the growing influence of opposition members. In relating these two phenomena to one another a question must be answered: Were the members whose interests were not those of the court deliberately and consciously developing and using ways of doing parliamentary business, for reasons of their own, or was the growth of new practices simply coincident with a shift of influence within the house and primarily a result of increased pressure of business? To this question the present chapter is addressed.

One may arrive at the firm conclusion that certain well-known criminals are responsible for a number of transgressions; a court of law may be able to establish evidence only of some more or less irrelevant crime, such as income tax evasion. A student of the parliament of 1604 is faced with some such difficulty, particularly when he tries to compare this parliament with those of Elizabeth. It may be said that beyond any reasonable doubt the volume of business was increasing between 1601 and 1610 and that the pressure upon the commons was becoming greater. The appearance of new forms and the increased activity of a new type of member are matters that may be disposed of by purely objective evidence. The establishing of a sure connection between them, however, is difficult. It is a problem in which one is justified in seeing around a few corners, since otherwise he cannot see at all. There must, of necessity, be some conjecture involved in arriving at a conclusion, but not too much.

The first point to be ascertained about this parliament is its degree of activity or busy-ness as compared with that of 1601. Of the various criteria for relative activity, several are unsatisfactory. The parliament in question was recorded in a different fashion and by a different clerical "system." It differed from its predecessors also in length and in continuity. The Thames and the Mississippi admit of comparison in length and volume, but hardly in "activity." Neither do these parliaments. The parliament of 1604 had four sessions, covering six years and four months. It numbered 437 days of sitting, in sessions of 88, 105, 120, and 124 days respectively. The shortest parliament of Elizabeth sat for 41 days, and the longest, covering ten years and eleven months, for 119. This protracted one was surpassed in actual days of sitting by one of but four years, which did business for 149 days. These figures have no particular significance in themselves, except as they show the impossibility of comparison on a basis of time.

If it were possible to learn the number of bills passed by the house in the various parliaments of Elizabeth, to find the ratio of these results to the actual days of sitting, and then to compare that ratio with a corresponding one for the parliament of 1604–10, something definite could be said. True, it could be said only that the house was disposing of more or less legislative grist in a given time, and it would still be a matter of conjecture as to whether the house was really working harder in one period than in another or whether the difference was due to the greater or less efficiency of privy councilors and other leaders. But even such a comparison cannot be made, since D'Ewes, who alone covers that part of Elizabeth's reign for which the statistics would be most significant, neglects in many cases to state what bills were passed.[1]

Suppose we try another tack. An attempt has been made to

determine from references to committee work, in D'Ewes and the journal, the number of subjects of legislation in each parliament and to relate it to the number of days of sitting. D'Ewes, however, is entirely unreliable for the necessary material covering the early part of the reign. It is evident, however, that his record for the last three parliaments is considerably fuller than for those preceding. On the assumption that he mentioned nearly all the bills referred to committees in 1592–93, 1597, and 1601,[2] a comparison has been made between the parliaments of those years and that of 1604, with the three normal sessions and the abnormal one of the 1604 parliament also shown separately.[3]

RATIO OF SUBJECTS OF LEGISLATION TO DAYS OF SITTING

	Days of Sitting	Subjects of Legislation	Ratio (Subjects to Days)
Parliament of 1592–93	41	43	1.05
Parliament of 1597	64	90	1.41
Parliament of 1601	45	72	1.6
Session of 1603–4	88	135	1.5
Session of 1605–6	105	127	1.2
Session of 1606–7	120	72	.6
Session of 1609–10	124	141	1.1
Parliament of 1604	437	475	1.09
Three normal sessions	317	403	1.27

The result is of interest. It shows a similarity, in point of activity, between the parliament of 1604 and its three immediate predecessors. The similarity also appears in a comparison of the ratio of statutory enactment to days of sitting.

RATIO OF STATUTES ENACTED TO DAYS OF SITTING

	Days of Sitting	Statutes	Ratio (Statutes to Days)
1558	76	42	.55
1562–66	149	86	.58
1571	46	41	.89
1572–83	119	85	.72
1584–86	71	49	.69

RATIO OF STATUTES ENACTED TO DAYS OF SITTING (*Continued*)

	Days of Sitting	Statutes	Ratio (Statutes to Days)
1586–87	43	11	.26
1588–89	46	24	.52
1592–93	41	27	.66
1597	64	43	.67
1601	45	29	.64
1604–10	437	226	.517
Three normal sessions	317	193	.61

The statute book takes into account, of course, neither the bills acted on by the house and dashed,[4] the bills passed the house and rejected by the lords, nor the bills passed both houses and rejected by the crown. But the tabulation showing the duration of parliaments and the bills that were made law between 1558 and 1610 indicates that, after a very irregular course, which is explained by affairs of state, the ratio settles down in 1593 to a fairly constant figure. If the parliament of 1604 is regarded as a unit, and especially if the 1606–7 session is disregarded,[5] it is almost constant.

Take these two compilations together (ratio of subjects of legislation to days and ratio of statues to days) and it appears that after 1593 a change may have taken place in the control and guidance of the house. Some sort of pressure may have been removed, and the removal of it may account for a new and fairly uniform "speed of production." A certain amount of work could now be done in a given time. This hypothesis strengthens the theory that, late in the reign of Elizabeth, the house was beginning that movement toward systematic organization which became so clear in the first quarter of the seventeenth century.

For the present, since we are talking about "degree of activity," let it simply be said that the house of commons of the first parliament of James was dealing in a given length of time with just about as much legislative material as had its three immediate predecessors. Although the house was not accomplishing more work per day, yet it was accomplishing more per year, and per decade. The pressure of business was increasing and was being met by the simple expedient of sitting more days in a year and more years in a decade.

No session in Elizabeth's reign was longer than 76 days,[6] and in every case but one the sittings either were held in the autumn and early winter or were held in the late winter and spring and terminated before June.[7] Summer sittings and protracted sessions were avoided, and business was hurried through to fit a preconceived notion of what constituted a decent and "convenient" session. Or it was left unfinished. The sessions of the parliament of 1604, on the other hand, ranged from 88 to 124 days in length. Three of the four lasted into July. The old notion of making the work fit the session had passed. During those long sessions there was more afternoon work. Although the afternoon sittings of the house itself show no great increase [8] and were mainly concerned with routine or miscellaneous business of small import,[9] the assignment of afternoon committee work became much greater, especially in 1610,[10] and there were even early morning committees before the house met.[11] Should it be objected that defects of record make it unfair to compare numbers and schedules of committees in the two reigns, it can be answered that the shift toward more elaborate committee work is detected between the early and late sessions of the parliament of 1604, for which the record is fairly uniform. Morning committees became more frequent in 1609 than formerly.

The relevancy of this long discussion of the length and activity of sessions may not be immediately apparent in a study concerned ultimately with the growth of a party. There is a bearing, however, on the main question. The house had more work to do, and it sat longer than its predecessors. Certain changes in procedure and committee work were made, and they must presently be examined. These changes had not made possible a speedier disposition of business, but they were altering the whole method of working and were opening up to the average member, and particularly, it seems, to the opposition leaders, new possibilities for activity and for obstruction.

In its formal aspects, the procedure changed little from 1601 to 1610. As before, each bill had normally three readings,[12] was not debated at first reading,[13] was committed or rejected at the second, was debated, recommitted, or engrossed at the time of its report from committee,[14] and was passed or rejected at its third reading.[15] It was becoming customary to dash a bill at its second reading,[16] and there is no record in this parliament of a bill that received more than three readings. Procedure was more formal and regular. This is of little interest in itself. But it seems to point to a shift of influence in the house, as will be explained.

There was an evident desire on the part of the house to give to old, well-worn usages the binding force of rules. In particular was this noticeable in the session of 1603–4. There were no less than twenty-three separate rules governing procedure entered on the permanent record for the parliament of 1604, eighteen of them in the session of 1603–4. A few of these rules were of little importance. Like similar rules in Elizabeth's time, they were aimed at increasing the decorum of the house.[17]

It is easy to make mountains out of molehills, especially when using very old records. In an assembly of 400 leading men of a great country—intelligent leaders and masters of their spheres, great and small—there are likely to be new ideas which are not necessarily aimed at upsetting anyone's authority or occasioned by any ulterior motive. It is naive to see plots and secret ambitions in every innovation. Yet it would be even more naive to miss the implication of the rules stated in the parliament of 1604–10 for the control of the speaker. An old rule was restated, allowing him to explain doubts but not to influence debate.[18] He could not refuse to read a bill, take it out of the house before the house was acquainted with it, or deliver it to anyone before the house had given leave. Most important of all, it was agreed, March 23, 1606/7, that the house might debate in the absence of Mr. Speaker. If these had been rules for the legislature of Missouri in the year 1821, they would attract no notice. But they were rules for the governance of the dignified presiding officer of a body bound by age-old precedents, a body which ever has proved itself slow to alter old forms, much as it may change its practice. The last of the rules mentioned was revolutionary. It, with the other four, was a plot against Speaker Phelips' power. He had been influencing debate and betraying the secrecy of business. He had absented himself in order to keep the house from sitting and to gain time. These rules were designed to curb, and even to shelve, stuffy Sir Edward. They were squarely directed against court influence. In some cases it is possible to identify the conspirators in this move, which must have brought a shudder of sympathy to Judge Crooke and a scornful recollection of the "good old days" to ex-Speaker Coke.

A third group of rules probably issued from the necessity of greater dispatch in dealing with the mounting load of bills. A matter once carried or lost could not again be called in question, but must stand as the judgment of the house.[19] A quorum of eight was sufficient to do business as a committee. If a man spoke irrelevantly or made a superfluous motion, the speaker could disregard him. A bill coming from the lords and generally "misliked" by the commons need not have a third reading, if the house had failed to commit it. After nine o'clock any bill could be put to the question. No bill could be committed *in toto* on third reading. A regular day each week was set for the committee of grievances. These rules speak for themselves.

A few other rules appear to have had no particular significance.[20] In fact, most of the rules [21] probably did nothing more than state the old form of procedure. If we except the important innovation of the committee of the whole, procedure in its formal aspect had changed but little. Practically, however, the house was beginning to work in a different way. The big development is that of the committee system,[22] the informal phase of legislative work.

It seems certain that there were more committees, in the absolute sense, in the three normal sessions (first, second, and fourth) of the parliament of 1604 than there had ever been before. It is likely that the session of 1603–4 had more committees in proportion to its length than any other. It cannot be proved, because the short cuts of D'Ewes's record make it impossible to tell just how many committees there were in any Elizabethan session. That the parliament of 1604 as a whole had less committees in proportion to its length than did the parliament of 1597 is certain. A comparison, from this angle, of all the parliamentary sessions from 1558 to 1610 shows pretty clearly that whatever change there was in James's first parliament was not in the direction of more committee work per day. The parliament of 1597 shows more committees per day than the parliament of 1604 or than any of its sessions save that of 1603–4.

Having failed to find anything sure about the trend toward more committee meetings in a given time, let us see if we can prove that more members were participating in committee work. We can not. Again it is because of the inexactness of the records of Elizabethan parliaments. It seems likely, as shown in the preceding chapter, that the size of committees was increasing in the last two parliaments of Elizabeth; [23] and from the general similarity noted in the parliaments of 1597, 1601, and the first two sessions of that of 1604, one is led to imagine that, within this period, committee work per day was along much the same lines from a statistical viewpoint.

The size of committees in the various sessions of the parliament of 1604 has been examined. The resulting tables, while they show little change in the number of named members,[24] show another trend of some significance.

SIZE OF COMMITTEES

Session	Total No. of Committees	Under 15 Members	15-30 Members	31-60 Members	61-100 Members	101-50 Members	Over 150 Members	Indeterminate Committees
1603-4	158	31	63	49	6	8	1	0
1605-6	132	20	55	38	10	9	0	1
1606-7	76	2	27	27	9	8	3	12
1609-10	162	40	56	45	14	4	3	39

In examining this matter of committees, an exhaustive count was made of the number of times every man served on a committee in the parliament of 1604. The result was entirely negative. It showed that the number of men serving in each of the four sessions was about the same, that the total number of committee services was practically constant, and that the number of men who served very frequently, frequently, and seldom remained about the same, except for the expected decline in the abnormal session of 1606-7.

In fact, the only real reward in this laborious search through the records of committee appointments, 1604-10, was found in the figures shown in the last column of the chart. By "indeterminate" committees is meant that type of committee containing "all lawyers," "all civilians," "all who will come," or "members for the clothing districts."

The tendency from 1605 on was marked. It was to throw open the work of committees, to make it free, to push the work of the house back into the committee room. This movement, like many others, had its root in Elizabeth's reign. The naming of large groups, such as "the knights of all shires," is the beginning of it.[25] The invitation to "all lawyers" is an extension of it. The words "all who will come" finally broke down all restrictions. The committee of the whole house was the culmination.

It was in the sessions of 1606-7 and 1609-10, especially the latter, that the idea of an informal extension of the business of the house into committee struck with force.[26] There were instances even in Elizabeth's reign of broad invitations to "all lawyers" and "all who will come," but they were exceptional.[27] In 1609–10 the practice had become frequent.

Apparently the first true "committee of the whole house" occurred on May 7, 1607. A few months before there had been a "Grand Committee of Union" sitting in the house itself in the afternoon,[28] and as early as November 29, 1606,[29] a motion was unsuccessfully made that the whole house be a committee. On December 1, 1606, there is a suggestion that a committee of the whole may have been operating, but the evidence is not clear.[30] On April 24, 1607, the device was attempted, but not successfully used.[31] The meeting on May 7 was very clear.[32]

A case of June 26, 1607, shows that the house could not easily become accustomed to the new procedure during the first session in which it was tried,[33] but during the session of 1609–10 there were 14 clear cases of its use [34] and a suggestion that the committee of the whole was used a number of times without any record.[35]

One must bear in mind that, in this analysis of procedure, we are trying to discover the period in which the direction of the business of the house passed into the hands of the house itself and into the hands of the generality of members and out of the hands of a small, powerful, court-controlled group. The "invention" of the committee of the whole house is obviously an important part of this change. Any increase in the use and importance of committees is bound to be a part of the same change. There is much evidence that such an increase was taking place in the parliament of 1604. When poor attendance at committees is cited as the prime cause for the slow progress of legislation [36] and when no one but a representative of a given committee is allowed to bring in a bill on a given subject,[37] it is clear that speaking of a "committee system" has considerable justification. Committee meetings were gaining in dignity,[38] and there is even record of their being so largely attended as to interfere with the work of the house.[39] Many subcommittees were also in use by 1610, although it is impossible to guess whether we have anything approximating a complete record of them, and of course because of their different nature they cannot be used in a statistical comparison with committees in the preceding reign. Their use was probably increasing in 1609–10.[40] Committees were sitting, at this time, in the mornings, during the time of the regular sittings, either in St. Stephen's Chapel or near it. We can tell this from the number of "committees adjourned" interspersed through the daily records.

This matter of the importance of committees would be clinched if it were possible to show an increasing tendency to act upon the recommendations of the committees without debate. Unfortunately it is impossible to show this. The mentions of committee reports in D'Ewes are too infrequent to admit of comparison with the entries in the journal from 1604 to 1610. From a few of the D'Ewes entries that are fairly clear, it appears that the recommendations were followed without debate. Yet even after 1603 we cannot always be certain what the clerk meant. When he says that a bill was reported and engrossed or negatively reported and dashed, does he necessarily mean that action was taken without debate? From the number of cases in which record of debate is interjected, it seems that the brief entries without comment indicate that action was taken directly. Assuming this to be the case, we can show, in a rather conjectural fashion, that action without debate, in the parliament of 1604, was a little more usual than debate upon or rejection of the reports.[41]

Much labor and many words have been expended upon the status of committee work by 1610. At the end it must be admitted that the result is only an impression. That impression is that committee work was the medium to which the leaders of the house were turning to accomplish their ends. Now we come to a very interesting bit of indirect evidence. *The known leaders of*

*the opposition were very active in committees. They certainly
would not have been increasing their activity in this direction if
the committee stage of legislation had been regarded as a per-
functory one.* Happily it is possible to find out a good deal
about these leaders and about the personnel of parliament in general.

The parliament of 1604 was in many respects different from
any preceding one. It had a definite opposition group, though
this could hardly be called a party. The influence of the crown
received a great rebuff. The commons answered the king's request for supply with a protracted and determined pressing for
redress of grievances and failed to satisfy the king's most ardent
wish, the Union with Scotland. It is therefore very natural to
inquire if the commons of 1604 differed radically from those
preceding in point of personnel.

One might expect to find a greater proportion of new members, especially among the leaders. Failing to find this, one
might reasonably look for some point toward the end of Elizabeth's reign at which there had been a noticeable shift in the
ratio of old and new members. Such a shift would probably indicate a removal of pressure from elections and the returning of
a larger group of men who were more closely identified with the
interests of their constituencies and of the kingdom at large and
less amenable to suggestion from the crown.

In point of fact, no such break is to be found. A fairly accurate
check is possible by means of the "Official List." Where exactly
the same name appears in the returns for a certain borough or
shire in 1597 and in 1601, for example, there is little doubt as
to the member's identity. This matter has been canvassed at
length. It has been found that between 1592 and 1604 there is a
fairly constant ratio among three categories: (1) members serving for the same constituency as in the preceding parliament,
(2) members who had sat before, but not in the preceding parliament, and (3) entirely new members.[42]

The outstanding leaders [43] in debate and committee in 1604 had, almost without exception, served in parliament before. Thirty-six of them had sat in the parliament of 1601.[44] Seventeen others were old parliament men.[45] Nine were new members.[46] With the exception of Crewe and Yelverton, the new members were leaders of second rate.

In one important respect the parliament of 1604 was, by Elizabethan standards, deficient. It had very few privy councilors.[47] Sir John Herbert and Sir John Stanhope were alone in the session of 1603-4. In 1606 Sir John Fortescue replaced Stanhope. In the session of 1606-7 Fortescue and Herbert again represented the council. In 1610 Herbert, Sir Thomas Parry, and Sir Julius Caesar were all of the house, but at no time were there more than three privy councilors, for Fortescue died before the appointment of Parry. Moreover, not one of these men was a first-rate leader. The slight activity of the council in the house was so noticeable that it attracted contemporary comment, in two extremely revealing letters.[48]

Despite the "paucity of councillors," the council had a way in which it provided for (or at least thought it provided for) the government's interests in the house. There were several very important henchmen to do the work. Bacon, first as "learned council" and later as solicitor general, was undoubtedly the most influential man in the house, next to the speaker. Sergeant Doderidge, solicitor general from 1604 to 1607; Sir Thomas Fleming, solicitor general to 1604; Sergeant Hobart, attorney general; Sir Henry Montague, recorder of London and "learned council"; and Sir James Ley, attorney of the court of wards— these were all active members. Then there were 34 men who held offices of secondary, though considerable, importance under the crown [49] and 56 with minor offices (such as clerkships) or executive offices of a somewhat impersonal nature (as sheriffs, lieutenants, captains, and commissioners). Eight members are known to have had some private connection with great men—

principally with Bacon. Eleven held some sort of monopolistic patents under the crown. Twenty-four were recipients of land or money grants or pensions. Three (Doderidge, Phelips, and Montague) were king's sergeants. Altogether 133 members can easily be found whose interests might be expected to lie on the side of the government.[50] In a few cases it happened that a man who had some slight connection with the government threw his influence to the other side,[51] but in general the wide distribution of offices among the members was calculated to be a source of strength to the king. It is most interesting to note that many of the pensions and grants were made during the time of the parliament, as if they were rewards for services rendered or bids for services expected. Whatever may have been the intent of those who planned parliament for James I, the event showed that such a miscellaneous and haphazard assortment of king's friends, of various grades of ability, was a poor substitute for the closely organized "core" of Elizabethan parliaments.

"The opposition which was the last Parliament to your Majesty's business, as much as was not *ex puris naturalibus* but out of party, I conceive to be now much weaker than it was, and that party almost dissolved. Yelverton is won; Sandys is fallen off; Crewe and Hyde stand to be Serjeants; Broke is dead; Nevell hath hopes; Barkeley I think will be respective; Martin hath money in his purse; Dudley Digges and Hollys are yours. Besides, they cannot but find more and more the vanity of that popular course; specially your Majesty having carried yourself in that princely temper toward them, as not to persecute or disgrace them, nor yet to use or advance them." [52]

A comment like the foregoing is worth a barrel of statistical evidence. It came from the pen of Sir Francis Bacon and refers to the opposition members of 1604–10. It lays to rest the question of whether there was an opposition party in that parliament. To such a party, in addition to those named by Bacon, may have belonged Nicholas Spray and Sir Edward Hext,[53] John Hare,[54]

Nicholas Fuller,[55] Sir James Whitlocke,[56] Sir Samuel Sandys,[57] Sir Henry Constable,[58] and Sir Christopher Piggott.[59] This much can be gleaned from scattering references outside the journal. The recalcitrants were too few, however, to make much of an impression in a body of over 400.

We are sure that there was a definite opposition in this parliament. We are also sure that there was considerable change in procedure. But can we find any connection between these two facts? Let us make an appraisal of the importance of these opposition members in the work of the house.

It is amazing that the clerk could cover so much paper and still continue to conceal so well the burden of members' speeches. In the record of 1604 hardly a speech can be definitely labeled as partisan. The journal for 1606–7 is nearly as ambiguous. Those for 1605–6 and 1609–10 are somewhat more revealing. It would be quite impossible to establish from the journal alone that Brooke or Crewe, Nevill or Spray, Yelverton or Sam Sandys, were members of the opposition. This, by way of digression, is in itself highly interesting. But these men were sufficiently active to be classed by their colleagues among the obstructionists. Where were they active? Apparently in the committee room.

But back to the matter of recorded speeches. In relying on them, one is baffled by finding contradictory evidence, as in the case of George Cotton, John Hoskins, and Sir John Sammes, who appeared to speak now on one side and now on the other.[60] Yet there are a few cases where the record of speaking makes it possible for us to identify a man as being of the opposition. We can prove what we already knew about Fuller,[61] Hyde,[62] Marten,[63] and Sandys.[64] They consistently took a popular stand on purveyance, subsidy, Union, and grievances. This is not surprising. But there are four men whose importance was evidently greater than their fame. Sir Walter Cope, although he was the recipient of favors from the government and was a friend of Bacon, spoke often against the court party on impositions, subsidy, and privilege.[65] Sir George Moore, a very active member of the house, officer of Prince Henry's household and later recipient of a large money grant from the king,[66] took the opposition side several times, in debate on the subsidy and purveyance.[67] Sir William Strode, a less important member, spoke several times against the government policy,[68] and Sir Herbert Crofts did likewise.[69] In the case of some 40 other members, definite utterances suggesting opposition are found, but the evidence necessary to identify them definitely with the opposition is lacking.[70]

What, after all, can be said of the opposition group? It certainly included Berkley, Brooke, Crewe, Digges, Hare, Hext, Hollis, Hyde, Marten, Nevill, Sandys, Spray, Whitlocke, and Yelverton. Probably it also included, at some time, A. Cope, Crofts, George Moore, and Strode. Then there were a score of lesser lights of whom we cannot be sure.

Next we want to find out in what way these men made themselves felt. A very detailed analysis, too cumbersome for inclusion, has been made to discover the activity of these men—in speaking, committee service, and reports from committee. These activities have been compared with the average number of speeches, committee appointments, and reports for all members of the house whose activities are recorded in the journal. This analysis shows several very interesting things.

With the exception of four men, Crofts, Marten, Moore, and Sandys, the members known to have been of the opposition were active in committee rather than in debate. This was an actual condition, and not a defect of record, for records of a number of much more frequent speakers are found in all the sessions. It is plain evidence that a man could make sufficient impression in committees to attract the attention of irritated courtiers. Did not Bacon refer to Nevill and Yelverton, Hyde and Hollis, Crewe and Berkley, as powers in the parliament of 1604? What could be clearer evidence of the importance of committee work?

Two of the opposition men, Digges and Spray, have almost no record, either in debate or in committee. What had they done to deserve the notice of Bacon and Phelips? Here is a riddle. Perhaps they were out-of-door agitators. Perhaps Bacon and Phelips were mistaken. Perhaps the record is faulty. One other man, Sir Edward Hext, falls in almost the same category. Save for a number of committee appointments in the first session, he would have hardly any record.

Four members, Hollis, Yelverton, Hext, and Hyde, have a distinct diminuendo in their records. Why is this? Possibly because of the conversion to which Bacon hopefully referred in 1614 they had "fallen off." In the case of Yelverton we know this to be true.[71] One step more—why were these men appointed to fewer committees as they weakened in the popular cause (assuming that they did so)? It certainly looks as if they had owed their many early appointments to some definite plan of execution in the popular ranks. This is only a suggestion—but it seems plausible.

Six men, Berkley, Crew, Crofts, Hare, Marten, and Sandys, had a marked crescendo in their records. Is this an indication of growing organization, or is it the result of a general increase in committee activity? The latter, I think, in the case of most—but not in that of Sandys. He stands somewhat by himself, as *the* popular leader of the end of the parliament. He reported more bills from committee in 1610 than any other man.[72] He alone made a fourfold increase in his speeches from the floor between 1604 and 1610. Of all the house, he is the easiest to picture—calm, plausible, diplomatic, shrewd—never waxing too violent or giving the impression of partisanship. If the opposition had a "brain," it was Sandys—and how very wrong was Bacon when he reported Sandys "fallen off"!

Sufficient has been said to show that these known leaders of the opposition were, with trifling exceptions, above the average in activity. Were they really among the leaders? Several of them were. Their importance may best be shown by a chart of the ten leading speakers and committee appointees in the several sessions.

LEADERS IN THE PARLIAMENT OF 1604

1603–4

Appointments to Committees		Speeches Made		Appointments to Committees		Speeches Made	
G. Moore	81	E. Hobby	22	Fuller	69	Marten	29
Wroth	78	Marten	21	G. Moore	61	Fuller	28
Wingfield	63	Hollis	15	H. Montague	52	Wingfield	23
F. Moore	63	Fuller	14	Heigham	51	Hoskins	22
Fuller	58	G. Moore	14	Yelverton	49	H. Montague	22
E. Hobby	57	Hastings	13	Wingfield	47	Sandys	18
N. Hyde	56	T. Hobby	12	Doderidge	46	G. Moore	18
Thynne	54	F. Bacon	12	Strode	45	Fleming	14
Yelverton	53	Wingfield	12	T. Smith	44	Strode	13
Marten	51	Sandys	11	Nevill	44	Yelverton	12

1606–7   1609–10

Appointments to Committees		Speeches Made		Appointments to Committees		Speeches Made	
Fuller	46	Fuller	10	Poole	88	Sandys	42
G. Moore	46	Marten	8	G. Moore	85	Fuller	37
Poole	44	Owen	7	Fuller	84	Crofts	30
Wingfield	41	Poole	7	Marten	72	Marten	29
Marten	35	Sandys	7	Owen	62	Hoskins	26
Barrington	35	Wentworth	7	H. Montague	56	G. Moore	23
E. Montague	34	Wingfield	6	Crofts	56	Poole	21
Heigham	33	H. Montague	6	F. Bacon	54	E. Phelips	20
A. Cope	30	N. Hyde	5	Caesar	51	Hastings	20
Oxenbridge	30	G. Moore	5	E. Montague	50	Caesar	18

This shows a very definite position of leadership for Moore, Fuller, Hyde, Marten, Yelverton, Hollis, Sandys, Strode, Nevill, and Crofts. When it is remembered that Wingfield, Heigham, Hastings, Hoskins, Poole, A. Cope, Owen, and Wentworth were among those whose speeches indicate a tendency to side with the opposition, it appears that, in the men of greatest activity in the house, judged by the criteria suggested, the neutral or court members were a minority of about 16 to 18. This condition is a very definite contrast to that in the last years of Elizabeth, when the position of courtiers in debate and committee was, while weakening, still somewhat preponderant.[73]

One more test may be applied to ascertain the importance of the small group in question. It proves too little merely to show that they were often appointed to committees. If, however, it is found that they were actually attending committees and bearing an increasing burden of committee reports, their leadership in committee work can be all but proven. In the absence of material bearing on the actual work in committees, we have no better gauge of their relative importance there than the record of their reports. The last line of the chart compiled is of most interest.

COMMITTEE REPORTS IN THE PARLIAMENT OF 1604–10

	1603–4	1605–6	1606–7	1609–10
Number of men reporting	52	47	29	36
Opposition men reporting	26 (50%)	19 (40%)	16 (55%)	17 (47%)
Total recorded reports	155	150	96	154
Reports by opposition men	59 (38%)	68 (45%)	69 (72%)	115 (75%)

It shows, if one further examines the record of individuals making committee reports during this parliament, a tightening grip of three men upon the committee stage of legislation. These men were Fuller, Marten, and Sandys.[74] The figures cannot be accurate, of course, because we cannot be sure exactly who the opposition were, but the men with large numbers to their credit are almost all known to have been on one side or the other, and mistakes in the cases of obscure members would not affect the result very much. Whatever new material may come to light, it seems extremely unlikely that the validity of this statement will be assailed: the opposition group in the parliament of 1604 was very important and increased its hold in the last two sessions. But is there good reason to believe that the opposition members were, in their efforts for supremacy, deliberately leaving an impression upon the practical workings of the house?

In a sense, a partial answer to this question has been made. Committees were still named in the old way,[75] and it was quite possible for any group with sufficient organization to secure representation on any committee. The opposition leaders secured their own appointment to enough committees to put them, not merely abreast with, but ahead of, the minions of the crown. That much can be, and has been, shown. Is it true also that practically every committee contained members of the opposition group?

It is, beyond a doubt, true. But it is also true that almost every one had also its smattering of courtiers. How could it be otherwise? Either side must be very blind indeed to allow its opponents to appoint all the committees. It would be a stupid waste of time to go through the thousands of committee names in an attempt to establish the preponderance of influence on every committee. We know so little of the "lineup" that any results would be valueless—especially since many of the meetings in 1610 were thrown open, and throughout the parliament there is no way of telling who actually attended. All that can be said from the appointments is that both sides had ample opportunity to make their impression on committee and that the important popular champions were appointed by name somewhat more frequently than were the important courtiers. That is, at any rate, a contrast to the Elizabethan arrangement.

Such being the case, it is bootless for us to examine the schedule of time and place for committee meetings in an effort to find evidence that one side was deliberately making it difficult for the other to attend. There was, of course, a good deal of overlapping and doubling up, but with so many partisans in either camp it is difficult to imagine that either the "patriots" or the "courtiers" could do much by such maneuvering. This much can be said: Sandys seemed to have some peculiar influence upon the schedule, for on at least three occasions in 1609–10 we read of his making a detailed and apparently authoritative announcement with regard to coming meetings.[76]

What then remains that can be shown about the strategy of

the opposition?—for it cannot have been wholly eloquence that made possible their effective obstruction. Needless to say, they were behind the outspoken assault upon the influence of speaker and courtiers.

In a number of cases, we cannot tell who were the prime movers. Who complained that the king had adjourned them in order to secure a more favorable division at a later day? [77] Probably several members. Who moved that, if one member complained of another to a privy councilor, the committee of privilege should examine it? [78] Who was it that boldly interrupted Speaker Phelips on May 24 and June 21, 1604? [79] Who were the ringleaders of disorder against whom the rule of June 20, 1604, was directed? [80] Who had the temerity to proclaim in open house that they had done enough for James by naturalizing his Scottish favorites? [81] Who turned off the insinuating self-confidence of some member of the king's council by the dramatic assertion that every member of the house was a member of the king's council and as much entitled to attention as any other? [82] Who moved the restrictions upon the speaker in withdrawing bills from the house, showing them to nonmembers, and refusing to read them? [83] Who moved that Bacon should not have leave to speak on May 14, 1604? [84] Who suggested that important members purge themselves of the suspicion of bearing tales to the king? [85] Who wished Mr. Attorney to be sent for with the mace, for leaving the house without permission? [86] Who suggested the election of a speaker *pro tempore*? [87] Who asked that Mr. Solicitor be called to the bar for his oral abuse of Mr. Noy? [88] How we should like an answer to these questions! But it does not greatly matter who the men were—we can be absolutely sure that they were of the little group of marked members of whom so much has been said.

The partisan speeches which serve to mark off "those who studied to please" from "such as continued according to their first opinion moved only out of Conscience" [89] are numerous and clear.[90] It is largely upon them (especially in the debates on sub-sidy and impositions) that the evidence for determining the op-position depends. There are a few welcome entries that tell of random but very purposeful shots at those who "sate in the high places"—shots by known marksmen. Fuller presses Sir Edward Hobby for his reasons in not signing the form of Union.[91] Sandys dares openly to define the prerogative.[92] Sir Edward Herbert "plops" (what a priceless word to find in the journal!) with his mouth at Mr. Speaker.[93] Sir Robert Twysden and Sir Anthony Cope press Phelips on the matter of bringing messages from the privy council.[94] John Tey openly upbraids the speaker for "clip-ping him off" and presumes to threaten him.[95] Fuller makes the revolutionary suggestion that the house might debate in the speaker's absence.[96] Crofts complains (in 1607) that courtiers are dominating the committees and asks that the Union be de-bated on the floor.[97] Lawrence Hyde moves against accepting the king's recommendation in a return case.[98] Sir George Moore opens the question of His Majesty's taxing members for their speeches.[99] Hoskins and Holt fearlessly speak of the bottomless gulf of the exchequer! [100]

All this is interesting in showing the attitude of the two groups toward each other. It still does not answer the question of whether or not there is a significant connection between new forms and the opposition. Which group, if either, was "using" the com-mittees, and especially the committee of the whole? We can see how Sandys delayed progress on the Union [101] and finally upset the applecart by reopening the whole question on March 7, 1606/7.[102] We can suspect that the addition of Poole to a naturalization committee was an astute move on someone's part [103] and that a closer study would reveal scores of such cases, if we only knew more of the importance and sympathies of mem-bers. But show any consistent method in using the committee sys-tem we cannot. We can observe that opposition members more frequently than others moved for additions to committees or for committee meetings,[104] but, after all, the cases are so random that they prove little. We can infer that the committee of the whole was a device unfavorable to the crown, since it took the speaker from the chair and removed many opportunities for hiding things from the house. We must let it go at that.

From various kinds of evidence things seemed to be coming into the open—the committee of the whole, committees open to all, and the like. Those who would work and attend could be powerful. But the opposition men seem to have been no more careful about their attendance than the other members.[105] As before, most of the members who went home were persons of little importance; nevertheless both "courtiers" and "patriots" are found running off for the gout or "necessary affairs." All this is further evidence of a situation to which I have already adverted—that there were two opposing groups in the house, but neither was well organized.

This general description of the parliament of 1604 has become somewhat particular. What were its main features?

The house was a body legislating very distinctly for the realm and for its several parts, for persons and communities as well as for the monarch. With a potential membership of about 421,[106] it possibly never contained at any one time more than 340 members.[107] Many of these were so inactive that their names are hardly to be found in the journals.[108] Attendance varied considerably from day to day—members, many of whom were lawyers, were busied with other interests. In sharp contrast to Elizabethan parliaments, the house contained few privy councilors, but numbered among its members several other important officers of the crown and a large group of relatively unimportant officials and beneficiaries of the government—a numerous, but heterogeneous and unorganized following of Majesty. Toward the end of the parliament, committee work evidently became more important, though it cannot be shown that there was a quantitative increase, as judged by the number of committees or the number of members serving on them. The volume of legislation was on the increase in an absolute rather than a relative sense. It cannot be shown that the house was able to deal with more matter in a given time, but it was accomplishing more work by sitting longer. The committee of the whole house was used for the first time. There was clearly an opposition group, whose members can be identified by their speeches and by outside references. Although lacking in organization and bearing no demonstrable relation to the changes in mode of practical procedure, it had leaders who were also leaders of the house, who were making committee work their particular sphere, and who were losing no opportunity to attack the influence of the court, in speeches that would have daunted the stoutest heart in the days when "Her Gracious Majesty's" dread disfavor loomed outside the walls of St. Stephen's.

There was an opposition group in this parliament, without doubt. That there was a *party* is not so clear. In fact, that there was such a party at any time before 1628 is not clear. Men who had once been in the opposition sometimes ended their careers as courtiers, and vice versa. This shifting of sides in the case of individuals is one of the things that make the study of the civil war period at once confusing and fascinating. The men who changed sides were not always, or even generally, renegades. They were sometimes embittered, like Coke, a man who started as a courtier and ended an archrebel. They were sometimes self-seekers, like Nicholas Hyde, who started off as a "tribune of the people" in 1604 and ended as lord chief justice of king's bench in 1628. They sometimes acknowledged, according to their lights, a higher loyalty, like the "patriot," Wentworth, who gave his life for his king.

It would be interesting to know how many of the opposition men of 1604 were destined to continue in the same cause and to become "charter members" of the revolutionary party. It would be interesting to know how many were to follow what then seemed the more prudent course of conservatism, and how many had their parliamentary careers cut short. Quite naturally, most of these men of the 1604 parliament were either dead or out of politics before the great test came in 1640. At any rate, we can say whether or not they continued to be opposition men and thus to have a part in the thing which I have called the "rise of the revolutionary party."

The great "patriot" names in the house of the 1620's are those of Sir Edward Coke, Sir Robert Phelips, Sir John Eliot, and John Pym. None of these were in parliament in 1610. Nevertheless, a few of the parliamentary veterans of 1610 were still there in the 1620's, and still active, though no longer the chief leaders. Ten fairly important ones among them can be identified, of whom Wentworth, Hackwell, Noy, Sir Edwin Sandys, Digges, and Crewe were the foremost. Wentworth, son of Peter Wentworth of Elizabethan fame, was a leading troublemaker in the Spanish question. He died in 1628. Hackwell, a "patriot" in 1610, was likewise a "patriot" in 1614, and the king burned his notes on impositions. Though made solicitor general to the queen in 1617, he was at it again in 1621 and was imprisoned for his words in parliament. Continuing in opposition, he took the Covenant and held office under the Puritans. Of all those of 1610, his record is the longest and the most consistent. Noy continued a "patriot" until 1631, when he rapidly changed sides and became attorney general. Meanwhile, he had been constantly in parliament (save for that of 1614) and attacked the monopolies in 1621, defended the five knights in 1627, and fought ship money in 1628–29. Sir Edwin Sandys, the adroit old veteran, continued in opposition until 1624, despite a land grant in 1614 and despite later erroneous talk about his change of heart. He was in parliament through 1626, but not active after 1624. Sir Dudley Digges was in opposition in 1614, notwithstanding Bacon's prediction to the contrary. Made ambassador to Muscovy in 1618, he returned to the attack in 1621, opened the fight on Buckingham in 1626, helped pass the Petition of Right in 1628, and, though called a "courtier" in 1624, remained a "patriot" until 1630. Thomas Crewe did not stand up so long. He was in opposition until 1621, but turned after that parliament. He was the crown's nominee for speaker of the house in 1624.

Along with these important opposition men in the 1620's were four minor figures who had been in opposition way back before 1610 and one, Sir Robert Cotton, the antiquarian, who strangely had shown no leaning to the popular side in 1604–10, but who in 1626 joined the attack on Buckingham and remained of the same persuasion until his death in 1631. John Hoskins, imprisoned in 1614 for his words in parliament, was likewise committed after 1628. Strode, never a strong figure, was still in opposition in 1625. His real contribution to political liberalism, however, was not himself but his son, who led in the uproar of 1629 and was one of the five members sought by the king in 1642. Sir Henry Poole, who made no daring speeches in 1614, returned to opposition in 1621 and was in royal disfavor after 1626. Edward Alford, always a frequent but not very trenchant speaker, was a critic of the court in both 1614 and 1621.

It thus appears that only a few of the popular leaders of 1610 had much influence in the 1620's. Some of them, however, had kept things going in 1614 and, though they later "fell off," saw new men come up to assume leadership, along with those few of the former leaders who remained active. Let us therefore see what happened to the "patriots" in 1614.

Of those mentioned above, all but Noy were present in 1614. Important parts were apparently taken by Hoskins, Wentworth, Edwin Sandys, Crewe, Digges, and Hackwell, while Strode, Poole, and Alford were less forceful, though still in the opposition. In addition there were 11 other men from the earlier parliament who lined up against the government. Five were of small importance, John Whitson, William Jones, Sir John Sammes, Sir Herbert Crofts, who spoke little and retired to a monastery

soon after the parliament, and Sir Maurice Berkley, whose sub-
sequent history is obscure, but who by 1627 was clearly a courtier.

From the others, Whitlocke, Samuel Sandys, Owen, Hyde,
Fuller, and Duncombe, some leadership came, but for the last
time. Whitlocke was made king's sergeant in 1620, sat in parliament in 1621 but did nothing, and was made a justice of the
king's bench in 1629. Sir Samuel Sandys was present in 1621
but did nothing. Sir Roger Owen, whose notes on impositions
were burned by the king in 1614, appeared no more. Nicholas
Hyde was not in parliament in 1621, defended Buckingham in
1626, and was made lord chief justice of king's bench in 1627.
Nicholas Fuller, the voluble speaker of 1604 and 1614, was
evidently "purged" in 1621. He had been elected "as a patriot"
by London in 1614, spoke nine fiery speeches, and appears not
in 1621. Duncombe, also a vehement speaker in 1614, got a
patent from the crown in 1618, and was not in the next parliament.

Thus it appears that of the 57 greater or lesser opposition
men of the parliament of 1604–10 only 20 occupied the
same role in 1614, and about 10 in the 1620's. What happened
to the rest? One died in 1610.[109] Twenty-three did not secure
reelection in 1614.[110] This is very interesting indeed. Did the
"purge" of the elections for the Addled Parliament eliminate
the rank and file of the embryonic party? Four other men were
returned, but gave no sign of their former opposition leanings.[111]
Seven others had definitely "fallen off" and inclined to the
crown.[112] Of these, one, Sir Walter Cope, made one independent
speech in 1614. But he had been made a master of the court of
wards in 1612, and in 1615 he became keeper of the armory
and master thereof in 1625. He refused ship money in 1636.
Yet as concerns parliamentary opposition he had "fallen off"
before 1614. Sir Henry Yelverton had deserted the opposition,
just as Bacon said he had, and spoke mostly in a neutral vein in
1614 and once for the court. He did not sit in the parliament

of 1621 and later became a judge in common pleas. Sir Henry Nevill sat in 1614 but did nothing. Sir John Hollis was "lorded at 10,000" in 1616. He had spoken for the court in 1614. Sir George Moore was made chancellor of the Order of the Garter in 1611. His speeches inclined to the court in 1614, and in 1616 he became lieutenant of the Tower. In 1621 he was present but passive, and in 1624 he received another sinecure. Anthony Cope inclined to the court in 1614 and became a contractor for chantry lands. He sat no more in parliament. Sir Edward Montague was present in 1614, made one speech for the crown and none against it. In 1616 he became lord chief justice, in 1619 received a sinecure and in 1621 (*parliamento sedente*) a barony, collected ship money in 1630, and was a royalist in the civil war.

It is very plain that King James accomplished his purpose of breaking up the opposition of 1604–10. Only 20 rebels out of the original 57 were in the house of 1614. Seven former opponents of the crown had been converted, 23 had been defeated for reelection. By 1621 others had been won away, and only 10 of the original number were still in opposition.[113] But this was only the first round of the fight. Other, and more formidable, recruits had made their appearance. But let us not anticipate. The intent of these concluding pages has been only to show that the life of the Puritan "party" was to a small degree continuous, even with respect to the persons who made it up, from the first parliament of James I.

III

THE ADDLED PARLIAMENT

IN 1614 the king clearly attempted, by pressure in the elections, to break up the opposition in the house. He partially succeeded, but other recruits and leaders appeared. Their influence was exerted in debate, apparently, more than in committees. They literally broke up the parliament, and after its dissolution many of them were disciplined. As concerns the main study, the Addled Parliament represents a step forward for the opposition. To prove this, it is necessary to discuss the parliament of 1614 in general, its procedure and personnel in particular.

"The City has chosen Sir Thos. Lowe and Mr. Fuller, and refused Sir Hen. Montague as being the King's Serjeant." [1] This tells a large part of the story of the parliament. King James's second parliamentary venture on English soil—there had been a parliament in Dublin since 1613—was even less happy in its outcome than was his first. The dangerous sparks of partisan faction in the four sessions of the parliament of 1604 had not escaped the attention of king and council. The plan adopted for extinguishing them had the opposite effect of fanning them to flame. By attempting, on a large scale, to influence the elections, the government irritated the house and precipitated a debate upon returns which degenerated into a policy of obstruction. The house was by no means "addled" in defending its own traditions and privileges. In defense of them it showed forth some masters of the art of filibuster. The commons wrangled over returns and insolently weighed the subsidy in the balance with public grievances. While courtiers tried to press forward the reading of bills, members worked themselves into a frenzy over a trifling speech in the lords that had reflected upon their dignity. When the king in wrath dissolved the house, but four public acts and four private had passed. The subsidy was not among them, and none of them became law.

Had the lords of the council taken a leaf from their own experience in dealing with the Irish house of 1613, they might have profited. The first session in Dublin had been concluded nearly a year when the English house assembled. The Irish house had been broken up by a factional fight over charges of corrupt and violent elections. It was barren of any real legislative activity. Its violence and failure were known in England and were even mentioned on the floor of the house.[2] In 1614, however, the same clumsy tactics that had worked so disastrously in Ireland were used in England, and with similar results.

These two parliaments stand in a curious chronological relation to one another. For practical purposes the English parliament of 1614 antedates the Irish one of 1613, because the entire productive period of the latter falls in the two sessions of 1614 and 1615, which held after the English house had been dissolved. The violent reception accorded the dubiously elected English members in Dublin, in 1613, may easily have affected the action of the "patriots" in the English house in their hue and cry against the "Undertakers," those members elected through crown influence who were pledged to advance the crown's policy in parliament. The more important interaction of the two was undoubtedly the effect of the Addled Parliament upon the actions of the Irish house, in its last two sessions of 1614–15. That phenomenon, however, is beyond the limits of the present study.

The English parliament sat for a total of 43 days, from April 5, 1614, to June 7, 1614. It was called for the usual purpose. It was expected that the king on his part should secure, in addition to the subsidy, the naturalization of Frederick the Palatine and that the commons should secure a voluntary redress of the grievance of purveyance.[3] "Dis aliter visum"—and none of these came to pass.

For no previous parliament can as much information on elections be gathered. Seven separate return cases,[4] involving 11 members,[5] were raised upon the floor of the house. This in itself is not necessarily an indication that the council made a deliberate attempt to pack the house, for men were by this time seeking membership in the commons as an honor desirable in itself. When the individual cases are examined, there seems to be rather dubious evidence that the contesting of the elections was between a crown candidate and an opposition candidate. It may have been, in several cases, a matter of one local dignitary against another.

In Northumberland, Sir George Selby was declared ineligible by the house, on the grounds that he was sheriff in Durham. There is no other evidence of his connection with the crown, but he was probably a member of that family which had long held a responsible place on the Council of the North.[6]

Sir John Saville, one of the knights for Yorkshire, had received a free gift from the king in 1607.[7] His case was dropped by the commons—it is merely mentioned as one of those to which attention was called by the constituencies.

Sir John Cuttes and Sir Thomas Chicheley, knights for Cambridge, appear to have been "Undertakers" and as such were challenged. Their election was supported, however, by the findings of the house. Neither of them was a man of importance, nor did either have any connection with the crown.

In the case of King's Lynn, the only information in the journal to account for the contested return is that one of the members returned himself as mayor. Neither Matthew Clerke nor Thomas

Oxenbridge, the members for the place, were men of any note.

Thomas Berry, of Ludlow, was expelled because he had returned himself as bailiff. He was an unimportant figure.

Complaint, upon some ground that cannot be determined, was made of Sir Robert Maunsell, knight for Carmarthen, but no action was taken. Sir Robert was a man of consequence in government, treasurer of the navy.

In the most interesting case of all, that of Stockbridge, in Hants, Sir Thomas Parry, chancellor of the duchy and a member of the privy council, was removed from the house for interfering with the election, and the two men wrongfully elected, Sir Henry Wallop and Sir Walter Cope, were ultimately expelled. Sir Walter was a master of the court of wards,[8] and a public registrar for commerce,[9] while Sir Henry Wallop was the son of the former lord justice in Ireland [10] and had himself been sheriff before this time in Hampshire and Shropshire.[11]

Certain it is that members openly charged on the floor and in committee that "Undertakers" had been active.[12]

A few invaluable scraps of evidence left by contemporaries outside parliament point much more clearly to the conclusion that the government made a deliberate attempt to influence the elections. At least there seems to have been a partisan issue. Sir Anthony Weldon, in his scurrilous little *Court and Character of King James I,* intimates that the lords were packed.[13] This is, of course, only indirect evidence on the matter of elections, but it reveals, if true, a policy with regard to parliament as a whole. John Chamberlain informed Sir Dudley Carleton that the undue exertion of pressure by great persons had worked to the disadvantage of the king in the elections [14] and described a scene in the election at Uxbridge in which an agent of Sir Francis Drury frankly stated the king's command with regard to the voting.[15] The same correspondence reveals that in the London elections Nicholas Fuller had won the day over Sir Henry Montague because the latter was the king's sergeant.[16]

There are fewer names on the roll for 1614 than for 1604, because parliament sat for a shorter time and did not require new elections to fill the places of men who had died. Yet somewhat more names of men connected in some way with court appear in 1614 than in the preceding parliament—133 in 1604 and 144 in 1614.[17] This, together with the large turnover of seats, to which more exact reference will presently be made, points again to a partisan rather than a haphazard campaign.

It has long been thought by students of English parliamentary history that the elections to the Addled Parliament were manipulated.[18] I am not aware that the matter of patronage among its members has been previously analyzed, nor does the present analysis [19] lay claim to completeness. The results of it simply bear out what has been suspected all along. The similarity in the descriptions of the Irish elections of 1613 and the English election in 1614 and the relatively large number of return cases dealt with in each house point with remarkable clarity to a government policy in the matter—a plan of attack adopted *after* the conclusion of the parliament of 1604 and applied (with ill success) in both Ireland and England.

This mass of unworkable evidence on the matter of elections requires at this point a word of comment. Any student of contemporary politics is aware that, even with the facilities of the modern press, official records, and statistics at his disposal, he can hardly hope to arrive at the whole truth with regard to electioneering processes. How much more hopeless is the task here! The entries in the journal, upon specific cases, certainly do not show a concerted effort on the part of the government. The journal for this parliament, however, abounds in deletions and ill-reported debate that baffles the student. The references of outsiders hint at a government campaign, but very clearly bear the earmarks of rumor. The Irish elections of 1613 confirm one's suspicions, but prove nothing. One stone has been left to turn—the talk in the house itself about the "Undertakers." [20] There was in the commons a group of men who believed that the government had tried to pack the house, or who affected to believe it, in order to obstruct business. Elections were an issue, regardless of the validity of the accusations. They were one of the "bones" flung in to disturb the session.

What kind of a house of commons resulted from these elections about which so much is said and so little known? The list, which is incomplete and not official,[21] bears the names of 433 members, after removing double returns. From the names of individuals mentioned by name in the journal as speaking or serving on committee, only 264 members can be identified, but it may be said with reasonable certainty that at least 400 men attended at some time or other, for there is a recorded division of 389.[22] The remarkable thing in the personnel of the house is that an unusually high proportion of its members were entirely new to parliament. Gardiner estimates—and all statements on this subject must be called estimates, even for the years for which returns are available—that 300 members were new men [23] and explains it in terms of England's resentment at arbitrary government and the supposed attempt on the part of the council to tamper with elections. An independent check of the list with those of preceding parliaments shows exactly the same figure. A total of 463 men [24] were returned, apparently, of whom 163 had been in parliament before, most of them in the one preceding. Here at least is the sharp break in the continuity of membership which was sought in vain in the attempt to explain the changes from 1592 to 1610. Assuming the estimates to be approximately correct, the Addled Parliament contained 65 percent new men,[25] as compared with 40 percent in 1604, 42 percent in 1601, 46 percent in 1597, and 40 percent in 1592. Gardiner's hypothesis that the elections were England's answer to tyranny would be strikingly upheld if it could be shown that the new men, as a group, did something to oppose the crown. As full an interpretation as is warranted by the evidence will presently be made of the activities of groups and individuals in the house. In passing, it may be said that the offenders of 1614 were mainly the same old leaders of 1604. The new members spoke very little and did not lay themselves open to the royal displeasure. The elections, and the talk about them, may have been of great importance in giving spirit to the opposition, but they did not give it new leadership.

The government was represented by 4 members of the privy council [26] and by a total of 142 members connected in varying degrees of effectiveness with the court.[27] The crown had practically the same sort of following that it had in 1604. Sir Ralph Winwood now, as principal secretary of state, instead of Sir Francis Bacon, was the spearhead of the official attack—and a blunt one he proved to be. The old "patriots" were badly shaken up by the elections and defections, though their chief leaders were still present.[28] The courtiers, swelled somewhat by the accession of a few second-rate officeholders, were worse organized than before. Bacon had become very petulant,[29] while Winwood was inexperienced and spoke seldom. The opposition was to hold the floor even as it had in Ireland the preceding year.

Upon assembling, March 5, the commons proceeded to a regular and orderly election of the man chosen by the council for speaker.[30] Almost immediately an attack was made on Bacon's eligibility, since he had been made attorney general since the last parliament. This dragged on for three days.[31] A number of contested returns were raised on April 9, some of which hung fire and were debated intermittently almost to the end of the session.[32] The Bills of Grace, prepared by the council and intended as a concession to the malcontents, were introduced April 11,[33] opening the way for an endless debate on grievances and especially calling attention to the government's failure to renounce the right to impose. On the following day, dramatically enough, Sir Hugh Middleton offered a bill against impositions,[34] and Secretary Winwood opened the debate on the subsidy.[35]

wever, would not long allow the matter of supply to
ntion and diverted the debate to a reconsideration of
nd grievances.[36] Now, from April 12 to May 9, fol-
hodgepodge of distracted debate on bills public and
pr.... on privilege, and on grievances.[37] Having failed to oust
Bacon on a technicality, the "patriots" succeeded in expelling
Parry, after a hot three days' partisan quarrel, for his alleged
complicity in a corrupt election in Stockbridge.[38] Then followed
further debate on privilege and the "Undertakers." [39] The
greatest "bone" of all was about to be thrown in. From May 25
to May 30 the house was almost exclusively occupied with its
own indignation at certain words of Bishop Neile of Lincoln,
who had impeached the loyalty of the commons in a speech
uttered in the house of lords.[40] On June 7 came the dissolution.
Shortly thereafter the king gave vent to his displeasure by tearing the bills in the presence of members of the house,[41] by
requiring Samuel and Edwin Sandys, Sir Roger Owen, Sir
Dudley Digges, Thomas Crewe, William Hackwell, and several
others not named to bring in their notes on impositions to be
burned,[42] by confining Sir James Perrott, Sir Edward Giles, and
Digges to London,[43] and by imprisoning John Hoskins, Sir
Christopher Nevill, Sir Thomas Wentworth,[44] and James Whitlocke [45] in the Tower, for their part in parliament.

Edged in between more exciting activities, a little legislative
work was accomplished. In fact, it is astonishing to discover how
much work had been laid out for this group of men who have
gone down in history as the parliament that accomplished nothing.
No less than 105 bills had a first reading, while 54 were read
a second time, and 9 a third. Eight were duly passed. In all,
67 committees were appointed, of which 58 were to deal with
bills.[46] In spite of the brave beginning in real work, it is per-
fectly clear that the interest of the house—at least of the articulate
part of the house—was not in the business of legislation. Of the
966 speeches recorded, only 318 were connected with bills, and

54 with the subsidy (which never was put in the form of a bill), while 438, or 45 percent of the total, dealt with returns, privilege, or the dignity of the house itself. A remnant of 156 defy classification.

Procedure, while tedious to trace, is a necessary part of the whole picture of party growth. It is much less important in 1614 than in the preceding parliament, since the new devices were less used by the "patriots," who relied chiefly on the filibuster to achieve their ends. Yet it must be briefly examined.

This parliament shows some rather marked changes in procedure, but changes whose importance it is difficult to estimate, because of the abnormal nature of the whole session. When a parliament succeeds in dealing with less than half of the work laid out for it and devotes a great part of its time to wrangling, it is obvious that the evidence bearing on procedure can be nothing more than a "sample." Especially in the interesting matter of committee work, tabulation is almost useless, since half of the bills never advanced to the committee stage and a relatively small number were reported back to the house.

The established rule for readings was adhered to. Debate followed the second reading and not the first. A single bill had two consecutive readings.[47] Commitment was invariably at second reading. As in 1604, there was no regularity with regard to the time at which a bill could be dashed.[48] It was voted as a rule that no motion should pass the house without a question [49] and that no bill should have its second reading before 9 A.M.[50] Aside from these and some temporary rules on the order of the day,[51] nothing of importance was spread upon the journal to affect procedure. Procedure seems to have approached a step further toward regularity, but there was a conspicuous absence of that interest in rules, especially governing the speaker's functions, which had characterized the session of 1603–4 and to some extent the whole parliament of 1604–10. Few petitions were presented by outside persons, and no provision had been made for hearing counsel at the bar or in committee, no doubt because few bills went beyond second reading.

It is futile, for reasons already stated, to compare the volume of committee work in 1614 with that of preceding parliaments. A ratio between committees and days of sitting could very easily be prepared, but it would have no meaning because parliament was broken off before it had fully organized itself for legislative work. Its few committees were appointed in the same old way as before,[52] reports were made as before, and the schedule of sittings, imperfect as it was left by the clerk, shows no significant change.[53] An analysis of membership and of the number of those serving on committees, although it is necessarily inexact, shows several interesting tendencies, interesting, that is, in comparison with a corresponding analysis of the last session of the preceding parliament.

COMMITTEES IN 1609–10 AND IN 1614

	Total No. of Committees	Under 15 Members	15–30 Members	31–60 Members	61–100 Members	101–50 Members	Over 150 Members	Indeterminate Committees [a]
1609–10	162	21%	35%	28%	9%	2%	2%	21%
1614	67	7.5%	25%	28%	6%	10%	1.5%	25%

	Total No. of Committees	Whole House	Men Serving	Average No. of Committees for Those Serving	Ratio (Men to Committees)
1609–10	162	0	325	11.2	2.00
1614	67	7.5%	246	5.3	3.72

[a] By "indeterminate" committees I mean those which included members designated in groups (as "all knights of the shires" or "all lawyers of the house"). In some cases the number thus included can be ascertained, so that the size of the committee, or at least its potential size, can be estimated. The "indeterminate" column, however, includes all those committees which included group appointments. Hence the columns total somewhat more than 100%. This has been done in order to show the trend in committee size and also the proportion of the committees that were constituted in this elastic fashion.

It cannot be said too often that countings and tabulations are not to be trusted in this work, when used alone. In this parliament, for example, there are several committees whose function is not stated, and several more whose function is stated but whose membership is not indicated. Then too, one cannot be sure that the parliament of 1614 would have continued to multiply its committees, had its life been longer, for already it had shown some tendency to assign several subjects to one committee,[54] a practice that had not hitherto been followed except in the case of the committee of privilege. In spite of all these doubts and unavoidable errors, the foregoing charts reveal several things.

The work of committees was spreading out, at least theoretically.[55] The ratio obtained by dividing the number of men serving on committees (or qualified by blanket appointment to serve on them) by the total number of committees was 2.00 in 1609–10 and 3.72 in 1614. That is, in proportion to the number of committees appointed in 1614 there were actually more men designated to serve, although the number appointed by name was much smaller than in 1609–10. At the same time, the average number of committees that each man serving was entitled to attend declined from 11.2 in 1609–10 to 5.3 in 1614. These two facts considered together tend to show that the process of taking more members into counsel in committees was going forward at the time that James I unceremoniously brought everything to a halt.

In keeping with this development, which was in reality a pushing of debate back into the committee room, is a very perceptible tendency to make the committees larger and more open. There is an increase from 21 percent to 25 percent in the number of committees thrown open to "all lawyers," "all who will come," or the whole house. For the first time specific subjects were committed, at the outset and before any select committees had worked upon them, to the committee of the whole house, with a definite time and place assigned. One other innovation looking in the same direction was the practice of appointing to a committee "all who had spoken."

It is, unfortunately, impossible to tell how many members attended committee meetings or who dominated them. There are no complaints, as there were in the preceding parliament, of a lack of quorum at committees. In fact, if one may judge by the divisions,[56] it would seem clear that there was a much livelier interest in the affairs of the house than before—perhaps because of the larger proportion of new members and undoubtedly because of the controversial and partisan nature of business. One other phase of committee work throws light on its importance. That is the practice of acting directly and favorably on the committee report, without debate. Out of 34 committee reports in 1614, 19 were acted upon without debate, and of the 15 upon which there was debate, only 4 were connected with bills. The others dealt with privilege, petitions, or the like. In 1609-10 there was a much higher proportion of reports on bills (in comparison, that is, with reports on other matters), and about 50 percent of them were debated.

A few scattering references strengthen the conviction that committees were being regarded more and more as the logical place for doing the real work on bills. Evidence and arguments were submitted to committees of which the house itself never heard.[57] The lawyers were urged, not necessarily to improve their attendance at debate, but to avail themselves of their wholesale appointment on the committee for impositions, that their technical knowledge might expedite the labors thereof.[58] Mr. Brooke urged that they debate the impositions no more, but leave it to the committees.[59] Much more frequently than ever before members interrupted debate with the motion that the matter in hand be referred to a committee. Bacon reported, April 11, from an afternoon committee of the whole house that most of the members had attended.[60] Apparently those "who will come" did attend at open select committees, for Edward Duncombe, on April 19, "Moveth, a Committee may have authority to speak, at a Committee, before another, not of the Committee." [61] The house had not, because of its use of the committee of the whole in the place of a select committee, abandoned the practice of suddenly "resolving itself" into that form in the course of debate. We find a good example of it on May 19.[62] Yet, unless much has been left out of the journal, there is good evidence that, though the committee of the whole house was used more than in 1609–10, it was by announcement and in the role of a select committee, rather than spontaneously and as a device for loosening debate at a regular sitting. Perhaps the house had not really "discovered" the device completely as yet. This is an interesting thought, in view of the total absence of the committee of the whole house in Ireland a few months later.

It has been suggested that there was in all probability a close connection between the rise of the commons to a place of importance in the government (along with the simultaneous rise to power in the commons of an opposition group) and the change in practical procedure which resulted in the increased use of committees. That aspect of the Addled Parliament will be examined in its place.

With regard to procedure itself, the following can be said. The spontaneous inclination to turn to the committee as a natural first step in proceeding upon all sorts of business, legislative and otherwise, stands out from nearly every page of the journal for 1614, and the work of the committees was accepted, in the legislative matters, with less debate and comment than ever before. In addition, a relatively larger number of members were taking part in committee work. The tradition that a few should be allowed to do all the work and serve on committees without end was declining, and at the same time committees were continuing to become more and more open—auxiliaries rather than ancillaries of the house itself. This is but a continuation of the development remarked in 1609–10.

All this is a mere matter of observation. A much more interesting task is that of examining the traces of initiative in the house and of leadership of the two distinct groups within it.

Although this study is primarily concerned with the rise of a partisan group within the house, the stirrings of the house itself are interesting and significant as a concurrent phenomenon. Any evidence in 1614 of the continuance of that corporate self-consciousness of past years should therefore be noted. This quality is especially interesting because, without any doubt, the Irish house of 1613–15 imitated it. It is, however, a force peculiarly difficult to appraise. Those displays of interest in the "liberties" of the house, which in other sessions gave a clue to the strength of feeling, were in 1614 mixed with partisan strategy and well-planned obstruction. Three incidents, or series of incidents, appear at first sight to betoken a lively concern for the dignity of the house itself, but become more complicated upon examination. They must be considered separately.

In primis, a number of return cases were dealt with, and so far as the journal tells, it might well be the same old story of the house "expressing" itself in a sphere over which tradition had given it exclusive competency. Other evidence, however, shows that in all probability there was a partisan issue in the whole matter of elections, especially in the one for Stockbridge, involving Parry, Wallop, and Cope. Yet when one looks to the individual speeches that concern Parry's part in the election, the interpretation along partisan lines meets a shock, in the discovery that government men, even Secretary Winwood [63] and Sir Thomas Lake,[64] joined in the attack on the chancellor of the duchy. This was one of those strange cases in which loyalty to the body of which they were members (and loyalty to certain axioms of good government) fought it out in the breasts of courtiers with a meaner loyalty to party, and won. In view of Lake's reputation, as well as the cases of Bacon, Coke, Cranfield, Essex, and Raleigh—all victims of a low code of political morality—one can hardly believe it. This, like the other return cases, was a party strife. At the end, courtiers shamelessly joined those who were howling for Parry's ruin, but only after they had discovered that the case had been so thoroughly aired that there was no hope of escape. They had best save what they could of their popularity and influence by a gesture for the right.

On May 16 a "Mr. Martyn" (not the Henry Marten who, as a member of the house in 1609-10, had been an active leader of the opposition) spoke at the bar as attorney for the Virginia Company. Exception was taken by Sir Edward Montague to the words spoken by Martyn about the house,[65] and there ensued a spirited debate upon the respect due the commons. Martyn was finally compelled to make his submission at the bar. Was this incident what it appeared to be, or was it a move to obstruct business? Or again, was it merely a matter of personalities? I believe it was the clearest case in the whole parliament of the house rising to maintain its dignity—and nothing more. It was introduced by a man friendly to the court, and members of the "patriot" faction seemed little interested in prolonging the debate, as they did later in the Bishop of Lincoln case.

The case just referred to concerned the interpretation put by Bishop Neile upon words spoken by Sir Thomas Wentworth. The ostensible purpose of the agitation in the house was to secure from the lord bishop a retraction of his offensive remarks, in order to clear, not Wentworth, but the house as a whole, of the aspersion upon its loyalty. This probably had very little to do with the whole matter. The case flared up for a few days, with "patriots" doing the bulk of the speaking, and then died down.[66] The house took up its legislative work again for a single day, but Sir Roger Owen would not let the old "bone" rest, while Sir Walter Chute, Sir Robert Phelips, Sir Maurice Berkley, Edward Duncombe, and other malcontents eagerly returned to the fretting of it.[67] The long discussion of the incident, the predominance of opposition members in the debate, and above all the direct allusions in the journal to a frank obstructionist policy of certain members [68] rob the whole affair of its color as a battle of principle and put it upon the level of undignified party tactics.

A number of petty incidents or speeches bear feeble witness to the group consciousness in question. The session was a disorderly one,[69] resembling that of 1601 or the first session in Ireland in 1613, and a few ineffective gestures for decorum were made.[70] There was a bit of righteous indignation at the courtiers' bearing of tales to the king,[71] but this may have been partisan in motive. Sir George Moore voiced a rather lofty sentiment when he spoke of the corporate responsibility of the house to the country.[72] The importance of the official record was several times alluded to,[73] but without effect, for it has survived for this parliament only in the most primitive form, expurgated and incomplete.[74]

In fine, the house was much less concerned with itself than it had been in the preceding parliament—much less concerned with what the house was than with what it could do for or against the prerogative. However, this fact may have escaped contemporaries, and even some members of the house. The returns cases, the Martyn affair, and the dispute with the lords had all the external characteristics of a determined fight for the liberties of the commons. If the Irish house in 1615 displayed some of these same characteristics, it is entirely possible that they were copied from the Addled Parliament quite as much as from the parliament of 1604. What was not as apparent then as now was the presence of those two groups in the house whose differentiation had been going on for years. The tactics of these groups in 1614 were different from their tactics in 1604.

From various sources one can identify a number of men on each side. By examining all sorts of correspondence and memoranda in the *Calendars of State Papers Domestic*, 142 members have been discovered who had some connection with the government.[75] The relations noted vary from principal secretary of state to clerkships or even financial transactions with the crown. Some of them, no doubt, were not of a very binding character. Not quite half of the offices or favors were conferred between the dissolution of 1610 and that of 1614—some 54 between the two parliaments and 12 during the Addled Parliament. It is certainly not within the scheme of this general study to make an interpretation of the large subject of patronage in parliament. Very probably an extensive canvass would uncover many more connections with the government than have been found in the *Calendars of State Papers*. My present concern is to find an answer with reasonable accuracy to a single practical question— the question of whether or not this group of officeholders and beneficiaries constituted a party within the house. The answer found in the record of members' speeches is clearly negative. Patronage did not succeed in building a party. Nearly all the members of the group of 142 were singularly passive in debate. Only 4 [76] of them showed sufficient partisan zeal to qualify them as leaders of the court faction. Eight more seem to have inclined somewhat to the official point of view in their speeches,[77] but even one of those was disciplined, after the dissolution, for some allegedly disloyal activity which is not apparent from the journal.[78] Five of the group [79] were outstanding leaders of the opposition, and 8 more [80] showed some leaning to that side. Not much can be said for the organization of the "defense." Bacon, Caesar, Lake, Winwood, Sir George Moore, Sir Edward and Sir Henry Montague—these were the only court men who spoke much. Of course, there were other court members who could be depended on in divisions, but we cannot tell who they were. They were an inarticulate quantity, and passive.

The leaders of the contrary-minded are easier to discover. From references outside the journal it is plain that Giles,[81] Digges,[82] Thomas Crewe,[83] Perrott,[84] Sir Samuel Sandys, Sir Edwin Sandys, Owen, Hackwell,[85] Phelips,[86] Sir Christopher Nevill,[87] Hoskins,[88] and Wentworth [89] were identified with the faction that opposed the government. From the record of speeches in the journal it also appears that Alford, Sir John Ashley, Sir Maurice Berkley, Christopher Brooke, Sir Herbert Crofts, Duncombe, Fuller, and Sir William Strode were "patriots." It will be of interest to see how they effected their obstruction.

The qualifying remarks that have been made about the importance of committee memberships apply to this parliament as to the others. Furthermore, leadership in committees was probably of less importance in 1614 because the whole legislative side of the parliament was stunted. Even so, if one side or the other was able to dominate in a form of organization such as that of the committees, it shows that that side had superior vigor and leadership. Moreover, if the parliament had continued, there is no doubt that a very considerable advantage would have accrued from the control of committees. Not knowing exactly what went on in the committee room, we cannot say with assurance that either group dominated there, but evidence points strongly to the superiority of the followers of Sandys and Fuller. The "patriots" were more successful in getting themselves appointed. Of course a number of committees were nearly open, but when the same score or so of men were appointed by name, time after time, these must have been the men who actually came and did the work. A list of the big committee men is significant.

MOST ACTIVE COMMITTEE MEMBERS

Court		Patriot			
G. Moore	23	Owen	29	Duncombe	15
E. Montague	21	Alford	26	Crofts	14
Winwood	15	E. Sandys	23	E. Hobby	14
Lake	14	Digges	21	Berkley	13
Caesar	13	Fuller	21	Phelips	13
Bacon	8	Hackwell	20	Crewe	12
A. Cope	7	C. Brooke	19	Perrott	10
Finch	6	Sammes	18	Wentworth	6
H. Montague	5	Horsey	17	Anderson	3
Chute	4	J. Ashley	16	S. Sandys	3
Reynolds	3	Hoskins	16	C. Nevill	2
W. Cope	1	Strode	16	Giles	1

The record of reports made from the committees to the house gives the best evidence available as to leadership in committees. Again, the leadership of the opposition is apparent. Out

MEMBERS REPORTING FROM COMMITTEES

Member Reporting	Sympathies	No. of Reports
E. Sandys	Opposition	8
Fuller	Opposition	7
Owen	Opposition	4
Davies	Doubtful	2
F. Moore	Doubtful	2
Poole	Doubtful	2
Bacon	Court	1
Finch	Court	1
E. Montague	Court	1
H. Montague	Court	1
Glanville	Doubtful	1
Mallett	Doubtful	1
C. Brooke	Opposition	1
Hackwell	Opposition	1
Hoskins	Opposition	1

of 34 reports, 22 were made by men of the opposition, as opposed to 4 by men of the court party. Over half of the total were made by three individuals, all of them very definite "patriots"—Fuller, Sandys, and Owen. Why should these three men, who were also among the most frequent speakers of the house, have been chosen to report? Presumably it was because their influence carried over into the committee chamber. It was no coincidence. The opposition men were dominating the committees due to the greater activity of their leaders. Sandys and Fuller were no more able than Bacon, but they had the advantage of being free from outside occupations. Besides, Bacon had lost his influence with members of the house,[90] and there were no leaders to take his place.[91]

The real work of this parliament, however, was not in committees, as was that of the parliament of 1604. It was on the floor. Here, again, the "patriots" shone. In a total of 966 speeches delivered, 171 were of sufficiently partisan nature that they can be classified as for or against the government. Of these, 109 were made in opposition, and 62 in support of the court policy. It is unsatisfactory to attempt a count of the speeches made by members of the two groups, because so few of the court followers are known that an exaggerated notion of the opposition influence would result. What can be made, however, is a list of the most frequent speakers, which again shows a considerable advantage for the opposition.

MOST FREQUENT SPEAKERS

Court Group	No. of Speeches	Opposition Group	No. of Speeches
G. Moore	33	Fuller	53
H. Montague	20	Alford	40
		Owen	30
		Digges	29
		Ashley	25
		E. Sandys	25
		Brooke	23
		Hoskins	22
		Duncombe	20
		Horsey	20

Enough has been said of the work of committees, of rules, and of the general history of the parliament to indicate that the speaking on the floor was the determining factor in the failure to achieve any positive results. In this speaking there was some strategy. Again the opponents of the crown bore off the palm. Speaker Crewe, like his unfortunate predecessor, tried to lend his weight to the service of the king, with indifferent success. He was distinctly a partisan, and later had his reward.[92] We know that on one occasion at least he interfered with a reading [93] and that on another he tried to prevent a division.[94] He was accused, probably with reason, of bearing tales to the king.[95] But Crewe was a weak presiding officer,[96] and his feeble attempts were not enough. Other courtiers tried repeatedly to keep the commons at work and especially to secure action on the subsidy.[97] Gardiner has traced with care the important speeches of the session. What he has not pointed out (and he needed not to remark it in his running account of the period) is the strategic quality of some of these speeches. It would be ridiculous to interpret the journal as an account of one long obstructionist campaign. Men of both sides worked together on a number of things, and the "patriots" frequently moved for the expedition of business. But the fact remains that it was Duncombe, Alford, and Owen who opened the attack on Bacon[98] and Owen who raised the hue and cry over "Undertakers" when Bacon was trying to press the bills of grace. When Perrott first introduced the subsidy debate, Fuller was the one who immediately warned the house to adopt Fabian tactics. When the subsidy debate was well under way, it was Owen again who interrupted with a question of privilege and Fuller and Brooke who interrupted on the following day. Alford was the man who moved to continue with other legislation, rather than give the right of way to the bills of grace. Thomas Wentworth (member from Oxford), Strode, and Fuller enthusiastically dragged out the old issue of impositions, almost at the end of the session, when the subsidy had been wearily reopened by Sir Thomas Roe and Moore.

These few moves were not accidental. The opposition men were not interested in obstructing all legislation. In fact, many of the public bills were brought forward by them. Their principal concern was to prevent the subsidy from passing unless they secured a satisfactory act on impositions.[99] Their obstruction was designed to wear down the courtiers—instead it resulted in a premature dissolution. Some contemporaries believed that there had been a plot from the outset to bring parliament to the same sort of conclusion actually reached. Hoskins was thought to have been "planted" by Northampton to throw in a "bone" and thus interfere with debate and exasperate the king.[100] Sir

Jerome Horsey and Samuel Sandys evidently felt that something of the sort had been attempted.[101] However that may be, it seems extremely unlikely that any considerable number of members had any such object in view. They would not talk of subsidy until they were assured of a *quid pro quo*. They would, and did, clutter up debate with irrelevant and hostile proposals and discussion to compass their end. The obvious leaders of the anticourt group were in the van. The journal, however, bears witness to a rather sincere effort on their part to proceed with business within this limit.

Of the general characteristics of this parliament little more can be said. It was a group of men relatively inexperienced, assembled under conditions that gave them from the start a suspicious attitude toward the government. It was a parliament primarily of speaking, rather than of committee work, and the influence was wielded by those who came forward in debate. Self-assertive and boisterous, it paid great attention, whether genuine or not, to the things that pertained to its own dignity. It lacked close party organization, so far as can be learned, but the opposition had become bolder and more influential. Obstruction was deliberately and successfully attempted by a small group whose collaboration may have been better planned than appears on the surface.

What of the "party" in 1614—its gains and losses of "members" and its tendency to acquire a more definite and discernible character? It has already been shown that the king succeeded fairly well in breaking up the opposition group of 1609–10.[102] Twenty-three of these men were defeated for reelection or for some other reason were not returned. One died. Four who were returned assumed a passive attitude, and 7 threw their weight on the side of the court.

What, then, was the nature of that group of men who, if not a party, were at least sufficiently determined and sufficiently cooperative with one another to bring the parliament of 1614 to

naught and to bring down the wrath of James upon its members?
Had we been able to sit for but an hour in old St. Stephen's
we could have known for certain who were the few men who
led the opposition—whose voices commanded attention and whose
opinions were not argued by the other "patriots." As it is, we
must rely upon such evidence as the number of speeches, the
displeasure of the king, and gossip. From these, something like
the following situation among the opposition emerges.

Twenty-two rather obscure members are found who spoke
once in a vein that favored the opposition, but who could certainly not be said to be clearly partisan.[103] In fact, 4 of them
also spoke in a contrary vein on occasion,[104] and even Secretary
Winwood made one speech apparently opposing the crown's policy. Twelve of these men had been in the preceding parliament,
and 10 were new. One of them, Nicholas Hyde, had been important in 1610. Very little can be concluded about speeches, except
in the records of those who spoke frequently and who spoke
almost always against the government. From these and from the
list of men whose notes were confiscated after parliament and
from the men who were imprisoned or who were mentioned in
outside writings as having been of the opposition came, we assume,
the leaders.

There were about 19 such men.[105] Five—Digges, Sir Edwin
Sandys, Hackwell, Fuller, and Sir Thomas Wentworth—had
been important leaders in the opposition of 1609–10. These,
then, were the continuing nucleus and central strength. Five other
men, who had been relatively unimportant figures in 1610, assumed a large burden of debate against the crown now. These
were Edward Alford, Sir Roger Owen, Christopher Brooke,
John Hoskins, and Edward Duncombe, recruits, as it were, from
the passive to the active wing. Five more, Sir James Perrott, Sir
Samuel Sandys, Sir Herbert Crofts, Sir Christopher Nevill,
Sir James Whitlocke, were minor figures in the parliament
of 1604, but clearly identified with the opposition in 1614—

less articulate than the preceding 5, but in the role of secondary leaders. Three more, Sir Edward Giles, Sir Robert Phelips, and Sir Walter Chute, were in parliament for the first time. One of them, Phelips, was destined to become a power in the opposition of the 1620's. Sir Thomas Crewe, whose defection was predicted by Bacon, evidently stood, at this point, midway in his descent from independence to grace. He spoke several times for the court, yet had his notes confiscated and burned after parliament. We shall no longer include him among the "patriots."

In addition to the major and minor leaders we can make out rather indistinctly a group of 8 "followers," clearly marked as partisan, but not very active—Sir Henry Anderson, Sir John Ashley, Sir Maurice Berkley, Sir Edward Hobby, Sir Jerome Horsey, Sir Henry Poole, Sir John Sammes, and Sir William Strode. All but Anderson and Ashley had been in the preceding parliament. Poole, once an active speaker, was relatively unimportant in 1614.

To summarize, the leadership of the hostile faction consisted of 5 unpurged and "unreconstructed" old parliament men, Sandys, Digges, Hackwell, Fuller, and Wentworth, joined by one new member of first-rate energy and ability, Phelips. Of the remaining 22 partisans, 17 were old parliament men, and 5 were new members. No quantitative estimate of gains and losses at this point can have much value in the exact sense. If 28 men of 1610 had been lost by defeat, death, or defection, 15 new members had swung to the popular side, and 5 rather unimportant figures of the preceding parliament had taken on greater responsibility in the "cause." It was now certain that James could not kill the opposition. While its recuperation was by no means phoenixlike, it at least survived James's very determined attempt to destroy it and, largely under its old leaders, proved even more effective in obstruction than the group of four years before.

IV

THE LOW POINT

OF CONCERTED OPPOSITION

1621

IN the muddled, turbulent 1620's much English constitutional history was made. The house struck a defiant posture, the image of which was to remain before the patriots of the angry thirties like the afterglow of a quickly extinguished light. The constitutional issues which, merging with religious ones, produced the civil war appeared in clear outline before 1629. They had not, however, become entirely distinct in the lifetime of James. It even seemed, at the point of his death, that a wiser treatment of parliament, learned from his costly early blunders, had checked the growth of the opposition and driven it into decline.

An appraisal of this falling off in 1621 and in 1624 requires some consideration of the general politics of the time and of the general history of the two parliaments. To show that procedure was not at this point very closely linked to partisan activity—as it certainly was not—requires that procedure be examined again and the negative evidence set forth.

The attitude of a single citizen toward his government is a mixture of sentiments colored by his varying opinions on divers problems and policies. The attitude of a whole people is an infinitely more baffling composite of thousands or millions of states of mind. The years that preceded the summoning of the parliament of 1621 illustrate this fact well. In some respects England was backing the crown. In many more it was, in the bulk of its citizenry, hostile. Foreign policy, religious prejudice, and corruption furnish the key to the unsettled times.

James had determined to assist his son-in-law in the recovery of the Palatinate. This looked like a vigorous anti-Catholic policy and was popular, for it gave promise of a return to the good old nationalist ideas of the days of Elizabeth, with sea fights and plunder and virile English bluster against a traditional foe. On the other hand, James had already conceived his role of the great peacemaker and was dallying with the idea of a Spanish marriage for Charles. In our day, this could be styled "un-English," and Englishmen of 1621 considered it so. The nation was also dissatisfied with various matters of domestic policy. It would have liked to see the recusants more severely dealt with. It was tired of being gouged by monopolists whose special privileges had been shamelessly purchased from the crown by deals over, or under, the counter. There was grave suspicion that functions of government, particularly in the courts, were being made the object of financial transactions. And finally, James's private life and court allowed room for adverse criticism by those Puritans who, for other reasons, were only too willing to believe ill of him. Parliament members brought with them to St. Stephen's all this mix-up of feelings. There were many things that needed legislative action. Many private bills were on their minds, and matters of trade policy, legal processes, and the like. They were not angry over elections as they had been in 1614. They were ready to support the king against the Catholics. Yet there were a number of grievances that they wished to see abolished.

As early as 1615 there had been talk of summoning a parliament for purposes of revenue.[1] But the guilty consciences of courtiers and the king's sour recollections of his last encounter seem to have killed the idea.[2] In 1616 the talk subsided,[3] only to revive in 1617.[4] In 1618, Contarini, the Venetian ambassador, reported that James, hard pressed for funds, was still reluctant to allow the representatives of his dissatisfied people to begin again their mouthings of high affairs of state.[5] It was a matter of necessity rather than choice that finally brought the house together on January 16, 1620/1. One is almost reminded of the advantageous position of the Short Parliament.

"The first Parliament somm opposed the King and broke that. The next the same men undertooke for him and broke that two. Take heed of such interruptions, but lett us all goe on so as may most redoune to his content, the kingdoms good, Gods glory." These hopeful words of Sir Lionel Cranfield were certainly tinged with irony as they were uttered November 21, 1621.[6] Yet on March 27 past, James had deigned to be jocular in his knighting of Speaker Richardson.[7] In May, Sir Edwin Sandys referred to the "Unitie talked of in all this Country and in Christendom between the houses and us and the King, and God forbid that ther showld be any breach betweene us." [8] But by the end of that same month disorderly outbursts were interfering with speeches,[9] a diarist made the laconic entry "Passionate speeches," [10] and the author of the Belassis diary discretely omitted the names of speakers from his record.[11]

This house of commons was not at all like that of 1614 in temper or activity. Although it left scarcely a trace upon the statute book, it was quite continuously busied with legislation. It quarreled over its privileges, but it did not deliberately obstruct business. It was called to finance the king's foreign policy. It had 101 actual days of sitting and imposed upon itself 19 afternoon sittings, more than any previous house had endured. The journal shows that at least 380 persons were actually present at some time or other.[12] The largest recorded division was 357.[13] An examination of the returns shows that 175 of the members had served in 1614 and that 205 had served either then or in 1604. The number of new members was thus a little lower than in 1614, when only 163 old members were returned.

Naturally, what the king wanted of parliament was money, although he later expressed himself as willing to "give the royal assent to anything really for the general good." [14] The only statutes resulting from the parliament were the subsidies of the clergy and the temporality.[15] This, however, was not the fault of the house. A considerable number of bills were passed, and a number more committed and given readings.[16] Upon examination of the number of committees concerned with legislation in this parliament, in relation to the days of sitting, it is found that 1621 had a somewhat busier parliament than that of 1604, the only other normal parliament of the reign up to this point.[17] Indeed, when one reads in the journal of the various things which distracted the deliberations, it is hard to see how so much activity could have been crowded in.

The chronicle of activities of the house is of little interest here except as it shows the temper of the members. There had been a little electioneering by the crown,[18] and the usual amount by the great families.[19] Return cases involving about a dozen constituencies were the object of intermittent discussion from the opening days of the session. But they were not a principal issue as they had been in 1614. Sir Thomas Richardson, sergeant at law, was chosen speaker. He was chancellor to the queen and turned out to be a persistent, but not very successful partisan of the crown. Though the two great issues of supply and the recusancy laws were raised immediately, the house insisted on wrangling over free speech, returns, and minor points of privilege until February 13, nearly two weeks. Then it settled down to work on bills, interrupted all through the session, however, by reform efforts of various kinds.

The abuse that consumed most time was the monopolies, especially those concerned with the licensing of inns and alehouses, the manufacture of glass and of gold and silver thread, and the sealing of wills. The house was in a reforming mood. Two members, Sir Robert Flood and Sir Giles Mompesson, were expelled for illegal monopolies. The discussion of Mompesson's case dragged on for days. The most spectacular incident of the parliament was the fall of Lord Chancellor Bacon by impeachment of the house, for corruption in office. But other disciplinary acts served to consume time and to convince the king that they had come there to pose rather than to legislate. Sir John Bennett was expelled from the house for accepting bribes as a master in chancery, and Thomas Sheperd for mocking the Puritans upon the floor of the house. The warden of the Fleet was examined and disciplined for abuses in his prison, and one Floyd, not a member of the house, was punished, after one of the most naively amusing debates on record, for jocular remarks made concerning Frederick and Elizabeth, the "winter" monarchs, in whose plight the foreign complications had had their immediate origin. This ridiculous case consumed almost as much time as did Mompesson's.

Meanwhile considerable legislative work had been sandwiched in. Recusants, trade in wool, logwood, tobacco, fish, and other commodities, the scarcity of money, fees in court, and various legal processes, together with the usual run of naturalization and land bills—these were only a few of the matters considered. Their further enumeration is pointless. The famous crisis that ended the parliament grew out of a controversial issue with regard to foreign affairs. When the house, by petition, insisted on pressing His Majesty concerning the Spanish match, James, in an outburst more characteristic of his earlier years, warned them to shun the matters that concerned the prerogative and redefined their privileges in a fashion that might have passed in 1590, but not in 1621. The house replied with that renowned protestation of their liberties which James tore from the record with his own hand. An impasse had been reached, and a speedy dissolution cut short the legislation with which the commons had been working. So ended a parliament whose beginning had held promise of accomplishment, whose procedure showed marked development, whose leaders exceeded in subtlety those of any preceding Jacobean parliament,[20] but whose stubborn insistence on English nationalism brought it into conflict with stubbornness as great as its own.

At this point, an obvious question demands an answer. Why was it that the courtiers in the house allowed the protestation to pass, not only without effective opposition, but even without much commotion? By reading between the lines of one of Chamberlain's letters to Carleton,[21] one may venture to supply the answer. "The King is extremely displeased with the protestation, and calls all his servants to account for not opposing it, but most of them plead absence." This piece of gossip is eloquent. The courtiers, sensing the situation with regard to foreign affairs, gave up their duty "as a bad job," foreseeing defeat, and adopted a policy of "suave qui peut" in order to escape the odium, on the one hand, of general unpopularity and, on the other, of neglect of their responsibility to the king.

It would be natural to expect that the house of 1621 would continue where the Addled Parliament left off in the development of an orderly and efficient form of procedure. Such was in fact the case. Bills had, as always, three readings and, with a single exception, were committed on the second.[22] Of 16 bills dashed, 12 were rejected at first reading, 3 at second reading, and one at the report from committee. A more orderly schedule for the work of the day and of the week was laid out. The committee of privileges was given a regular hour of meeting every Tuesday and Thursday.[23] Saturday afternoons were set aside for the reading of private bills, and the committees for private bills were evidently relegated to the same short space later on. Earlier, the hours nine to ten daily had been set aside for reading of both public and private bills, and it was further ordered, "no bill to be put to pass, till past Nine of the Clock; and Notice to be given, a Day before, that Bills shall be passed the next Day." Apparently none of these rules were consistently followed. A number of other orders of the house found their way into the record, but seem to have been of little, if any, significance, being mainly concerned with matters of decorum. The very fact that the house was interested in the dignity of its procedure is not as important now as in the parliament of 1604, for in 1604 their interest was a new thing. The house had "arrived" before 1621, and one need not be troubled with its rules unless they have some intrinsic significance.

It is interesting to note here, especially in view of a similar activity in the Irish house of 1634, that the house, acting presumably in its legal capacity as the remote descendant of the great council, entertained a number of miscellaneous petitions.[24]

As the task is approached of analyzing the great bulk of committee statistics which may be extracted from the journal, it is necessary to keep in mind a few simple objectives in order to avoid the accumulation of a mass of stupid figures lacking even an academic interest. Was the committee still continuing to supersede debate upon the floor? Were the committees becoming the property of more or fewer members? Were committees more or less frequent?

As nearly as can be determined from the sometimes inexact wording of the journal, no less than 169 committees or subcommittees were appointed, 81 concerned with public bills, 38 with private, and 50 with nonlegislative matters of various sorts, such as privilege, messages, and grievances. This, with respect to the length of the parliament, represents greater committee activity than in the parliament of 1604.[25] A few more men served on committees than in any session of the parliament of 1604.[26] The average number of committees on which each man served was much higher in 1621—15 as opposed to 11.2 in 1609–10. The reason for this, of course, was that the committees were larger.

It will be interesting to learn whether the added committee work was distributed about the house or whether it was borne by a few. An examination of each man's record shows that the former was the case. The number of men who served on less than 10 committees advanced from 67 percent to 77 percent, while that of members serving on many committees declined.[27] This change is hardly remarkable, however. The one big difference in committee work in the parliament of 1621 is the much more extensive use of the committee of the whole house. Not only are there frequent references to individual instances of its use,[28] but there is also the very interesting record of a regularly scheduled committee of the whole to meet every Wednesday afternoon.[29] No doubt many afternoon meetings were unrecorded. The essential point is clear, namely that in order to expedite business committees were used more than ever before in place of formal debate upon the floor.

If it could be found that increasingly committee findings were acted upon without debate, further evidence of this trend would exist. As a matter of fact, the proportion of reports acted upon without debate was about the same as in the parliament of 1604, although it should be noted that there was, as a rule, much less debate on the reports of committees concerned with legislative work than with those of other committees. Fortunately it is not necessary to rely entirely upon an analysis of figures in arriving at these conclusions relative to committees. Members complained of the burden of committee work and of the excessive growth of committees. Dr. Gooch was perhaps voicing a general feeling when he observed that "some were chosen hand over head into committee whereby they have more businesses than they can dispatch," [30] for shortly thereafter Sir Edward Montague charged that "we are not attentive enough to

Bills, too hastie in Committinge Bills, not endureinge debate which is more proper and proffittable in the House than in a Committee." [31] On the other hand, some members disliked the frequent use of the committee of the whole, holding that select committees were a device deliberately developed and enlarged for expediting business and that the house should stick to them instead of constantly falling into informal general debate.[32] It is obvious that, by this time, the house felt itself considerably bound by the reports of committees. Mr. Mallett said, "The Committee rejected it and lett (not) the house receive it." Mr. Alford, although arguing on the other side, showed what the usual custom was when he remarked, "That we may not thinke it any discredit for any Committee for to have that called into the house and considered that theay have reiected. I have seene it so in a bill reiected by the Committee and after passed in the house but lett this sleepe." [33]

It is difficult to tell definitely how committees were chosen. From the order of May 17, 1621, "No one man to nominate above two upon a committee," [34] it appears that random calling of names was still the general practice. There may have been another method of assignment, however, for in the spring of the same year Sir Robert Phelips moved, "That every one of this house that stayes in towne may bringe in their names to the clarke on Munday that they may be distributed to three committees." [35]

The chairman of a committee was chosen by the committee when it sat and not before,[36] but whether there was a regular election or only a sort of choice by acclamation is not clear. It is easier, from the account of such an election on February 5, 1620/1, to believe that the choice was informal.[37]

When all is said, the parliament of 1621 was not very different in forms and procedure from its predecessors. More profit may be derived from a study of its parties and its passions. By studying the fortunes of its members over a long period of

years, considerable information has been accumulated.[38] Yet it
is information that must be used with the greatest caution, for
several reasons. In the first place, there is great uncertainty in
the identity of persons. The seventeenth-century Christian no-
menclature ran excessively to Johns, Thomases, Georges, Fran-
cises, and Henries. Even in this single parliament there are several pairs of men with exactly the same names, not to mention
the possible scores outside parliament. Then there is the very
grave and certain danger that not all the pertinent data have
been found regarding patronage. Most dangerous of all, however, is the tendency of a student to look for a hard and fast set
of prejudices and ambitions which never existed. It does not
necessarily follow, because a man received a favor or office from
the crown, that he surrendered his free will.[39] Nor did a single
rebellious speech or gesture mean that a man was forever cut
off from the springs of royal favor and alienated from the king's
cause.[40] Above all, it is necessary to remember that, in 1621,
there were still, in a strict sense, no parties. With allowance
made for the usual amount of timidity and ambition and bra-
vado, members were, to a considerable degree, so many free
lances. They were men, many of them proud and strong men,
who felt it their duty and interest to debate and legislate for the
good of England and their parish, whether they held of the
king or no. One would hardly say, however, that these obvious
grounds for doubt should be allowed to throw out the whole
evidence of the patronage record. They only make necessary a
large admixture of common sense in dealing with the statistics.
Had the times been less troublous and the prejudices less shifting, the interpretation could be more confident.

For 146 members no information of a significant nature is to
be found. Twenty-one others are mentioned only as participants
in some kind of rebellious gestures or as victims of the royal
displeasure. Some 294 at some time held an office, large or small,
or received a benefit from the government. It is pertinent to ask

how many of these had established such relations in the year
1621 or before. There seem to have been about 135, as opposed
to 106 in 1614. Of these, 21 were important people. There had
been only 10 such men in 1614 and 4 privy councilors. There
were 8 privy councilors in 1621.[41] This fact probably had much
to do with the smoothness in the early days of parliament. There
were some 50 men of less importance, patent holders, pensioners, political aides and the like, whose indebtedness to the court
party is obvious. Sixty-four other members, army officers,
sheriffs,[42] incumbents of petty clerkships, have been noted. In
some cases their identity is not certain, and in many the importance of their relation to the government is dubious. The bulk
of them, however, might reasonably be expected to vote on the
right side. The increased number of office and pension holders
over those of 1614 is significant, particularly the increase in the
number of privy councilors and other important people. James
seems at last to have learned the Elizabethan technique in this
matter and to have accomplished his purpose without the commotion that ruined the preceding parliament.

It is difficult indeed to establish the importance of the offices
and favors bestowed on members of this parliament after 1621.
Between this date and the beginning of the civil war, 29 of them
were found among England's great officeholders. Sixteen had
not held important office before 1621. There were 68 more
whose connections with the crown were clear, but less important.
One hundred forty-two held unimportant offices or entered upon
some minor relationship. All together 159 men, who had been
in no way connected with the crown in 1621, established some
relation therewith during the next two decades. This seems to
indicate one of two things. More exactly, it indicates two separate things—one in the case of some men, another in the case
of others. Some of them the king's counselors tried to win to a
position of loyalty during the turbulent twenties and thirties.
Others no doubt attained office or received favors because they

were ambitious or had the crown's point of view. If they were safe men in 1625 or 1632, it is more than likely that in the ordinary business of parliament in 1621 they could also be counted on, although there is no way in which to prove it.[43]

This assumption is based on rather tenuous evidence. Yet it seems entirely reasonable when we consider that both the journal and the diaries of the parliament show that, until the unhappy incident of the protestation, there was a noticeable spirit of cooperation and an absence of bad feeling and obstruction. There were many, very many, members in 1621 whose sympathy lay with the crown. But there was even less of a "party" spirit than in 1614. Even those who had tasted royal favor did not feel bound by it—or it would have been impossible to raise a rebellion out of a group so extensively beholden to the existing government. This confused state of affairs had, of course, a bearing upon the leadership of the assembly in speaking and committees.

In the clerk's record, 3349 speeches are recorded for 1621. They were delivered by 259 men. But 21 men delivered 1741 of them, or 52 percent. These leaders of debate were: Sir Edward Coke (224), Sir Robert Phelips (144), Edward Alford (140), Sir George Moore (93), Sir Robert Naunton (84), Sir Dudley Digges (83), Sir Henry Poole (78), Sir Edwin Sandys (78), Sir Lionel Cranfield (77), Sir Edward Sackville (76), Sir Thomas Coventry (74), Sir Edward Giles (67), Sir James Perrott (65), Sir Thomas Wentworth (63), William Hackwell (62), William Noye (60), Sir Edward Montague (56), Sir Thomas Crewe (55), Sir Francis Glanville (55), Sir William Strode (55), Sir Thomas Rowe (52). The speeches of none of these men were of a predominantly partisan character. From their records before and after 1621 and from their speeches, we may roughly classify Phelips, Alford, Poole, Sandys, Wentworth, Hackwell, Noye, Rowe, Giles, Strode, and

Coke [44] not exactly as leaning toward the popular side, but at least leaning away from the royal side. Digges,[45] Naunton, Coventry, Cranfield, and Sackville were, of course, "studying to please," while Moore, Perrott, Crewe, Glanville, and Montague defy classification. Phelips, who spoke eight times against the court party never for it, is the closest approach to a "patriot," yet even he, in most of his speeches, used such moderation that no partisan intent could be ascribed to him. Naunton and Coventry exhibited the most consistently conservative attitude, but they too, on most occasions, spoke with disarming reasonableness, if we may believe the clerk and diarists.[46]

Speaker Richardson was several times criticized for partisan action. The house had come a long way from the days of Puckering, Williams, and Coke, for member after member rose to berate the presiding officer for making motions abortive,[47] for adjourning the sitting in order to sidetrack discussion,[48] or for jesting at the expense of members.[49] The humiliation of Speaker Finch was still eight years ahead, but the office to which he was to bring a dubious grace was already highly suspect.

Neither side could claim a clear leadership in debate—nor indeed were there two "sides." Yet the three men who spoke most frequently, Coke, Phelips, and Alford, inclined toward the "reform" point of view, even though they probably did not regard themselves as members of any party or group in the house. What of the interesting matter of committee work?

The men who took the most active part in committees were: Sir Edward Coke (75), Sir Henry Poole (70), Sir George Moore (64), Thomas Crewe (55), William Noye (55), Edward Alford (51), William Hackwell (51), Sir Edwin Sandys (45), Sir Edward Montague (43), Sir Thomas Lowe (42), Sir Nathaniel Riche (42), Sir Thomas Coventry (40), Sir Jerome Horsey (40), Sir Francis Barrington (36), Sir Robert Phelips (36), Sir Dudley Digges (35), Sir William Strode (35), Sir

Thomas Edmondes (33), Francis Glanville (33), Sir Lionel Cranfield (32), Sir Fulke Greville (32), Sir Thomas Rowe (32), Robert Heath (30).

This is substantially the same as the list that was compiled for frequent speakers. All but 7 of the men who did a great deal of committee work also spoke often,[50] and all but 5 of those who dominated the floor were also active in the committee room.[51] The honors were fairly even as between "patriots" and "courtiers." Of the 23 men, 9 were very clearly of the court persuasion,[52] and 2 more, [53] whose speaking records are colorless, inclined in that direction. Only 3 may be classified as outspoken "patriots," [54] but 9 others,[55] although apparently bound in some measure by favors to the crown, played the independent ingrate. Thus it appears that 11 of the leading committee men were for the court and 12 were inclined to oppose it. The combined committee appointments of the 11 "courtiers" total 442, while those of the 12 "patriots" total 565.

There is some evidence to support the theory that the chairmanship of committees may be determined by noting the men who reported the bills back to the house.[56] If we may assume that it was the general but not binding rule that the chairman report, we can gather from the journal considerable material on committee influence.[57] The reports of 133 bills or other matters are included in the journal account. They were made by 43 men. Seven men made 83 of the reports: Coke (26), Hackwell (12), Glanville (11), Coventry (10), Moore (10), Poole (9), Phelips (5). With the exceptions of Phelips and Moore, they all reported for 7 or more different committees. Regardless of whether they were the chairmen of their committees or not, they were certainly the leaders in committee work.

When all these statistical scraps are assembled, they point to the fact that the parliament of 1621 was led, both in the house and without, by a mixed group of men—a few courtiers, a very few rash patriots, and quite a number of independent gentlemen who were willing to cooperate with the great Authority, yet were not afraid to break with it. This essentially sound situation, so different from that obtaining in James's first two parliaments, might finally have vindicated Jacobean statecraft, had not the incident of the protestation interfered.

1624

Viewing the heroic days of Pym and Cromwell and Strafford from our remote vantage point, one seems forced to the conclusion that the terrific clash of spiritual and governmental ideals could never have been resolved without a bloodletting and the successive triumphs of one fanatic faction over the other. Again, however, one is tempted to wonder if Prince Henry, had he lived, might have succeeded where Charles failed. Could England in 1642, as in 1789 and 1848 and even as in our own day, have restrained the fires of change to smolder, while on the continent they were ablaze? A close examination of James's last parliament (and after all it was in parliament that the revolution started) shows that the representatives of the commonalty had never since the days of Elizabeth been more reasonable. Feeling was friendly on both sides; speeches were moderate; charges of bad faith were few.[58] The legislative output was considerable. No such untoward incident as the protestation marred the session.

It would be naive to assert that any particular parliament of this period was free from coercion with respect to its elections. The parliament of 1624, however, seems to have been about as free as any. Certainly it was distinguished by an absence of bitterness arising from such pressure. "The elections are hopeful, little attention being paid to great men's recommendations. The Prince has failed to get Sir Fras. Cottington chosen." [59] Sir William Pelham "hopes the nether House of Commons will be compounded of honest, religious gentlemen. The country augurs good, because there has been less labour than usual to bring in particular men." [60] There was some electioneering activity, of course. Naunton was chosen by Cambridge at the king's request.[61] Sir Dudley Digges failed of election in Kent because he was suspected of royalist sympathies.[62] As usual, Lord Zouch was active in Kent, and question of his practices was raised.[63] Several members were expelled from the house for irregularities in their elections.[64] Though the matter of elections was jealously watched by the house,[65] there is definite evidence, as already cited, that good relations with the crown were unaffected.

If any particular passion marked the parliament of 1624, it was the hatred of recusants—hardly a new sentiment. The members were summoned for the same old reason, need of money for James's foreign policy. Again the king was interested in Germany and land operations, while parliament was bent on a sea fight with Spain. Relieved at the breaking of the Spanish treaties, but alarmed at the prospect of a French marriage, parliament compromised by granting a subsidy, a small one. Its members removed the bitter memories of their resentment in 1621 by discussing foreign affairs to their heart's content. They added 35 statutes to the rolls, including a bill against monopolies. The big sensation of the session was the impeachment of Middlesex. James was presented with a number of grievances before the dissolution, but the tone of all the meetings was distinctly friendly, at least so far as can be judged from the journal account.[66] Gardiner concludes that the parliament was of great importance in the crystallization of parliamentary forms, but that its efforts were marred by lack of self-control.[67] Yet, compared with all other seventeenth-century parliaments before the civil war, it seems quite restrained.

The parliament of 1624 sat from February 12 to May 29 of that year, a total of 79 days and 21 afternoons. As usual, there is some difficulty in determining how many men attended. The "Official List" of returns indicates 489. Twenty-two names are encountered in the journal which are not in this list. Three-hundred sixty-four men are mentioned by name in the journal.

The largest recorded division is 329.[68] By using the Official List as a basis for comparison, it appears that 304 of the 489 listed there for 1624 were old parliament men and that 249 of them had served in 1621. Thus, as the membership of this body is compared with that of its predecessors, it seems to have been a more experienced body than any thus far in the seventeenth century.[69]

By every possible criterion, it was more active than any other held in the reign of James. Thirty-five statutes resulted from its deliberations, whereas nothing but the subsidy received the royal assent in 1621. Ninety-two bills were passed by the house, as opposed to 41 in 1621. Ninety-nine bills had their third reading, 121 were committed (as opposed to 78 in 1621), 152 had a second reading, and 169 were once read. The ratio of committees for legislation to days of sitting was 1.78 as compared with 1.09 in 1604 and 1.18 in 1621. Obviously the kingdom got more work out of this group of men than out of any before, even though James received less subsidy than he wished. Sir Humphrey May, chancellor of the duchy, "never rejoiced so much in any Parliament." [70]

Aside from some development in the work of select committees, there are but two changes in procedure which distinguish the two last Jacobean parliaments from one another. In 1624 the committee of the whole was used more extensively than before,[71] and a greater resort was made to the house in petitions.[72] This latter practice was not new in 1624. But its increased frequency attracts the interest of students of the Irish parliament, since in 1634 that body made large use of the petition, evidently to circumvent the restrictions placed upon its activity by Wentworth's ruthless application of Poynings' Law.

Although it sat for a shorter period than the parliament of 1621,[73] the parliament of 1624 had more committees.[74] A few more members participated, if we may judge by the names recorded for select committees.[75] The distribution of work seems

to have been very much like the distribution in 1621, save that
Sir Henry Poole and Sir Edward Coke were more prominent in
1624 than were any members in 1621, each serving on more than
80 committees.[76] As in 1621, nearly half the committees contained unnamed members, "all who will come," "all lawyers,"
"burgesses of all port towns," or the members of this or that
shire or group of shires.[77] Of course it is not possible to discover
how many, either of these members or of actually named members, attended meetings. The differences in committee work be-
between the two parliaments are minor. The members of the privy
council were less frequently appointed to committees in a body
in 1624, and, as already mentioned, the committee of the whole
house was evidently used more frequently.[78] Although nothing
can be determined with certainty from the journal, it seems that
even more than formerly the committee had taken the place of
debate upon the floor of the house. By far the bulk of the committee reports were acted upon without debate.[79] The uniform
flatness of the recorded speeches and the care of the clerk in recording committee meetings and changes attest the same thing.
Before the reign of Charles began, the select committee and committee of the whole house had become the normal instruments
for doing business. Their operation is more clearly visible in 1624
than in 1621 because in 1624 there were fewer distractions and
the house could really go about the business of legislation more
seriously than at any time since 1610.

The patronage record for this parliament is striking for its
similarity to the record of 1621. Aside from the somewhat larger
number of members whose names appear nowhere in records of
patronage and discipline, the figures tally rather closely. About
the same number of recalcitrants appear in each parliament.[80]
The total of men who at some time were indebted to the crown
was about 294 in 1621 and 280 in 1624.[81] Those whose connection antedated 1624 were 136; the members in 1621 whose connection had already been established at that time totaled 135. To

be sure there were only 5 members of the privy council in the house in 1624, as opposed to 8 in 1621.[82] But the parliament of 1624 contained 17 other courtiers of first importance,[83] and the parliament of 1621 only 13. Of the remaining members who were in some way beholden to the government, it has been estimated that there were 109 in 1624 and 114 in 1621. It appears that these two parliaments were made up of just about the same kind of men, mixed in much the same proportions.[84]

Equally interesting is the record of leadership in 1624. There still were no clear-cut "parties" although there was, as before, a distinct difference in the attitudes of different members.

Only 857 speeches are recorded in the journal. These were delivered by 137 men. A third of the total were delivered by 7 men, Coke, Phelips, Alford, Heath, Glanville, Sir George Moore, and Sandys. Of these leaders, all but Moore and Heath had been or were to be in some degree hostile to the crown. Alford spoke against the court in 1621. Coke was accused of sabotage in the same parliament [85] and was so much in disfavor in 1624 that the council had tried to get him out of parliament by sending him to Ireland. Glanville later opposed ship money.[86] Phelips was in disfavor in 1621 and was to be again in 1629.[87] Sandys was imprisoned after the parliament of 1621 and certainly was not in favor in 1624.[88] Heath was the only real courtier of the group, and in the matter of speaking he was a poor fourth, with only 29 speeches recorded, as against 71 for Coke, 59 for Phelips, and 51 for Alford. The independent or hostile members did most of the speaking. Yet, with the exception of two spirited speeches by Phelips, none were of a partisan or violent nature. These men were in no way guilty of obstruction.

In committee work these 7 men also took a leading part, although they did not head the list. Those most frequently mentioned for committee service were: Sir Henry Poole (85), Sir Edward Coke (83), Robert Heath (58), Sir John Saville (52), Edward Alford (47), Sir George Moore (47), William Noye

(47), Sir Nathaniel Riche (47), Sir Thomas Estcourt (43), John Pym (42), Sir John Stradling (40), Sir Guy Palmes (39), Sir Francis Barrington (38), Sir Dudley Digges (38), Heneage Finch (38), John Glanville (38), Sir Walter Pye (37), Sir Peter Hayman (36), Sir Robert Phelips (34), Sir James Perrott (33), Sir Thomas Hobby (32), Sir Edwin Sandys (31). In this group of 22 men, 13,[89] including the 2 with by far the largest records, were or were to be hostile to the crown, or at least independent. Five [90] were as obviously courtiers. Four [91] are difficult to place.

From the regularity with which certain members reported for certain committees, it is rather clear in this parliament who the chairmen were. For example, Sandys always reported from the committee on trade, Noye from repeal of statutes, Coke from grievances, John Carville from reforms in chancery, Glanville from privilege. The 6 who reported most frequently were Coke (37), Sandys (25) Glanville (23), Heath (12), Noye (9), Phelips (9). In this group it will be seen that Heath was the only consistent courtier and that all the others were men who, early or late, made themselves objectionable to the crown.

From these tabulations an interesting conclusion can be drawn. Although the independent members, inclined to be refractory, dominated the work of 1624 more than that of 1621, the parliament was infinitely more harmonious and productive. There seems but one possible explanation, and that is the attitude of King James. When these men were aroused in 1621 and in 1629 they gave trouble. When their liberties were respected in 1624 they were no "party," but only a group of sober and loyal subjects. We are led again to speculate upon the fate of England in the mid-century if some wise monarch had succeeded James I.[92]

It is but natural that the men who had been growing in the direction of a party should become more difficult to classify in 1624, when we reflect upon the reluctance with which some of them brought themselves to open opposition even after 1640.

The "party" may be said to have been almost dormant in James's last two parliaments. For that reason there is no hope of securing a full count of members. Yet, since some of the old "patriots" came to life again after 1625 and were joined by new confederates, it is pertinent to follow the continuity of personnel in the house, with party matters in mind.

Casualties to the old "party" were heavy in 1621. Of 49 greater and lesser "patriots" of 1614, 22 failed to be returned. These included Hoskins, Owen, Fuller, and Duncombe, who had been leaders in 1614. Four more who were returned seem, at this point, to have gone over to the conservative position.[93] Eight more, who had been among the leaders seven years before, showed no partisan zeal now,[94] though several of them continued to be very active in debate and committee work.[95] Of the minor figures of the 1614 parliament, 3[96] became very active, but showed no partisan spirit. Four more left no record at all,[97] and 5 continued after the parliament to be of the "patriot" turn of mind.[98] Four of the old leaders of 1614 were still leaders, and still recalcitrant. Sir Edwin Sandys, Hackwell, and Sir Robert Phelips were all disciplined by the government for their part in parliament, and Sir Edward Giles introduced the great protestation. Thus only about 9 of the old opposition men did much in 1621.

Yet a survey of the parliament roll of 1621 reveals a curious thing. This relatively quiet assembly was the one in which first appeared some of the really great parliamentary leaders. Sir Edward Coke, the most active debater and committeeman of 1621,[99] while motivated mainly by personal considerations at that time became in 1625 a firebrand. The later "King Pym," Sir Harbottle Grimston, Glanville, and Christopher Earle were present. All together there were 31 men who were to come into open opposition, and several of them were to feel the crown's displeasure ere the civil war. But this is coincidental rather than significant. The fact is that very few men spoke out in 1621. The nascent party languished. In 1624 it almost died. Even Coke, Phelips, and Pym were cooperative. From a general historical standpoint this is extremely significant. It tends to weaken the argument for the inevitability of the civil war as a great class struggle and to build up the importance of the policy of Charles I. James I, by increasing political astuteness and timely concessions, had just before his death anesthetized the revolutionary movement. His son's mistakes quickly revived it.

V

THE REVOLUTIONISTS APPEAR

HAD the new king appreciated the potentially formidable character of parliamentary opposition or had he estimated correctly the popular temper with regard to Buckingham, he might not have launched his reign upon so desperate a course. His first parliament produced little for him. It did immense harm to England. It was, in a sense, King Charles's Rubicon. Before it, there was a chance of cooperation, but after it, none. Strangely enough, this parliament, so tragically significant in English history, is of little interest to the student of parliamentary institutions. The development of those practices and tendencies which have been the object of investigation in the earlier chapters cannot be traced here for two reasons. First, the parliament itself was abnormal, disturbed not only by the animosities of the hour, but by an epidemic of the plague. Members fled the city, and the final fortnight of sitting took place in the various college halls of Oxford. Secondly, the record is meager and carelessly kept. There can be no doubt of this, for whole days are omitted, and on many occasions the second or even third reading of a bill is noted when no first reading has been recorded. The record is more interesting than that of either 1621 or 1624, but it defies analysis. Questions of leadership and procedure cannot be discussed with profit.

The meetings were, however, so extremely important that they cannot be passed over. A few of the facts concerning the parliament [1] bear directly upon this study and are of sufficient interest to recount, since they indicate the turn matters were taking as between the king and his people in parliament assembled.

First in interest are the very small turnover of seats and the unusually low number of new members. The "Official List" notes 481 returns. Of these, 299 had also been returned in 1624, and 59 others had sat in earlier parliaments. It has been said by an eminent authority that there was great canvassing for seats; [2] John Chamberlain gave the same impression to his friend Sir Dudley Carleton; [3] and the Venetian ambassador informed his government of what would in our day be called a two-party election.[4] For various reasons, however, it seems unlikely that Ambassador Pesaro's impression was correct. The election contests described by Chamberlain turn out to be purely personal ones. The return cases dealt with by the house were of the same nature. Most important of all, it appears that the house resembles that of 1624 even more closely than the latter had resembled that of 1621. The number of old members has been noted. The patronage list, so far as it can be trusted, shows the same thing—namely that the election was not a hotly contested issue between king and people. At least, if any attempt to shut out courtiers was made, it was unsuccessful. We have only to consult the returns to prove it. The house contained 7 members of the privy council [5] and 14 other men who had held offices of the first importance before 1625.[6] The total number of members who were at some time connected with the administration was a little smaller than in 1624, yet more of the members in 1625 had already established that connection than was the case in 1624.[7] Practically the same number of men who enjoyed no favor from the government, but incurred the royal displeasure, is noted in each of the two parliaments.[8]

Again, then, there was a parliament which, from its personnel, might be expected to cooperate in a friendly fashion with the king. Although we may discount heavily the courtier Rudyard's fulsome eulogy of Charles, delivered early in the session,[9] we may safely assume that no great trouble was expected.[10] Indeed, the king gave early and unequivocal notice that he desired the friendship of his commons,[11] accepted their paltry subsidy with much better grace than it was offered,[12] and in the face of a growing hostility promised to call another parliament to deal with general matters of reform.[13] The parliament failed neither because of Charles's hostility to it nor because of its hostility to his general policy, but because of the intense bitterness toward Buckingham [14] and lack of confidence in him.

Just as the whole Puritan revolution was a minority movement, so the opposition which wrecked Charles's first parliament was a minority movement. The meeting might have been successful had not the plague produced a "lean house." It is an interesting example of the interaction of personalities and fortuitous circumstances in molding the destinies of a nation. Since some of the men who led the fight against Buckingham were to figure largely in the ill-starred parliaments of 1626 and 1628, they are worth singling out for observation, even as they marked themselves by the few speeches that were recorded in the journal. And when that observation has been made, this institutional study may pass on to the more profitable annals of the parliament of 1626.

The main issue in 1625 was the subsidy—whether it should be given and in what amount. Because of the clerical defects already noted and the cryptic nature of some of the recorded speeches, it is difficult to determine how much partisan intent is to be imputed to the speakers. More especially is this true because the matter of adjournment, upon which a great deal of strategy depended, could be, and was, affected by genuine apprehension of the plague on the part of some of the members and by willingness to embarrass the king on the part of others. Again, opposition to the proposed modest subsidy arose both from those who wished to postpone the grant until a more respectable sum could be offered and from those who wished to bring pressure to bear upon the government. With all these complications in mind, it is still possible to enumerate some members whose utterances were unfriendly to Charles and Buckingham.

Coke and Phelips were the leaders. Coke was insistent that the grievances of 1624 be accounted for [15] and that the expenditure of the former subsidies be scrutinized. His parting shot, on August 10, was a veiled attack on Buckingham, so worded that none could mistake its object. Phelips, from whatever motive, fell in with the idea of an early adjournment, first suggested by William Mallory, and advised that the king be made to raise money by some means other than the subsidy. He opposed the tonnage and poundage bill on principle and sharply criticized the government's policy with regard to religion. None of the other members spoke often in a critical vein. Mallory, after suggesting the early adjournment, opposed the subsidy and marked himself as an opponent of the court. Sir Thomas Wentworth did likewise. William Rolle showed a disposition to take advantage of the king's financial difficulties, and perhaps Strode did also, but a speech of his on August 6 shows him as opposing the subsidy more for its small amount than out of ill will. Sir Miles Fleetwood, Sir Nathaniel Riche, and Sir Thomas Hobby were definitely hostile, as were Glanville, Sir William Spencer, and Sir Thomas Grantham. Gardiner holds Sir Francis Seymour largely responsible, with Phelips, for the blocking of an adequate subsidy, but this is hard to understand, since the small subsidy advocated by Seymour was supported by May, Edmondes, and Weston, apparently as a strategic move. There can be no doubt, however, that Mr. Maynard meant no good when he proposed one subsidy and two fifteens.[16]

From the passing, shifting lists of men who could be identified as opposition members before 1625, 19 are found on the roll for that year.[17] As already remarked, any trend toward party organization had been arrested in 1621 and 1624. Yet in this score of men appear 8 names that give an important continuity to the opposition movement. Wentworth, Sir Edwin Sandys, Coke, Digges, Poole, Giles, Alford, Phelips, were present—in fact, all the really important ones of the recent parliaments with the exception of Hackwell and Noye. Not all of them took part in debate, so far as we can judge by the scanty record. Coke, Phelips, and Wentworth spoke, along with the hitherto "minor patriots" Glanville, Strode, and Grantham, while 9 new men were heard from as opposition speakers—Mallory, Sir Samuel Rolle, Sir Miles Fleetwood, Sir Nathaniel Riche, Sir Thomas Hobby, Sir William Spencer, John Maynard, Sir Guy Palmes, Sir Francis Seymour, none of them destined to be of too great importance in the parliamentary cause.

More interesting by far is the discovery on the roster of the names of 8 men who in 1640 became the vital core of the revolutionary party.[18] In 1625 they were not yet active. But fifteen years later, when the "old patriots" of 1625 were all gone, these parliamentary youngsters of 1625 were the real powers. John Pym, Sir Henry Belassis, Sir John Eliot, Sir Walter Earle, John Hampden, the younger Strode, John Crewe, John Glanville, all were present in 1625. In fact, with the exception of Cromwell, Sir Arthur Hazlerigg, Denzil Holles, and Nathaniel Fiennes, the great men of the Long Parliament were beginning to gather, though their importance was not yet known.

The old leaders were aging. The new were coming up. Ever since the parliament of 1610, despite change and defection, there had always been a continuing nucleus. Now the nucleus was undergoing change.

1626

The dissolution of his first parliament was by no means a confession of Charles's inability to operate the constitutional machinery of England. But before financial necessity impelled him to another attempt at parliamentary economy, events for which he was unquestionably responsible had further damaged popular confidence in him. The expedition to Cádiz was a fiasco. It would have been ludicrous, had it not involved so much suffering and expense. Its failure was not taken by the king as evidence of the fundamental incompetence of Buckingham's administration. It resulted only in a widespread irritation. The king's insistence on interfering with the domestic religious affairs of France had prevented an alliance with Richelieu which might have ended the Thirty Years War. As it was, although no crisis existed when parliament was called in February 1625/6, foreign policy had been badly bungled, and finances were in their chronic state of insufficiency. Charles's confidence was naive. He still hoped to make Buckingham a popular minister and in some way to secure parliamentary benediction for a yet-to-be-devised solution of the international religious puzzle, at which both he and his father had made feeble and futile stabs. He tried to secure a friendly parliament by the elephantine subtlety of making the leaders of opposition sheriffs. Sir Edward Coke, Sir Robert Phelips, Sir Francis Seymour, Sir Guy Palmes, Sir Thomas Wentworth, and Edward Alford were disqualified in this way.[19] He also reverted to James's early policy of tampering with elections.

From the debates themselves it is impossible to discover how far the electioneering was purposefully directed by the government, since the return cases discussed dealt with personalities and technicalities rather than with the general fact of interference or with its motivation. Moreover, the tampering in this instance, probably because it was not very successful, did not engender any great bitterness, as did the chicanery of 1614. It was forgotten in the furious personal hostility to Buckingham. Nevertheless, from sources outside parliament, one can see that the interference was considerable. The people of New Romney and of Bridport apologized to Buckingham for not electing his candidates, excusing themselves on the ground that his instructions came too late.[20] Sir John Hippesley, evidently the duke's principal agent in Kent, reported failure in the Hythe and Dover elections and in that for the knights of the shire.[21] In the latter instance, the failure is rather remarkable, because the defeated candidates were no less personages than Sir Richard Weston, chancellor of the exchequer, and Sir Edwin Sandys, the popular veteran of five preceding parliaments.[22] Kent seems always to have been a victim of pressure in elections, and one might be inclined to discount the importance of evidence from that quarter, were it not confirmed by a general observation in Ambassador Pesaro's dispatch of February 5, 1625/6 to the Doge and Senate.[23]

This was a long but unproductive parliament. Between February 7 and June 15 it sat 98 days, with 20 afternoon sittings. Its utter failure, from a standpoint of legislation, was a gloomy fulfillment of the evil omen of Charles's first parliament. No statutes resulted.[24] Only 13 bills had their third reading.[25] One hundred four second readings are recorded.[26] Only 122 bills had even a first reading.[27] A total of 139 committees were appointed, of which 65 dealt with public bills, 35 with private bills, and 39 with other matters. The ratio of committees for legislation to days of sitting is 1.02.[28] The attendance at sittings of the house was good.[29] The activity of committees was considerable, judged by the large number of reports [30] and the very evident preoccupation of the clerk with announcements of committee meetings.[31] There was evidently some great stumbling block for Charles's program. It requires no very careful search to reveal that the stumbling block was the duke of Buckingham.

Although the explosion against Charles's favorite did not come immediately, there was some unfriendly feeling from the start. Sir John Eliot opposed action on the subsidy pending a thorough survey of past grievances, particularly naval mismanagement.[32] The government's speaker, Sir Heneage Finch, was elected, however, without question, and the several return cases were disposed of apparently without much rancor. A bootless discussion of the seizure of a French vessel occupied considerable

time early in March, and at the conclusion of this matter the real
attack on Buckingham began. For this first attack Clement Coke
and Dr. Samuel Turner fell under displeasure, and Coke was
confined to his lodgings.[33] Meantime the house had been stead-
ily busied with the work of legislation and with an unusual number of privilege cases of a routine nature, involving court actions
of various kinds.[34] The business against Buckingham evidently
smoldered and grew without much talk upon the floor. At least
the clerk, who was rather timid in recording debate, made little
mention of it. Sir Benjamin Rudyard, at that time an obvious
courtier, wrote to his friend Sir Francis Nethersole on March 19,
"the points (of recent business) being so 'dangerous,' as we dare
not speak here freely amongst ourselves." [35] Sir Dudley Digges,
on March 14, voiced the general willingness to engage in war
with Spain—and the general distrust of Buckingham—by moving for "a War at Sea, for Defense and Offense, by the voluntary
joint Stock of Adventurers out of all Counties of England; to
be encouraged by a settled Course in Parliament, and by Privileges to be granted to them, without much Prejudice to his
Majesty's settled Revenue . . ." [36] This whimsical motion was
not heard of again.

At exactly what point the comprehensive inquiry into Buckingham's administration was entrusted to a committee is not clear,
though the attack was hinted at as early as February 18.[37] It was
probably some time after the ides of March, following an unsuccessful attempt to secure information from the council of war.
The charges against the duke, eight in number, were prepared
by April 24. He was indicted for incompetence, plurality of offices, corruption, extortion, and extravagance.[38] To this broadside
was later added a charge of tampering with James I's health
during his last illness.[39] For their part in presenting these charges
in the impeachment proceedings, Sir John Eliot and Sir Dudley
Digges were imprisoned.[40] With the failure of impeachment, the
house turned to condemn the illegal collection of tonnage and

poundage.[41] Another gesture against Buckingham was made possible by his election to the chancellorship of Cambridge, which the house hastened to condemn, to the great irritation of the king.[42] When it became apparent that a hopeless deadlock had developed and dissolution appeared imminent, a remonstrance against illegal taxation and against the duke's administration was presented to Charles.[43] Parliament was immediately dissolved and the publication of the remonstrance forbidden.[44] The Venetian ambassador gloomily wrote to his government that an impasse had been reached from which he could see no escape.[45]

As in the study of previous parliaments, we must plunge for a while into the details of procedure, to see whether or not it had any bearing on partisan activity. The result is negative, save for one matter, the use of the committee of the whole in the attack on Buckingham. That is significant.

In the main, there is little to distinguish the procedure of 1626 from that of 1624. The period of rapid development of a mechanical kind was over. The readings, rejection of bills, and action upon committee reports were entirely regular, except in the case of four first readings which were immediately followed by second readings, a custom ordinarily reserved for the bill for the general pardon. As usual, an exact study of procedure is hampered by the short cuts of the clerk in keeping his journal. His negligence is particularly striking in 1626, because of his known omission of various exciting verbal passages—passages of which one may have exact knowledge from outside sources. Even this defect tells something.

It tells of emphasis on committee work. This was the thing that engaged the clerk's attention. He might omit nearly all the speeches from the floor,[46] but he was very careful to record time, place, and membership of committees, along with all changes of the same. More than ever before the business of legislation had departed from the floor to the committee chamber. More than ever the report of the committee was followed by action—engrossing or recommitting. This condition makes it very interesting to discover how the burden of committee work was distributed. Again, a good deal of reading between the lines is required, for the actual membership of committees is obscured by the inclusion of those vague categories "all knights of shires," "all lawyers who will come," "all merchants who will come," "all who come to have voice." Even after the original select committees had been named, their membership might be suddenly thrown open. This was probably due to irregular attendance. The plague was not entirely over, and, for whatever reason, many members had left town, though curiously enough, as noted earlier, several large divisions were taken late in the session.

The only possible way to estimate the committee burden is by a study of those named. This shows that 299 men served on 139 committees. In 1624, 351 men had served on 193 committees. That makes the burden of service fairly even for the average man serving, with a somewhat greater burden in the more active parliament of 1624.[47] The matter may be more accurately analyzed, however, by ascertaining how many men bore an excessive load, how many a moderate one, and how many had a very light committee assignment. Again, the proportions are very similar to those of 1624. Several of the men who had served on many committees in 1624 were necessarily absent, and others had filled their places. As in the last Jacobean parliament, 4 men served on over 50 committees. There was some increase in the proportion of those serving in the middle categories—those on from 10 to 50 committees. This recalls a comparison of 1621 and 1624, when the same trend was noted. It could hardly be called a general spreading of committee work, but rather an increase in the number of those moderately, though not excessively, occupied with the work of committees.[48]

The following of a regular schedule for committee meetings was nothing new, but it seems to have been pursued more systematically than before, both in the work of select committees and in that of the committee of the whole house. The record of meetings of the latter is more full than for any preceding parliament. In most cases the committee of the whole was used for discussing the highly controversial matters arising from the conflict between Buckingham and the commons. There is no alternative to the assumption that it became, in 1626, a device deliberately employed to expedite the attack on the duke's government. As such, it is comparable to the exploitation of new forms in the parliament of 1604.

With the approach of the great schism of 1629, the matter of leadership and individual records becomes more interesting than ever. The electioneering for this parliament of 1626, evidently not very successful, had not greatly altered the complexion of the house. There was a very high proportion of old members. Three hundred sixty-five had probably served before. Two hundred ninety had served in, or been returned to, the parliament of 1625.[49] Of all the members, 270 were, had been, or were yet to be, indebted to the government. This represents a continued, if not very marked, falling off. In 1624 there had been 280, and in 1621, 294. At the same time it is significant to note that although the total number of beneficiaries in 1626 was smaller, the number who had already established their connection at the time the parliament convened was much higher.[50] This tendency was probably due to the fact that the government had now for some time been consistently building up, or attempting to build up, a following among the kind of men likely to be returned to parliament. No doubt also a good deal of pressure, impossible for the student to discover, was exerted to secure their election. It was the same old policy that James had followed, with ever-increasing success. It was followed in the parliament of 1628. Moreover, a number of members in 1626 must have conducted themselves "loyally," inside parliament and out, for in addition to the 151 who had already been befriended in 1626, another 119 were given similar treatment before 1640. But the uncertain effect of such honors was becoming more and more clear. Seventeen of the men who had received them before 1626 were later found in the opposition.[51] On the other hand, 7 of those who had opposed the government before 1626 were later rewarded. Changes of mind are difficult to treat statistically. All that can be said is that the house was composed much as it had been in the latter days of James and that its members, in times of stress, acted as any such group of men would act under similar circumstances. In most of the categories explored, the similarity between 1624 and 1626 is striking.[52] Since this is true, and particularly since Coke, Phelips, and several other firebrands were not present in 1626, the parliament should have been as harmonious as that of 1624. It would have been, had it not been for Charles's evil angel, the well-hated duke.

One more aspect of the parliament remains to be studied, that of leadership. Was it mixed, as in 1624? Was there much sign of party? These questions can be answered definitively. Influence was very mixed, and the evidence of any close organization is not impressive.

Very little can be learned of leadership in debate because little can be learned of the debate itself. Of the 6 most frequently recorded speakers, 3 were crown sympathizers [53] and 3 were, or later became, critics.[54] This evidence is so incomplete, however, that it signifies little.

Of the 119 committee reports recorded,[55] 74 were made by 12 men. Of these, 3 were quite colorless members with no pronounced leanings or connections.[56] Seven more were clearly opposition men.[57] The remaining 2 were as clearly courtiers.[58] Pym and Digges were certainly among the leaders in speaking and reporting from committees, and both were, and had been, critics of the government.

In the matter of committee membership, there is a similar even division. Those serving the most frequently were the two courtiers, Moore and Stradling, and the two noncourtiers, Poole and Barrington. Of the leading 19 in committee service, 8 had records that would tend to make them court sympathizers,[59] 10 fall in exactly the opposite category.[60] One appears to fall nowhere.[61] In short, the record holds a tantalizing paucity of evidence, not only of any clear partisan split, but even of the monopoly of leadership that can be observed to some degree in earlier parliaments and more clearly in 1628.

What then does this whole parliament reveal in the way of institutional development? It shows a house elected and guided, as was the last house of James, in accordance with the principles of Tudor statecraft, but with an absence of that fear which had repressed members before 1603. It failed, not because of any concerted effort of an opposition group or because of stupid Stuart parliamentary bungling, but because of the disturbing hatred of a personality. None of its members were yet uncompromising foes of the crown. The house was now developed as to its procedure, but it still lacked parties. The parliament of 1628 was to fill the cup of antagonism to such abundant overflowing that the interparliamentary hiatus of 1629–40 must see the growth of parties. In fact, a party really came into being in the parliament of 1628.

The subject of partisanship, however obscure in 1626, cannot be thus easily dismissed. Something, if not much, can be learned of the fortunes of that which has from time to time been rather inaccurately referred to as a "party." Very much the same thing happened as happened in 1614. Charles eliminated several of the chief leaders, and only 22 men appear on the list who can be identified as former partisans.[62] All of these, except Noye, Harley, Peak, Saville, and Walter had been in the preceding parliament. But enough of the old group were left to provide leaders. Sandys, Digges, Wentworth, Poole were there, and, emerging from the "silent brothers" of 1625, were two important figures, Pym and Eliot, and one more who was to be troublesome in 1628, Clement Coke. Judging from the very spotty recording of speeches in the journal, we may add to these 24 recalcitrants 9 more who could be so classified by this time.[63] The opposition had ceased to wane; it was waxing once more.

1628

The general historians of Charles's reign have painted an interlude of dramatic passions between the parliaments of 1626 and 1628. They have shown the inevitablity of war with France, as Charles ignored the promises of the marriage treaty and persisted in his ill-conceived determination to use Buckingham as the instrument for relieving continental Protestants by a naval expedition against the Isle of Rhé. They have shown that such an expedition, in view of its conflict with popular notions of the war, the hatred for Buckingham, and the ill-found personnel of the armed forces, would have been difficult enough, even had not the English populace been chafing under the abuses of arbitrary taxation, martial law, and quartering. All this is of great interest in assigning to this two-year interval its place in the struggle for English liberties. It reveals a little *inter-parliamentum* something like that of 1614–21 and of 1629–40, a timid attempt to abandon constitutionalism before the determination to embrace absolutism had hardened. Here, however, it is only appropriate to inquire how the events of these months affected the elections for, and temper of, the parliament of 1628. They influenced both mightily.

Never since 1614 had the laboring of elections produced such a furor. What James I had learned of the folly of open electioneering Charles's counselors cast to the winds. It was a desperate last chance, and every effort must be made to secure a docile house. As a result, an abnormal number of election cases were brought before the house, and an abnormal amount of official correspondence is discovered bearing on pressure and manipulation.

A curious duality attaches to the evidence on elections in 1628. Fifteen separate cases of election controversy came before the house. In addition, contemporary correspondence discloses a number of cases of pressure and irregularity. But the two sources do not overlap. The journal sheds very little light on the motivation of electioneering, and in most cases the members involved in contests were persons of no strong leanings for or against the king. In Cornwall, Sir John Eliot and William Coryton were opposed for knights of the shire as enemies of the king. They were seated by the house, and Lord Mohun, responsible for the alleged slander, was rebuked.[64] In Yorkshire, Sir Henry Belassis and Sir Thomas Wentworth, both at that time inclining toward the cause of liberty, were seated as knights of the shire,[65] and for Newport Medina in Cornwall, Nicholas Trefusis, who opposed the forced loan in 1627, was seated in place of a rival returned by the sheriff.[66] In several cases [67] men mildly in the court favor were seated. There certainly is no evidence of any clear policy of the house to exclude the king's friends because of indignation at election practices.[68] On the other hand, there was an abnormally large number of election cases, and they dragged on through the whole session,[69] as if they were somewhat of an issue. It is more than likely that some significant common denominator in all these cases has been obscured by the very niggardly habit of the clerk in recording. In five cases [70] the issue involved was that of the right of the commonalty to the franchise. This clearly bespeaks an attempt of great ones to control parliament. Yet it does not necessarily bespeak a connection between great ones and the government. One extremely interesting case, however, that of Taunton,[71] shows the hand of royal tyranny. It was alleged that troops were quartered on the town as a punitive measure, because of the election of the wrong representatives. As is so often the case, the information in the journal alone would be insufficient to prove anything very impressive about Carolinian electioneering. It fits so well, however, with what people were saying outside that a rather convincing impression of a controlled election results.

Secretary Conway was active in his solicitation of votes. At Yarmouth, Newport, and Newton,[72] Andover,[73] Southampton,[74] and Evesham,[75] his fine hand was busy among the local gentry. There is just a shred of evidence that he met some opposition.[76] That he was pursuing some consistent policy with an eye to a loyal parliament can be neither doubted nor proved.

Secretary Nicholas was another busy letter writer. For Dover he pushed Buckingham's candidate, Sir William Beecher.[77] In Cambridge University he was the active agent.[78] He tried to swing the knights of the shire for Essex, but Edward Nuttall reported to him that Sir Francis Barrington and Sir Harbottle Grimston were elected, by means of a very irregular creation of freeholders.[79] Both these gentlemen had refused the forced loan. Here at least is evidence of that recalcitrance among the people observed by Contarini in his report to the Doge and Senate.[80] Sometimes a very cordial response was made to the suggestions of Nicholas.[81] Buckingham himself urged Sir Edwin Sandys upon Sandwich. Quite likely it was this very influence that lost Sir Edwin the election.[82] The court dictated the elections in Essex,[83] with what result has been marked.

There was doubtless an endless amount of this correspondence which has not survived. For the Venetian ambassador was mightily impressed, both with the efforts of the court to carry the elections and with the determination of the people to prevent it.[84] How little would we know of many important matters were it not for the Venetian ambassador!

A ticklish business was Charles's dealing with parliament. It is small wonder that he spared no pains to get a loyal one. One John Hope wrote in January that he wished "the Duke better than to trust to a Parliament which hates him. If there be a Parliament, fears whether they will give the King more than will do his work by halves." [85] Contarini reported a little later to his government that members of the council, urging Charles to do the inevitable and summon parliament, had guaranteed that if he consented nothing would be said about Buckingham.[86] Sir Robert Aiton probably had gauged the atmosphere acutely when he reported to the earl of Carlisle a very ominous suspicion abroad [87] that Charles was not trusted as he had been two years before.

Yet this parliament was not stiff-necked as had been the Addled Parliament. It meant to legislate, if we may judge by its activity. In the end, the continuance of abuses outside stampeded it into a revolt of despair.

The parliament of 1628 sat for 116 days, with 19 afternoon meetings. There were two sessions. The first lasted 85 days, from March 17, 1627/8, to June 26, 1628, and the second 31 days, from January 20, 1628/9, to March 10, 1628/9. Except for the long break from June to January, the meetings were continuous.

This was a tense parliament, and in one sense an active one. It produced no statutes and devoted a relatively small part of its time to legislation. Thirty-two bills had a third reading (13 in 1626), 70 were read twice (104 in 1626), and 95 had one reading (122 in 1626). The proportion of legislation completed in the house (but never enacted into law) was much higher, therefore, than in the previous parliament. The distribution of committees, however, will show that in 1628 the house was largely concerned with nonlegislative matters. One hundred forty-nine committees were appointed (139 in 1626). Of these only 64 dealt with legislation (100 in 1626), while 85 dealt with other matters, such as petitions, investigations, grievances, privileges, drawing up of petitions. There had been but 39 such miscellaneous committees in 1626. The ratio of committees on legislation to days of sitting was only .55, while in 1626 it had been 1.02.

Attendance was sporadic and comparatively good. Only 36

members were licensed to depart, but many more absented themselves, for on June 23 all were forbidden to depart without license.[88] There was an attempt to hold members in attendance,
and much more mention made of this matter than usual. The
reason is clear. Some timid members were drifting off, due to
fear of the impending clash with the king. The safety as well
as the influence of the house demanded that all hang together
in the crisis. So Mr. Sawyer was compelled to explain his absence
on May 19, and it was announced that the house would be called
on April 10, with a £10 fine to be levied against absentees. On
May 1 the sergeant was sent for all lawyers and other members,
for a committee of the whole. The door was locked and the key
"sent up." As a result of these efforts, some fairly large divisions,
ranging as high as 405 on May 13, are recorded.[89]

Even from the cold record of the clerk the charged atmosphere of this parliament can be sensed. Its remonstrance and the
uproar of its final adjournment are well known. But all through
its sessions it was touchy and nervous. Its time was abnormally
taken up with privilege and election cases, with examining complaints about the abuses of soldiers, and with violation of the
liberties of the king's subjects. It was jumpy about the recusants.
Some members were afraid and wished to depart; others tried to
hold them. The importance of secrecy, as a matter of individual
self-protection, was strongly emphasized, and toward the end of
the first session it was voted that all members should be free
from having spoken anything undutiful in this parliament.[90] The
house as a whole was thoroughly aroused, prudently looking to
its safety, but still willing, at long last, to be defiant.

As in 1626, the house showed no striking change in procedure.
Past trends strengthened. The reading of bills was entirely regular. On one occasion there is record of a bill that was committed
on first reading,[91] but in all probability the clerk simply failed
to note that it had its first and second readings together.

In committee work it appears that more men shared the labor

in 1628 than in 1626. Four hundred thirty-four men served on
138 committees, while in the preceding parliament 299 men had
served on 139. No high degree of accuracy can be claimed for
this count, because of duplication of committee lists in the journal and the extensive mention of subcommittees. After discount-
ing this, however, it is very clear that there was an extension of
these responsibilities. An analysis of the committee assignments
shows that 7 men [92] shouldered the heavy burden carried by 4
in 1626 and that apart from this increase in concentrated leadership the trend was toward greater distribution of the work.

Never had committee work been as continuous or systematic.
The committee of privilege met each Tuesday and Thursday at
2 P.M. in the star chamber.[93] A schedule for the committee of
the whole house on various subjects was set up with meetings
once or twice a week.[94] In addition, the house very frequently
resolved itself into committee of the whole for specific purposes,
including deliberation on the liberty of the subject, the king's
message, the Petition of Right, the subsidy, the remonstrance,
tonnage and poundage, privilege, and several matters not recorded. Sometimes the committee of the whole chose a select
committee to continue its work. The great increase in the use of
the committee of the whole calls for some explanation. Having a
majority, the aggressive "patriots" were determined to use their
advantage in keeping discussion in the open and upon vital matters and in pushing through with dispatch.

The make-up of this parliament was very interesting. Two
hundred sixty-three members had sat in 1626, and 375 had sat in
parliament at some time. These figures correspond rather closely
with those of 1626, but not exactly. There were fewer men of the
last parliament, but more from earlier parliaments than had
been the case in 1626. Fifty-seven men of 1625 who had not been
returned in 1626 were elected, and similarly 24 from 1624, 13
from 1621, and even 16 from the Addled Parliament of 1614.
Of these old members, brought back after an absence from the

house, 65 appear to have been of the court persuasion, and only
14 of the "patriots." The new men, elected for the first time in
1628, show 40 courtiers and 12 patriots. This seems to be further,
very clear evidence of a vigorous contest in the election and of
the lively effort made by the government to control seats. Despite these efforts, however, there was a steady drop, from 1621
on, in the number of court-minded members.[95] The number of
men who at one time or another opposed the government increased both in 1628 and in 1626.[96]

As in 1626, the record of speeches, other than committee reports, is so sparse that it is impossible to tell whether the king's
friends or his critics did the most talking. Only 25 members are
recorded as speaking. Five of them were courtiers, 7 were minor
beneficiaries, and 7 were "patriots." No conclusion at all can be
drawn from this as to leadership.

But when the reports from committee are analyzed, the story
is different. Nothing could be clearer than that the members
opposed to the crown and zealous for the liberty of the subject
were running the committees. The reports recorded in the journal number 124 and were made by 37 men, of whom 19 could
be classified as "patriots." But 86 of the reports, or approximately two thirds of the total, were made by these 19 men. More
than that, nearly all the important ones were made by them.
Reports from the committees on grievances and privilege were
made by Sir Edward Coke, Eliot, Earle, and Hackwell. The
committee on the Petition of Right was reported by Littleton (at
that time against the government), Herbert, Hoskins, Noye, and
Selden. All the reports of the important committee on religion
were made by Pym. Every one of these men was, at least up to
this time, known as an adherent of the popular cause. Practically
no reports of any important committee were made by any other
men. Five men made 55 reports, or about two fifths of the
total.[97] Since 1603 the committee system had taken over procedure, and the popular party had taken over the committee sys-

tem. Very naturally, an analysis of committee membership in this parliament shows the same thing.

It would avail little to study the committee service of each man, for 435 out of the 475 members are recorded as serving. A total of 3231 committee assignments, by name, were distributed among 435 men. But of these there were 7 who served on more than 50 committees.[98] All but one of them, Sir Nathaniel Riche, were at the time of this parliament marked as former critics or active opponents of the crown or as champions of liberties. Nineteen members served on from 30 to 49 committees,[99] all but 3 "patriots" of some hue.[100] The 16 "patriots" among these active committee men accounted for 840 committee assignments, and the little group, numbering 4 percent of the house membership, accounted for 26 percent of the committee service.

This evidence and that yielded by the record of committee reports give concrete proof of what has long been known of the actions of the house in 1628 and 1629—that the business was being done in committees and that the king's opposition had captured the new mechanism.

Our analysis has revealed a shifting group of men, suffering from vicissitudes and changes of mind, who with some consistency had come to hold the political views that in the 1640's were to divide the advocates of parliamentary government from those adhering to the old conception of monarchy. We have readily admitted the difficulty of uncovering completely the men who spoke and voted in accordance with this new line of political thought. Moreover, even in the 1640's, there were so many shades of opinion, and so many changes of it, that it is hard to pin down the membership of what we have chosen to designate as the revolutionary party.

These things being so, our conclusions have been based on much circumstantial evidence. We are intent on the answer to this question: Did a party nucleus come together in the house of commons prior to the dissolution of 1629? From the control that the opposition members gained over affairs in 1628–29 it is clear that such was the case.

But who were these men? Their names are found in two categories of members in the house of 1628: (1) those who were already known to have been in opposition or were in trouble between 1629 and 1640 and (2) those who sat in the Short and Long Parliaments and are there known to have espoused the popular cause.

Some 60 men of the 1628 parliament have been identified and connected, at some time and in some manner, with the opposition, at least to the extent of expressing themselves freely in parliament. Most of them, of course, are much more clearly identified. Thirty-one of them sat in either the Short or the Long Parliament, or in both.[101] They included Sir Walter Earle, Grimston, Pym, Strode, Alford, Henry Belassis, John Glanville, and John Hampden. Among the 60 were 16 who were to stick through and sign the Covenant in 1643.[102] Here indeed was a solid nucleus. There were also in the house of 1628 at least 13 who were in trouble with the government between 1629 and 1640,[103] and 7 of these sat in parliament in 1640.[104] Thus the Short and Long Parliaments [105] contained at least 38 men from the parliament of 1628 who had in some public way been marked as opposing the government. In the years 1640–42, 15 other men [106] who had been in the parliament of 1628 openly showed their attachment to the popular party. When the Covenant [107] was signed in September, 1643, the names of 50 more parliament men of 1628 appear.[108] In the parliament in 1640, then, when at long last the Puritan Party can be said to have come into existence, there were 103 party men who had also served in the parliament of 1628.

The statistics on the Short and Long Parliaments, like the others garnered in the course of this study, are admittedly estimates. My belief is that they are conservative estimates. Through them, however, it has been possible to trace the contribution of the first two parliaments of James I in developing those parliamentary usages that made effective the activity of the opposition. The passionate meetings of 1626 and 1628, too, were important in shaping up the strong men of the 1640's. From a scattering, hesitant, timid beginning the parliamentary opposition to the Stuarts grew into effective, organized partisan action.

NOTES

CHAPTER I: FIRST STIRRINGS
IN THE HOUSE OF COMMONS

1. The records of Elizabethan parliaments are as interesting as they are tantalizing. For a description of them, see the Bibliography.

2. D'Ewes, p. 486a. Letters, in citations to D'Ewes and the Commons Journal (hereafter cited as C.J.), refer to the column, *a* to the first and *b* to the second, on the pages.

3. All the figures cited in this paragraph are derived from D'Ewes, pp. 454a, 511a, 347b, 309a, 453a.

4. He noted it often. See, for example, D'Ewes, pp. 39a, 335b, 355a, 463b, 665a.

5. *Ibid.*, p. 625a (speech of Sir Edward Hobby).

6. Burnet, *History of the Reformation*, II, 252.

7. *Acts of the Privy Council, 1571–75*, p. 15; *ibid., 1586–87*, pp. 227, 241–42 (separate cases); *ibid., 1597*, pp. 361–62; *ibid., 1601–4*, pp. 248, 251; *Loseley Manuscripts*, pp. 242–43.

8. For example, in 1586–87, the sheriff of Norfolk was forced to hold a new election because he had returned the wrong men (*Acts of the Privy Council, 1586–87*, p. 241). See also the warning in 1601 to combat certain elements and prejudices in the electorate in the interests of a certain gentleman (*ibid., 1601–4*, p. 248; *Loseley Manuscripts*, pp. 242–43).

9. D'Ewes, p. 393a.

10. At an election in Norfolk in 1586 there is record of 3,000 people voting (*ibid.*, p. 396).

11. *Ibid.*, p. 430a: "as in some not returned at all, some others returned erroneously, and for some places for which none hath been returned heretofore, and some returned superfluously, as two for one place and one for two places, and other corrupt courses . . ."

12. *Ibid.*, p. 237b; see also p. 241a.

13. *Ibid.*, p. 220b.

14. *Ibid.*, p. 594b.

15. *Ibid.*, p. 393.

16. *Ibid.*, p. 453.

17. *Ibid.*, pp. 393a, 431a.

18. For these two episodes, see D'Ewes, pp. 490a, 684a.

19. *Ibid.*, p. 339a.

20. *Ibid.*, 474, 476.

21. *Ibid.*, p. 485 (Cecil).

22. *Ibid.*, p. 497a. "All the Privy Counsellors" said that the man had been committed by Her Majesty herself—therefore, they should not seek privilege.

23. *Ibid.*, pp. 342b, 407b.

24. Fortescue's admonition against proceeding in certain bills (1597), and Cecil's defense of Raleigh (1601).

25. Usher, *The Institutional History of the House of Commons*, pp. 205–8.

26. A typical description of the election of a speaker is found in D'Ewes, p. 469.

27. This ridiculous mummery was not ended until 1858, at the suggestion of Disraeli.

28. Smith, *The Commonwealth of England* (1621 ed.), p. 38.

29. C.J., I, 73; D'Ewes, p. 121.

30. D'Ewes, pp. 158, 242a.

31. Townshend, p. 205.

32. D'Ewes, p. 127a.

33. *Ibid.*, p. 306b; also C.J., I, 134b. (Speech of Cope, March 16, 1580/1).

34. This and the ensuing information on the speaker, in this paragraph, is derived from D'Ewes, pp. 410–11, 393b, 394b, 478–79, 176a, 656–57, 369, 438b, 284, 490b, 686, 470, 257a, 500a.

35. The proportion of speeches of courtiers to all recorded speeches is as follows: *1571*, 50 percent; *1572*, 46 percent; *1584*, 56 percent; *1586*, 46 percent; *1588*, 40 percent; *1592*, 51 percent; *1597*, 55 percent; *1601*, 42 percent. In the parliaments of 1558 and 1562 the recording of speeches by the clerk was so small that no conclusions at all can be drawn.

36. The various parliaments took cognizance of privilege cases as follows, if the records are accurate: *1558*, one case; *1562*, five; *1571*, three; *1572*, two; *1584*, four; *1586*, one; *1588*, two; *1592*, three; *1597*, three; *1601*, eight.

37. D'Ewes, pp. 236–41.

38. *Ibid.*, pp. 241–44.

39. *Ibid.*, p. 558.

40. Townshend, p. 303.

41. For various references to this disorder, see D'Ewes, pp. 623, 633, 640, 651, 673, 675, 683–84; Townshend, p. 209.

42. This is no mere generality. It is proved by counting the number of times the queen sent messages to the commons in 1601 as compared with the number in 1572–83 or in the short session of 1586.

43. D'Ewes, p. 633.

44. A careful statistical study of this phase of parliamentary development has been made, but, save as it justifies this short conclusion, it has little interest. Bills were passed or rejected after a number of readings in full house. Although this number came, in the reign of James, to be regularly set at three, it varied in Elizabeth's time. In the main it was three, although several cases of a fourth reading are recorded (see D'Ewes, pp. 89b, 134b). The Queen's Pardon passed on first reading (*ibid.*, pp. 134b, 309b, 455a, 595b; Townshend, p. 29). Usually readings were separated by at least a day, but instances are not lacking of two and even three readings immediately consecutive, or at least on the same day (Townshend, pp. 21, 22, 23, 26, 317; D'Ewes, *passim*). There might be "speaking to the bill" at any of the readings, and it might be "dashed" or rejected at any of them, although the greatest casualties were coming, toward the end of the reign, to be at second reading. The total number, by a count of those given by D'Ewes, is: first reading, 13; second reading, 41; third reading, 36; fourth reading, 1. In the last parliament of the reign, when forms of procedure were taking shape, 24 bills were dashed on second reading, 7 on first, and 8 on third.

Various things might happen to a bill in Elizabeth's time. A bill was read by the clerk, at the command of the speaker, sometimes on the motion, or at the request, of a member. There might or might not be debate at this point. Soon the bill was read again and, upon motion and vote of the house, either ordered engrossed or committed. If both motions failed, the bill was dead. There was usually debate at second reading, and occasionally counsel of interested parties was allowed to present a case at the bar, although this was sometimes done immediately before third reading. Some days after second reading, the bill was read again and acted upon. It was before this (usually) final reading, of course, that the committee reported it back, with or without amendments or recommendations. If it was agreed upon, either *viva voce* or by a division, it was sent to the lords, very often, although not invariably, by one or more members of the privy council, accompanied by an indeterminate number of members. If it was not agreed to, the bill was dead. In the case of bills sent from the lords, the committee step was normally omitted (see D'Ewes, pp. 186b, 252a), although there were exceptions to the rule (*ibid.*, p. 369b). Later usage demanded that commitment be only after the second reading, but this had not become established in Elizabeth's reign, though it was growing. Usher has tabulated the commitments to 1580: 55 on first reading, 13 on third, and 147 on second (Usher, p. 226). After 1588, commitments on any other reading than the second were extremely rare.

Bills were sometimes committed more than once. What went on in committees is not very clear. The committees improved upon wording, rejected bills entirely and drafted new ones in their places, drafted new measures at the express command of the house, or returned bills with amendments and with recommendations that they pass or be rejected. Sometimes they made no progress and returned bills without change or recommendation. It does not appear that bills were often "killed in committee."

As to the organization of committees, we are in the dark. In many cases the record gives the name of the man to whom the bill and the list of committee members were delivered by the clerk, but this man probably was not the chairman, since he was often an obscure member, and often the report from committees was by another man. "It liked the committees after their resolution to choose one amongst all, to give an account of their proceeding; and that is myself . . ." (Secretary Cecil, in 1601; see Townshend, p. 202). Evidently no committee chairman was designated at the time the committee was selected.

45. The recording of speeches in the journal becomes fuller as the reign progresses: *1558*, 4; *1562*, 4; *1571*, 94; *1572–83*, 85; *1584–86*, 120; *1586–87*, 75; *1588–89*, 99; *1592–93*, 181; *1597*, 168; *1601*, 324.

46. He recorded 168 in 1597 and 324 in 1601, despite the fact that the parliament of 1601 was a month shorter than that of 1597 and perfected only 29 bills as opposed to 43 in 1597. The ratio of the number of speeches recorded to the number of speakers recorded for 1592, 1597, and 1601 respectively was: 2.6 to 1, 2 to 1, 3.7 to 1.

47. Cecil (principal secretary of state), Fortescue (master of the wardrobe), Haman (queen's sergeant), Harris (queen's sergeant), Heneage (vice chamberlain), Knollys (treasurer of the household), Raleigh, Wooley (Latin secretary), Wroth (like Raleigh high in favor at that time), Yelverton (queen's sergeant). Of these men, all save Harris and Haman were also leaders in debate, as has been already noted.

48. Henry Finch, "Mr." Hext, Edward Hubberd, Edward Lewkenor,

and Robert Wingfield were men of little fame. Fulk Grevill, though a courtier, held no important office and was certainly second rate. Sir Francis
Moore was a distinguished lawyer, but had no court connection. Sir Edwin
Sandys, known so far only as a lawyer and writer, was yet to show his stature
as a politician.

49. Sir Francis Darcy and Sir George Moore were unimportant figures.
Sir Moyle Finch was the unimportant scion of an old and important family.
Sir Edward Hobby was a courtier, but not an important one. Sir Francis
Hastings, like Sandys, was a man of ability, presently to throw his weight
on the side of opposition.

50. Usher, *The Institutional History of the House of Commons*, pp.
205–8.

51. Townshend, pp. 306–7.

52. See D'Ewes, pp. 644a, 677a; Townshend, pp. 216, 222, 229.

53. Townshend, p. 224.

54. *Ibid.*

55. The number of privy council members in the house, as nearly as can
be determined from a comparison of returns and council attendance lists,
was: *1558*, 8; *1562–66*, 10 (8 at any one time); *1571*, 5; *1572–83*, 9
(6 at any one time); *1584–86*, 7; *1586–87*, 8; *1588–89*, 8; *1592–93*, 5;
1597, 3; *1601*, 5.

56. D'Ewes, pp. 393 (twice), 403a, 469a; *Acts of the Privy Council*,
1558–70, pp. 310–11; *ibid.*, *1575–77*, p. 73; *ibid.*, *1588*, pp. 416–17.

57. D'Ewes, pp. 88a, 652–53, 86a, 444a, 124–25, 131a, 220b.

CHAPTER II: DISCOVERY
OF SOME INTERESTING POSSIBILITIES

1. For example, D'Ewes states that, at the last day of the parliament of
1597, 48 bills were "quashed" by Her Majesty and 43 made law (p. 596).
There must have been some bills passed by the commons and rejected by
the lords, so that the house must have acted favorably on more than 91 bills.
A careful examination of D'Ewes for this session reveals only 50 cases in
which the passage of a bill is noted. This throws out D'Ewes's evidence on
the whole point. Unfortunately, the parliament of 1597 and that of 1588–
89 (p. 455) are the only ones for which D'Ewes tells of the negative action
of the crown.

2. This seems to be a reasonable assumption since the number of cases
discoverable in the parliaments has a ratio to the statutory enactment which
is nearly uniform and is very similar to that of the sessions of the first parliament of James I:

	Subjects Mentioned	Statutes	Ratio (Statutes to Subjects)
1592–93	43	27	.63
1597	90	43	.47
1601	72	29	.40
1603–4	135	71	.52
1605–6	127	56	.44
1606–7	72	33	.46
1609–10	141	66	.47

3. The session of 1606–7 was almost entirely taken up with the consideration of the union with Scotland. Hence it did not resemble the others and cannot be considered normal.

4. This phase has been noted but seems to have little bearing on the matters of general interest. For the three last parliaments of Elizabeth and the first of James the bills dashed were: *1592–93*, 4; *1597*, 16; *1601*, 23; *1603–4*, 47; *1605–6*, 32; *1606–7*, 13; *1609–10*, 21; entire parliament of *1604*, 113.

5. For reasons already mentioned, the session of 1606–7 spent 120 days in argument with only 33 statutes resulting, a ratio of .28, as compared with .81, .53, and .50 for the other three sessions.

6. That of 1559.

7. The first session of the parliament of 1572–83 is the one exception; it ended June 13, 1572.

8. The figures are: *1597*, 3 afternoon sittings; *1601*, 8; *1603–4*, 10; *1605–6*, 8; *1606–7*, 4; *1609–10*, 10.

9. In the session of 1603–4 the afternoon sittings were mainly devoted to first readings (C.J., I, 165b, 178b, 194b, 207b, 224a, 241b). In the later sessions the work became more miscellaneous—appointments, orders and reports of committees, privilege cases, and even third readings (C.J., I, 295b, 301b, 313b, 381b, 389b, 450b, 452a, 453a). "The Titles of Twelve Bills, Yesterday in the Afternoon the first time read, published to the House by Mr. Speaker" (C.J., I, 196b, May 2, 1604). This looks like a small, very routine afternoon sitting, to expedite business.

10. There is a sharp increase in this session of the number of notices of committee meetings entered in the journal. See C.J., I, 392–454 *et passim*.

11. C.J., I, 169b, 329b, 339a, 351a, 352a, 390b, 400a, 407b, 408b, 409a, 412a, 417a, 418a, 423a, 424a, 425a, 429a, 432a, 435b, 439b, 441a, 444b, 446b, *et al.*

12. One exception was the bill for His Majesty's general pardon, which had but one. The readings were usually on different days, though in the

case of a bill with strong backing there might be two on the same day. See Salisbury's bill, C.J., I, 330a; see also p. 444b.

13. This was not invariable. A bill might even be committed on its first reading (C.J., I, 300a).

14. Bills were sometimes debated at this point and might be dashed (C.J., I, 183b, 205b, 234b, 236b, 237b, 272b, 279b, 286a, 292a, 386a, 434a, 441a). Dashing at this point became less frequent in the last two sessions.

15. Provisos and amendments might be recommitted at this point, but not the body of the bill (C.J., I, 424b).

16. As the 1604 parliament wore on, members became reluctant to waste their time, and that of the committees, with bills that were not likely to pass. The number of bills dashed at second reading became greater.

	1st Reading	2d Reading	Com. Report	3d Reading
1603–4	9	20	5	10
1605–6	6	11	4	9
1606–7	0	7	1	4
1609–10	4	11	2	3

17. Examples are the rule requiring silence when the speaker addressed the house, that requiring members to remain in their places until he had left the chamber, that concerning discipline for disorderly members, and that prescribing the form in which new bills should be submitted (C.J., I, 244a, 371a, 243b, 187b).

18. This and the following references in this paragraph to the limitation of the power of the speaker are based upon passages in C.J., I, 187b, 212b(twice), 223b, 353b.

19. The rules in this group are found in C.J., I, 162a, 168a, 175a. 304a, 408b, 424b, 427a. The rule on speaking irrelevantly was often repeated (C.J., I, 172a, 177b, 214b).

20. The house might adjourn itself (C.J., I, 150a). A ratio of 2 to 1 should be maintained at conferences with the lords (C.J., I, 154b). No double question should be put upon the passing of a bill, though it might be put double at the time of committing (C.J., I, 240a). If two stand to speak to a bill, the opponent shall speak first (C.J., I, 232a). When alteration of a law in being is required and a question put, the Yea sit still and the No go out (C.J., I, 240a). A man may change his opinion in a division, after an oral vote (C.J., I, 303b). Provisos and amendments to a bill recommitted (in part) at its third reading must be penned at the table of the house and not in committee (C.J., I, 304a).

21. With the exception of the rule regarding debate in the absence of

the speaker and the standing order regarding the committee of grievance.

22. This expression is admittedly used in a loose sense. It seems academic, however, to deny the existence of a "system" when bills were being more or less regularly reported back from committees with definite recommendations and acted on without debate or comment, usually along the lines of the committee recommendation.

23. See pp. 20–21.

24. In the case of such entries as "the knights of all shires," it was possible in most cases to secure, without much doubt, the number of persons involved. (Such groups as "all lawyers" and the like are discussed in later paragraphs in the text.) The chart compiled, therefore, is fairly accurate. The laborious task of tracing and crediting with a committee membership every individual member listed in some other way than by his name has not been attempted. The problem to which this chapter is chiefly addressed is the relative activity of the members, and it is clear that the honors are so evenly distributed in these nameless appointments that the result would not be much affected.

25. The entry "the first knight for every shire" can be found as far back as 1587 (D'Ewes, p. 409b). This classification was used 14 times altogether in Elizabeth's reign, although in many more cases the knights of specific shires, burgesses of port towns and of particular boroughs, and even "all citizens of cities" (a group of about 39) were named.

26. In 1603–4 there was not a single example of these general invitations. In 1605-6 there was one (all lawyers, April 30, 1606, C.J., I, 303a). In 1606–7 there were 12 cases in which the lawyers were appointed (C.J., I, 326b, 346a, 364a, 366a, 374a[2], 374b[2], 375a, 378a, 387b, 389a). In 1609–10 there were 22 cases in which the lawyers were appointed (C.J., I, 394a, 398b, 404b, 408a, 408b, 410a, 413b, 416a, 417a, 419a, 420b, 422a, 426a, 426b, 428a, 429b, 432a, 432b, 434a[2], 440b, 448a) and 17 invitations to "all who come" (pp. 394a, 398b, 413b[2], 421a, 425b, 426b, 428b, 429a, 429b, 435b, 442b, 444b, 447b, 449a, 450a, 450b).

27. In 1597 (D'Ewes, p. 553) there is a case of "all the Lawyers" being appointed to a committee, and again (p. 557b) "any other that will come." These are the only cases that I have found.

28. Dec. 19, 1606 (C.J., I, 329a); Feb. 20, 1606/7 (p. 339a).

29. C.J., I, 326b.

30. C.J., I, 327a: "The Court did this Day arise at Ten a Clock; being remembered of their Meeting at One a Clock, upon the grand Committee touching the Instrument of the Union, in the Parliament-House."

31. Bowyer, *Parliamentary Diary, 1606–1607*, p. 102: "The Committee sent word that they would come downe into the House (if so it pleased the House) and conferr with the Company, not as in the House, but by way of Committee: This the Speaker having received from them by the Serjeant, did deliver to the House, and the House alloweing thereof; The Speaker added, That himself in this Case was to departe the place, with which allowance he did, and the most of the Company departed with him; a few staied untill after eleven of the clock expecting the coming downe of the Committees, and then likewise departed, and after them the Committees followed."

32. C.J., I, 371a: "Affirmed, that if Mr. Speaker were absent, the whole House might be a Committee, and thought fit to commit this Bill to the whole House, Mr. Speaker only excepted."

33. C.J., I, 378b: "And moved, that Mr. Speaker might depart, and the Committee being compounded of the whole House, and now together, and the Business of the House very little, might (for saving of time) presently enter into consideration of their Charge: Which, after some Dispute, whether it were fit, or no, being without Precedent, seldom moved, and carrying with it no Decorum, in respect of Mr. Speaker's ordinary and necessary Attendance upon the House till Eleven a Clock, grew to a Question; viz. Whether the Committee should now sit, or in the afternoon. And Resolved, upon Question, They should meet in the Afternoon, and not now."

34. C.J., I, 414a, 429b, 430a, 434b, 436a, 441b, 443a, 444b, 445a(2), 447a(2), 453a(2).

35. C.J., I, 441b, March 15, 1609/10: "A Committee of the Whole House:—to sit every other day."

36. C.J., I, 169a, April 12, 1604. It was for this reason that a committee quorum of 8 was ordered.

37. C.J., I, 177a, April 19, 1604: "The House thought fit, that the Bill for Continuance &c. should not be brought in by any but the Committee for Continuances, which was to be named."

38. C.J., I, 289a, March 25, 1606: "The Clerk to attend at the Committee." (This was evidently an ordinary committee, for the first suggestion of a committee of the whole does not come until the following autumn.) C.J., I, 412a, March 17, 1609/10: "The Clerk to attend, and to say Prayers in the Morning, at the Great Committee for Wards." (This, of course, may have been a committee of the whole, but it does not affect the case.)

39. C.J., I, 377b, June 1, 1607: "This day Mr. Speaker, with the

Officers, and sundry Members of the House, being assembled, sat in the House from Eight a Clock until Eleven; and then did arise, and depart, without Motion made, or Bill read.

"The great Committee for the Bill touching hostile laws, sat in the mean Time, in the Court of Wards."

C.J., I, 378b, June 4, 1607: "this Forenoon the great Committee, for hostile Laws, sat in the Court of Wards; and nothing in the mean time done in the House."

40. The references noted are: *1603–4*, 3 (C.J., I, 153b[2], 253a); *1605–6*, 5 (pp. 260a, 263b, 265a, 276a, 299a); *1606–7*, 4 (pp. 340a, 346a, 350a, 355a); *1609–10*, 14 (pp. 400a, 409b, 413a, 414a, 414b, 415a[2], 417a, 433a, 433b, 435b, 440a, 441b, 448a).

41. In tabular form:

Session	Number of Reports Recorded	Action without Debate
1603–4	126	79 (63%)
1605–6	133	77 (58%)
1606–7	86	46 (53%)
1609–10	152	81 (53%)

42. In tabular form:

Parliament	Same Constituency as in Preceding Parliament	Different Constituency	Other Old Parliament Men	Total Old Parliament Men	New Members
1592	106	71	102	279	184
1597	80	71	75	226	129
1601	90	52	123	265	193
1604	83	70	93	246	170

(The biggest break is obviously between 1592 and 1597.)

43. I have selected a list of 61 "leaders" of this parliament. In the spelling of these names I have in general used the form which appears in the list of returns. In some cases I have indicated in parentheses the most common variant. The variant is sometimes the form (e.g., Hoby, Montagu, Phillips) under which later generations of the families have chosen to be known. In a few cases Christian names cannot be found. The list is as follows: Edward Alford, Sir Francis Bacon, Sir Nathaniel Bacon, Sir Francis Barrington, Sir Henry Beaumont, Sir Maurice Berkley, Giles Brooke, Sir Julius Caesar, Sir Gamaliel Capell, Sir George Carew, Sir Anthony Cope, Sir Walter Cope, Sir Charles Cornwallis, Thomas Crewe,

Sir Herbert Crofts, Sir John Doderidge, Sir Thomas Fleming, Nicholas
Fuller, Sir Edward Grevill, William Hackwell (Hakewill), John Hare,
Sir Francis Hastings, Sir John Heigham, Sir John Herbert, Sir Henry
Hobart, Sir Edward Hobby (Hoby), Sir John Hollis, John Hoskins,
Nicholas Hyde, Sir Robert Johnson, Sir Edward Lewkenor, Sir Thomas
Lowe, Henry Marten (Martin), Sir Robert Maunsell (Mansell), Sir
Edward Montague (Mountague, Montagu), Sir Henry Montague, Francis
Moore, Sir George Moore, Sir Henry Nevill, Sir Roger Owen, Sir Robert
Oxenbridge, Sir Thomas Parry, Sir Edward Phelips (Phillips), Sir Henry
Poole, John Prowze, Sir Thomas Ridgeway, Sir Edwin Sandys, Sir Nicholas
Saunders, Sir John Saville, Sir John Scott, Sir Thomas Smith, George
Snigg, Sir William Strode (Strowd), Lawrence Tanfield, Sir John Thynne,
Mr. Whitson, Sir Robert Wingfield, Sir Robert Wroth, Humphrey Wynch,
Mr. Wyseman, Henry Yelverton.

44. F. Bacon, Barrington, Berkley, Caesar, Carew, A. Cope. W. Cope,
Crewe, Crofts, Fleming, Hackwell, Hare, Hastings, Herbert, Hobart,
Hobby, Hyde, Johnson, Lewkenor, Marten, Maunsell, E. Montague,
H. Montague, F. Moore, G. Moore, Nevill, Owen, Saunders, Snigg,
Strode, Tanfield, Thynne, Wingfield, Wroth, Wynch, Wyseman.

45. Alford, N. Bacon, Beaumont, Brooke, W. Cope, Doderidge, Fuller,
Grevill, Heigham, Parry, Poole, Ridgeway, Sandys, Saville, Scott, Smith,
Yelverton.

46. Brooke, Capell, C. Cornwallis, Hollis, Hoskins, Lowe, Oxenbridge,
Prowze, Whitson.

47. The gap in the *Acts of the Privy Council* between 1604 and 1613
makes it difficult to check on council membership. The dates of privy
council members in the house were:

Sir John Herbert. Throughout the parliament.
Sir John Stanhope. First session only.
Sir John Fortescue. Returned Feb., 1605/6. Died Dec. 23, 1607.
Sir Julius Caesar. Returned July 5, 1607. Served till end of the parlia-
ment.
Sir Thomas Parry. Returned Jan. 4, 1609/10. Served to end of the
parliament.

A complete list of privy councilors in the house, 1604–29, is found in
Willson, *The Privy Councillors in the House of Commons*, pp. 99–101.

48. Birch, *The Court and Times of James the First*, I, 59–60, letter
of Sir Edward Hobby to Sir Thomas Edmondes, 1606: "Whereby it seems
that the former day's work, first propounded by Sir Thomas Ridgeway,

and seconded by such like (for I must tell you, that I think the State scorneth to have any privy councillors of any understanding in that House) came short to expectation and necessity."

Ibid., II, 176, John Chamberlain to Sir Dudley Carleton, June 17, 1612: "For the king, being given to understand that he is ill served in parliament by reason of the paucity of councillors and officers of the household, that were wont to bear great sway in that House, is minded to reduce it to the form it had in the late queen's days . . ."

49. Such as masters of requests, officers of the queen's or prince's household, barons of the exchequer, and master of the jewels.

50. No claim is made for the exhaustiveness of the foregoing analysis. It is based largely upon the *Calendars of State Papers*. The list of these men will be found in Appendix A.

51. Such as Hollis and Hare.

52. Spedding, *Letters and Life of Bacon*, IV, 370. A letter of advice from Bacon to James, just before the parliament of 1614.

53. *Calendars of State Papers Domestic* (hereafter cited as C.S.P. Dom.), 1603–10, 292 (xviii, 115), Sir Edward Phelips to Salisbury, Feb. 25, 1605/6: "The House displeased with the proceedings concerning Hare. Their heat on the Bill against Purveyors. One of the seedmen of sedition Nich. Spray asks leave of absence, and another Sir Edward Hext is going away soon."

54. Sir Edward Hobby, writing to Sir Thomas Edmondes, March 7, 1605/6, referred to Hare and Hyde as "like tribunes of the people," in connection with their speeches on purveyance (Birch, *The Court and Times of James the First*, I, 60). See also C.S.P. Dom., 1603–10, 348 (xxvi, 43), Feb. 4, 1606/7.

55. He was fined £200 by the commissioners of causes ecclesiastical, presumably for his speeches in parliament (C.S.P. Dom., 1603–10, 382 [xxviii, 90], Nov. 14, 1607). But it is hardly necessary to prove that Fuller was one of the opposition by reference other than his own speeches recorded in the journal.

56. He claimed for himself the initiative in opening the grievance of impositions and tells how it brought him into disfavor (Whitlocke, *Liber Famelicus*, pp. 24, 32–33).

57. C.S.P. Dom., 1603–10, 559 (xlix, 26), Ralph Lord Eure to Salisbury, Nov. 13, 1609. In describing the irregular election of Sir Samuel Sandys, Eure refers to him as a strong opponent of the jurisdiction of the Council of Wales.

58. He also was committed, presumably for speeches in parliament (C.S.P. Dom., 1603–10, 403 [xxxi, 26], Chamberlain to Carleton, Feb. 11, 1607/8).

59. Piggott was expelled the house and sent to the Tower for a rash speech with reference to the Scotch, delivered by him in the house, Feb. 16, 1606/7 (C.J., I, 335, 336).

60. C.J., I, 402b, 439 (Cotton); 266b, 399a, 449a (Hoskins); 430b, 438a (Sammes).

61. C.J., I, 261b, 266b, 276b, 282b, 297a, 353b, 430b, 448a; *Parliamentary Debates in 1610*, pp. 37, 58–61, 143.

62. C.J., I, 166b, 261b, 289b, 397a, 402b; *Parliamentary Debates in 1610*, pp. 109, 130.

63. C.J., I,, 266b, 274a, 427b, 438a; *Parliamentary Debates in 1610*, pp. 55, 89.

64. C.J., I, 186a, 266b, 272a, 275a, 280b, 289a, 448a, 453b.

65. C.J., I, 289b, 297a, 427b.

66. *Dictionary of National Biography.*

67. C.J., I, 231a, 278a, 438a, 448a.

68. C.J., I, 272a, 282a, 397a.

69. C.J., I, 427b, 438a, 448a.

70. Alford, N. Bacon, Beaumont, Berkley, Brooke, A. Cope, Cotton, Duncombe, Dyett, Hackwell, Harley, Hastings, Hedley, Heigham, Hollis, Holt, Hoskins, L. Hyde, Irby, James of Newport, Jones, Leveson, Maynard, Mercer, E. Montague, Nevill, Noy, Owen, Paddy, Peak, Piggott, Poole, Sammes, Saville, Tey, Twysden, Wentworth, Whitlocke, Whitson, Wingfield.

71. On June 29, 1610, Yelverton made a speech justifying the impositions. This is supposed to mark his turn from the "patriots" to the "courtiers." (See *Parliamentary Debates in 1610*, p. 85; also Birch, *The Court and Times of James the First*, I, 121.) Yelverton was appointed solicitor general in 1613, and attorney general in 1617.

72. Fuller was a close second, and Marten a poor third.

73. See Chapter I.

74. The steady importance of Fuller, increasing markedly at the end of the parliament, the sharp decline of Bacon after 1604, and the equally sharp rise of Marten and Sandys in 1609 show a spectacular change of influence in favor of the "patriots." The record of the "first ten" committee reporters follows.

	1603–4	1605–6	1606–7	1609–10
Sir Francis Bacon	24	7	6	4
Sir John Doderidge	0	13	0	0
Giles Brooke	1	1	0	12
Nicholas Fuller	10	19	12	22
Sir Henry Hobart	1	11	4	3
Henry Marten	1	2	5	17
Francis Moore	17	2	0	2
Sir Henry Montague	1	14	5	10
Sir Henry Poole	0	3	5	10
Sir Edwin Sandys	3	3	5	28

75. Bowyer, *Parliamentary Diary, 1606–1607*, p. 2 (Jan. 24, 1605/6): "Mr. Fuller moved That no man should name above two Committees to a Bill, affirming that such is the Order of the House: Which was denyed, and his Motion rejected as frivolous."

C.J., I, 172b (April 16, 1604). Mr. Marten suggested that there be three urns, containing names of knights, citizens, and burgesses and that a young boy should put his hand in and draw out names. This was not generally agreeable to the house, but a committee was named to devise a better system. (It was apparently an impartial committee—at least a very mixed one.)

76. C.J., I, 409b, 413a, 414a.

77. C.J., I, 376a (May 27, 1607). The allegation had attracted sufficient notice to cause James to deny it in the house through Speaker Phelips.

78. C.J., I, 277a (March 4, 1605/6). This was apparently entered as a rule.

79. C.J., I, 224b, 244a.

80. C.J., I, 243b.

81. C.J., I, 231b (June 2, 1604).

82. C.J., I, 226 (May 25, 1604).

83. C.J., I, 212b, 223b.

84. C.J., I, 209b (May 14, 1604).

85. C.J., I, 197a (May 2, 1604).

86. C.J., I, 368b (May 4, 1607).

87. C.J., I, 354a (March 23, 1606/7).

88. Bowyer, *Parliamentary Diary, 1606–1607*, p. 80 (March 14, 1606/7). He was actually called to the bar.

89. Bowyer uses these picturesque words in his account of the division on the subsidy, March 16, 1605/6 (*ibid.*, p. 49). I am not at all sure,

however, that he means by them to make a distinction between two parties.

90. Especially in the *Parliamentary Debates in 1610* edited by Gardiner.

91. Bowyer, *Parliamentary Diary, 1606–1607*, p. 168 (Nov. 27, 1607).

92. C.J., I, 396a (Feb. 17, 1609/10): "The true Scale of the King's Prerogative was, when in Concurrence with the publick Good:—In some Things inherent and inseparable."

93. C.J., I, 451–52 (July 18, 1610). The speaker, incidentally, got small satisfaction either from Sir Edward or the house and in the end was "worse satisfied than before."

94. C.J., I, 427b (May 11, 1610).

95. C.J., I, 175 (April 17, 1604). Tey was censured for his rashness.

96. C.J., I, 353b (March 23, 1606/7).

97. Bowyer, *Parliamentary Diary, 1606–1607*, p. 246 (March 28, 1607).

98. *Ibid.*, p. 15 (Jan. 31, 1605/6).

99. C.J., I, 370b (May 7, 1607).

100. Bowyer, *Parliamentary Diary, 1606–1607*, pp. 77, 79 (March 12, 14, 1605/6).

101. *Ibid.*, pp. 168–69 (Nov. 27, 1606). By counsel of procrastination, for further conference and commitment.

102. This was probably the most dramatic act of the whole parliament—certainly one of the shrewdest. See Bowyer, *Parliamentary Diary, 1606–1607*, pp. 192 (March 7, 1606/7) *et seq.*

103. C.J., I, 333 (Feb. 13, 1606/7). It is very clear from Poole's speeches that he was rather violent against the Scots (C.J., I, 328–30).

104. For samples, see C.J., I, 208a, 238a, 276a, 291b, 301a, 375a, 387a, 428a, 429a, 436a, 443b, 444a, 445a.

105. Of 78 cases (during the whole parliament) in which leave to depart was granted, 13 concerned men apparently on the court side, 16 concerned their opponents, and 48 concerned members of small influence—for the most part obscure persons whose names hardly appear elsewhere. The attendance was poor throughout the parliament. See C.J., I, 300a, 326b, 343b, 344a, 346b, 364a (attendance "not above three-score," April 20, 1607), 376a, 381a, 403b, 412b, 437a.

See also records of very small divisions: C.J., I, 246b (98 on June 26, 1604), 292a (84 on April 20, 1606), 300b (50 on April 24, 1606), 376b (121 on May 29, 1607), 434b (92 on June 1, 1610), 439b (64 on June 15, 1610), 450a (30 on the afternoon of July 14, 1610). These divisions were of course abnormal, for there were several over 300 (C.J., I, 176b, 199a, 205a, 240a, 403a), and the greater part of the others were over 200 (26 as opposed to 20 between 100 and 200). A total of 60 divisions has been noted. (Three of the small divisions were not noted as they occurred on the same day as others cited.)

106. According to the "Official List," 395 members are sure, 9 are doubtful, and 17 returns are missing.

107. Division for June 15, 1604 (C.J., I, 240a).

108. The greatest number of names is to be found in the journal for 1603–4. It is 356. Other members either failed to attend or took a very insignificant part in the business of the house.

109. Sir Francis Hastings.

110. Nathaniel Bacon, Sir Thomas Beaumont, Giles Brooke, Sir Henry Constable, Sir Anthony Dyett, John Hare, Sir Robert Harley, Hedley, Sir John Heigham, Sir Edward Herbert, Sir Edward Hext, Holt, Lawrence Hyde, James of Newport, Sir John Leveson, Henry Marten, Mercer, Sir William Paddy, Peak, Sir Christopher Piggott, Nicholas Spray, John Tey, Sir Robert Twysden.

111. Irby, Maynard, Sir John Saville, Sir Robert Wingfield.

112. Sir Walter Cope, Sir Henry Yelverton, Sir Henry Nevill, Sir John Hollis, Sir George Moore, Anthony Cope, Sir Edward Montague.

113. These computations cannot, of course, claim completeness or, for that very reason, full accuracy. They are undoubtedly accurate enough to support the main conclusions.

CHAPTER III: THE ADDLED PARLIAMENT

1. So John Chamberlain wrote to Sir Dudley Carleton, March 3, 1613/4 (C.S.P. Dom., 1611–18, 225).

2. C.J., I, 461b, Secretary Winwood, speaking April 12, 1614: "That the last disorderly Parliament there awakened Tyrone, who now treateth with the Pope, to come next summer."
See also C.J., I, 483a. Hackwell, in reporting the disorder at a committee meeting, compares it to the physical violence practiced at the time of Sir John Davies' election as speaker of the Irish commons of 1613.

3. C.S.P. Ven., 1613–15, 100–101, letter of Antonio Foscarini to the Doge and Senate, March 21, 1613/4.

4. C.J., I, 457b, 458a, 461a, 464b, 468a, 468b, 477, 480, 485b.

5. Sir George Selby, Sir John Saville, Sir John Cuttes, Sir Thomas Chicheley, Matthew Clerke, Thomas Oxenbridge, Thomas Berry, Sir Robert Maunsell, Sir Thomas Parry, Sir Henry Wallop, Sir Walter Cope.

6. See Appendix A. Sir William Selby is listed as a commissioner of the Border in 1605.

7. C.S.P. Dom., 1603–10, 364.

8. C.S.P. Dom., 1611–18, 157.

9. C.S.P. Dom., 1611–18, 14.

10. See *Calendar of Patent Rolls, Ireland*, Henry VIII, Edward VI, Mary, Elizabeth, *passim*.

11. *Dictionary of National Biography*.

12. Notestein, Relf, and Simpson, eds., *Commons Debates, 1621*, VII, 634, May 9, 1614: "The afternoone, a committee touchinge undertakers."

". . . and with more it was farther alledged that noble men engrossed the burgesshippes, some 8, some 10."

"The effect of Mr. Ashlyes speache was, that Sir Reynolds Moors told him of a merchant that said there were undertakers, he denied it but it was approved to his face by Sir John Crompton, besides. Prince Henry did expostulate with Sir Thomas Overburye wherefore he was so greate with some men who answered that they were to doe the kinge good service in the next parliament."

13. *The Court and Character of King James I*, p. 16: "Now did the great Mannagers of the State (of which Salisbury was chief) after they had packed the Lords, begin to deal the government of the Kingdom amongst themselves . . ."

14. Spedding, *Letters and Life of Bacon*, V, 20; Birch, *The Court and Times of James the First*, I, 300, Chamberlain to Carleton, March 3, 1613/4: "Here is much justling for place in Parliament, and letters fly from great persons extraordinarily: wherein methinks they do the King no great service, seeing the world is apt to censure it as a kind of packing."

15. Birch, *The Court and Times of James the First*, I, 235, Chamberlain to Carleton, March, 1613/4: "Upon Saturday last there was a great concourse at Uxbridge for choosing Sir Julius Caesar and Sir Thomas Lake, knights, for Middlesex. Sir Walter Cope stood not, but Sir Francis Drury had a man there, who, getting up upon a table, told the assembly that his master meant to have stood, but was forbidden by the king. Wherefore, he desired all his well-wishers to give their votes to Mr. Chancellor, and for the second place, to do as God should put in their minds."

16. *Ibid.*, pp. 301–2, Chamberlain to Carleton, March 3, 1613/4: "Upon Tuesday, the city chose Sir Thomas Low for their knight, but will in nowise hitherto admit Mr. Recorder, alleging only that he is the king's serjeant. Mr. Fuller is their first burgess, whose choice is as much subject to interpretation as the refusal of the others . . ."

17. Figure compiled from Appendices A and B.

18. See Gardiner, *History of England, 1603–1642*, II, 228–29: "Under these circumstances, the ministers of the Crown were induced to take steps to procure a favourable majority, to which they had thought it unnecessary to resort ten years previously. How far they went it is difficult to say, with the scanty information which we possess."

19. In Appendix B the available information on patronage, experience, and royal discipline of the members of parliament in 1614 has been assembled.

20. See the long debate on this subject in the journal for May 2, 1614 (C.J., I, 470–71).

21. A list is included in *Parliamentary Accounts and Papers* for 1878 (XVII, xxxvii–xli), but it was not compiled like the others from the returns, which were found to be missing when the work was undertaken by order of the house. It is based upon a list found among the Duke of Manchester's Papers, No. 143.

22. C.J., I, 505a, June 1, 1614. Fourteen men are mentioned in the journal of whose returns there is no mention in the list.

23. *History of England, 1603–1642*, II, 230.

24. This takes account of missing and double returns.

25. That is, *potential* members, as judged by the returns.

26. Sir Julius Caesar, Sir Thomas Lake, Sir Thomas Parry, and Sir Ralph Winwood. After May 11 there were but three, due to the expulsion of Parry, because of the Stockbridge election.

27. Compiled from Appendix B.

28. See pp. 51–53.

29. See his tactless and defiant speech on the Bills of Grace, April 20, 1614 (C.J., I, 470a), and also his insulting condescension of May 10, in connection with the returns case involving Sir Thomas Parry (C.J., I, 478a).

30. Birch, *The Court and Times of James the First*, I, 236, Chamberlain to Carleton, March, 1613/4: "Randolph Crew is already designed speaker."

31. C.J., I, 456–60. Bacon was allowed to keep his seat, but it was ordered that in future the attorney general should be ineligible.

32. Final action was not taken in the Stockbridge case until May 31 (C.J., I, 458b).

33. C.J., I, 458b.

34. C.J., I, 461a.

35. C.J., I, 461b.

36. C.J., I, 462.

37. One whole day, May 5, seems to have been consumed in debate on impositions (C.J., I, 472–74).

38. The whole point of this case was evidently a partisan one, for Cope and Wallop, being found illegally elected, were expelled, and Parry, a member of the privy council, was not saved by his exalted position and suffered the same fate (C.J., I, 477–81).

39. C.J., I, 485.

40. C.J., I, 496–505.

41. Birch, *The Court and Times of James the First*, I, 346, Rev. Thomas Larkin to Sir Thomas Puckering, Sept. 11, 1614: "Nay, to show his majesty's further indignation against it, he publicly, in the Banqueting House at Whitehall, tore all their bills, a day or two after the said dissolution, before their faces."

42. Nichols, *Progresses*, III, 5; Birch, *The Court and Times of James the First*, I, 322, Chamberlain to Carleton, June 9, 1614.

43. Birch, *The Court and Times of James the First*, I, 324, Larkin to Puckering, June 18, 1614. This reference also mentions one Hoyley and a Dr. Sharpe and Sir Charles Cornwallis, none of whom were members.

44. C.S.P. Dom., 1611–18, 237.

45. C.S.P. Dom., 1611–18, 186.

46. These figures and the following ones on speeches are based upon an analysis of the journal.

47. That for the count palatine, April 11, 1614 (C.J., I, 459b).

48. Two were dashed at second reading (C.J., I, 465b, 476a), two at first reading (C.J., I, 483b, 495a), one at third reading (C.J., I, 493b).

49. On motion of Hackwell, April 13, 1614 (C.J., I, 464a).

50. On motion of Sandys, April 11, 1614 (C.J., I, 458b).

51. Such as that of May 23, requiring the house to sit every day at 7 A.M. and to begin reading bills at 8 A.M. (C.J., I, 495a).

52. Sir James Perrott, on April 12, suggested a more equitable manner of naming, but it came to nothing (C.J., I, 461b).

53. The clerk posted announcements of committee meetings in a conspicuous place (C.J., I, 468a). There were not as many meetings as there had been in the last session of the 1604 parliament.

54. The bills for Assignment of Debts, Right of King's Subjects to Plead Not Guilty and Weights and Measures were assigned to select committees, originally appointed to deal with other matters.

55. Committee appointments and committee attendance were of course two quite different matters.

56. Of the four divisions reported, three were over 300: *May 23, 334*

(C.J., I, 493b); *May 31*, 305 (C.J., I, 503b); *June 1*, 389 (C.J., I, 505a).

57. Sir Herbert Crofts complained, April 15, that this was a violation of the liberties of the house (C.J., I, 466a).

58. C.J., I, 467b (impositions), 469a (French company patent).

59. C.J., I, 487a, May 16.

60. C.J., I, 459b.

61. C.J., I, 468b.

62. C.J., I, 490b: "This being thus ordered; Word was brought, that the Lords were arisen, and gone: Whereupon Mr. Speaker left his Chair; and Sir Edw. Sandys taking the Clerk's Chair, Mr. Bawtry argued the matter of the King's Right of imposing."

63. C.J., I, 479b, May 10. This was the first speech that Winwood had made on the case, though it had been debated for two days. By this time the house had shown itself overwhelmingly hostile to Parry.

64. C.J., I, 479a, May 10. Lake spoke before Winwood and evidently gave him his cue.

65. C.J., I, 488a.

66. C.J., I, 496b–503b, May 25 to May 31.

67. C.J., I, 504, June 1.

68. C.J., I, 497b, May 25, 1614: "Sir Jerome Horsey:—That continues Interruptions all this Parliament. This Bone, among the rest, thrown in by a Devil, if a Bishop may be a Devil. That the Speech of an honourable Person in this House hath rubbed them, and they now winch."

C.J., I, 500b, May 27, 1614: "Sir S. Sands:—That hath been Thirty Years past in Parliament.—More Bones cast in this Parliament to divert the good Proceedings of the House, than in all the Parliaments he hath known.—"

69. References to heated debate, disrespect to the speaker, disorder at committees, and the like, abound. See, for example, C.J., I, 464a, 465b, 472b, 473a, 475b, 483b, 497a.

70. Among these gestures were the punishment of an intruder in the house (C.J., I, 484b), the fining of members for loitering in the entry (p. 501a), and a motion for better respect to Mr. Speaker (p. 464a).

71. See speeches of Sir Maurice Berkley, Sir George Moore, and Edward Alford on this subject (C.J., I, 463a).

72. C.J., I, 462b: "Sir G. Moore:—Liberty of Speech every Man's Right here; but Interpretation in best Sense, Favour of the House.—Sent hither from all the Commons of the Kingdom.—Our principal Care to speak from the Commonwealth that continually speaketh to us."

73. Sir Edwin Sandys "Moveth, the Committee for Privilege may consider of a safe Course, for keeping the Journals, and other the Memorials and Records of this House. That may consider of a fitting Place to keep them in, and not to come into the Hands of Executors" (C.J., I, 465b, April 15).

Later the committee of privilege was assigned the weekly perusal of the journal—but must have failed in its duty (C.J., I, 501b; see also p. 491a).

74. As before stated, the whole record for several days is missing, and in a number of cases deletions of critical passages have been made. See, for example, C.J., I, 460b (deletion of Ashley's defense against charges of misinforming the king), and p. 503a (Sir Edwin Sandys' defense against a charge of abusing Sir Dudley Digges).

75. See Appendix B. This includes some references to appointments made after 1614, as an indication of the probable sympathies of the man in question at the time of the Addled Parliament. Such speculation surely is open to question, however, for some of the later officeholders were patriots in 1614, as Hoskins. Most of the references are to earlier appointments or grants.

76. Sir Francis Bacon, attorney general; Sir Julius Caesar, chancellor of the exchequer and privy councilor; Sir Thomas Lake, privy councilor; Sir Ralph Winwood, principal secretary of state and privy councilor. Sir Thomas Parry, while he served on a number of committees, made no impression in debate upon the floor and was expelled May 11.

77. Sir Walter Chute, Sir Anthony Cope, Sir William Cope, Sir Henry Finch, Sir Edward Montague, Sir Henry Montague, Sir George Moore, Sir Carey Reynolds.

78. Sir Walter Chute is reported to have been confined in the Tower for his part in parliament (Turner, *The Privy Council of England, 1603–1784*, I, 203, Chamberlain to Carleton, June 9, 1614).

79. Sir Dudley Digges, Edward Duncombe, William Hackwell, Sir Robert Phelips, Sir Edwin Sandys.

80. Sir Henry Anderson, Sir Maurice Berkley, Christopher Brooke, Sir Herbert Crofts, Sir Edward Hobby, Sir Jerome Horsey, Sir John Sammes, Sir William Strode.

81. Birch, *The Court and Times of James the First*, I, 324, Larkin to Puckering, June 18, 1614. "Sir Robert" Giles was among those confined to London for parliamentary activity.

82. *Ibid.* Though Digges spoke often, it would be difficult from the journal to tell on which side he counted himself. This outside reference settles it, at the same time bearing witness to the weakness of the journal.

83. Crew had been assigned a legal point in the investigation of the king's right to impose and was one of those whose notes were confiscated and burned after parliament (*ibid.*, p. 322, Chamberlain to Carleton, June 9, 1614).

84. Sir James Perrott's speeches seem to incline to the court side, but he must have done or said something that is not recorded for, with Giles and Digges and a man named Hoyley, not a member, he was confined to London after the dissolution (*ibid.*, p. 324, Larkin to Puckering, June 18, 1614).

85. The notes of all four were confiscated (*ibid.*, p. 322, Chamberlain to Carleton, June 9, 1614).

86. *Ibid.*, p. 326, Chamberlain to Carleton, June 30, 1614: "The master of the Rolls [Sir Edward Phelips] that was in great favor with the king, hath lost his conceit about this business, for there be many presumptions that his hand was in it, his son [Sir Robert] being so busy and factious in the House, and Hoskins etc."

87. He was sent to the Tower (S. P. Dom., James I, lxxvi, Chamberlain to Carleton, June 9, 1614, cited in Turner, *The Privy Council of England, 1603–1784*, I, 203).

88. *Ibid.* He is referred to as "Hopkins."

89. *Ibid.*

90. Besides the references to Bacon's petulance, already cited, there is a curious little entry by the clerk, for May 10, that indicates a certain undercurrent of ridicule: "Mr. Attorney the Heir apparent of Eloquence.—"

91. Sir George Moore was, all things considered, the most active man of the party, if it may be called such.

92. He was made lord chief justice ten years later.

93. C.J., I, 502a: "Mr. Fuller tendereth a Bill against the Chancery, which was pressed by divers to be read; but Mr. Speaker desired the Respite thereof till To-Morrow; Whereupon Mr. Alford—." (Alford's speech was evidently a complaint that the clerk saw fit to delete.)

94. C.J., I, 456b (this concerned the attack upon the eligibility of Bacon): "Hereupon the House calling to the Question; Mr. Speaker desired them to stay a while, to see whether any other would speak; and then, being pressed to put the Question, desired to know the Pleasure of the House, if the first Question should not be, Whether the Question should be, without first a Search of the Precedents. To which Exceptions were taken; telling Mr. Speaker, he ought not to divert the Question."

95. C.J., I, 500b. Crewe defended himself on this point, admitting that

he had taken notes from the clerk's book, when sent for to the king, to give an account of proceedings in the house.

96. No other speaker since 1558, with the exception of Crooke, had as little success in maintaining order and decorum.

97. C.J., I, 463a (Maunsell), 470a (Sir H. Montague and Bacon), 474a (Lake), 506a (Sir George Moore).

98. References for the balance of this paragraph are as follows: C.J., I, 456a, 470a, 462a, 463a, 463b, 469a, 506a (the Wentworth mentioned was the member from Oxford, not Sir Thomas Wentworth).

99. This idea is expressed so often in debate on the subsidy that it needs no reference.

100. Gardiner, *History of England*, II, 246–47. The source of this rumor is not stated by Gardiner, and I have been unable to find a primary reference for it. There is no doubt, however, that it is based upon a reliable documentary reference, else it would not appear in a work of the character of Gardiner's. The suggestion is borne out by the remarks of Horsey and Sandys.

101. C.J., I, 497b, 500b.

102. See pp. 51–53.

103. Sir Thomas Bromley, Sir Henry Bulstrode, Henry Button, Matthew Davies, John Glanville, Sir Francis Goodwyn, Sir Thomas Grantham, Rice Gwyn, Nicholas Hyde, Sir William Jones, Thomas Mallett, Mr. Mervin, Sir Hugh Middleton, Sir Henry Montague, Francis Moore, Sir Robert Rich, Sir Thomas Roe, Sir Thomas Smith, George Thorpe, Sir William Walter, Sir Richard Weston, John Whitson.

104. Montague, Moore, Roe, and Whitson.

105. The 19 may be grouped as follows.

> *Confined to London after parliament:* Sir Dudley Digges, Sir Edward Giles, Sir James Perrott.
>
> *Identified by their speeches:* Edward Alford, Christopher Brooke, Edward Duncombe, Nicholas Fuller.
>
> *Imprisoned in the Tower:* John Hoskins, Sir Christopher Nevill, Sir Thomas Wentworth, Sir James Whitlocke.
>
> *Notes confiscated and burned:* Sir Thomas Crewe, William Hackwell, Sir Roger Owen, Sir Edwin Sandys, Sir Samuel Sandys.
>
> *Referred to as suffering king's displeasure for their activities in parliament:* Sir Walter Chute, Sir Herbert Crofts, Sir Robert Phelips.

CHAPTER IV: THE LOW POINT
OF CONCERTED OPPOSITION

1. C.S.P. Ven., 1615–17, 34, 37, 45, 53. Foscarini, Venetian ambassador, to the Doge and Senate: "If he wishes to use it [money appropriated by parliament] for things useful to the kingdom and honourable to the crown, he will never be in want of it" (C.S.P. Ven., 1615–17, 57).

2. C.S.P. Ven., 1615–17, 37, same to same: "The calling of parliament encounters the usual opposition of those who having excessive sums from the king think they will be compelled to render account for it, and also of those who are dependent on the Spaniards and receive pensions from them, who are very numerous."

3. C.S.P. Ven., 1615–17, 165, Donato, Venetian ambassador to Savoy, to the Doge and Senate.

4. C.S.P. Ven., 1615–17, 572, Lionello, Venetian ambassador, to the Doge and Senate.

5. C.S.P. Ven., 1617–19, 417.

6. Notestein, Relf, and Simpson, eds., *Commons Debates, 1621*, III, 425, Barrington diary.

7. *Ibid.*, V, 328, Smith diary: "And then, merily speakinge that he would punish our thankes with killinge of our Speaker, drew out a Rapier and knighted him before us all."

8. *Ibid.*, III, 192, Barrington diary.

9. *Ibid.*, III, 344–46, Barrington diary.

10. *Ibid.*, II, 406, anonymous "X" journal.

11. See *Ibid.*, V, 185, 186.

12. The returns, according to the "Official List," show 458 names. Of these, 24 were elected in the place of other members, but the list is obviously incomplete.

13. C.J., I, 541.

14. C.S.P. Ven., 1621–23, 186, James to Speaker Richardson, Dec. 3, 1621. This statement, of course, was made *parliamento sedente*.

15. In the Statutes of the Realm, IV, Pt. II, it is noted that in addition to the two subsidy bills an act containing the censure against Mompesson, Mitchell, and Bacon was found, but there is doubt whether it ever received the force of a statute. It is not included in the Statutes at Large.

16. The figures compiled from the journal are as follows: public bills passed, 26; private bills passed, 15. Other bills advanced to the committee stage: public, 55; private, 23; total, 78.

These figures do not agree with the memorandum of Pym (Notestein,

Relf, and Simpson, eds., *Commons Debates, 1621*, IV, 418, Pym diary, Nov. 20, 1621):

"The Bills were reviewed and appeared in this state, vizt. Publicke Bills:

Of such as were past both Houses	9
Past this House and sent to the Lords	10
Past this House but not sent up	4
Lying under Committment	29
Past Committment and Engrost	6
Once read	43"

17. In the parliament of 1604 the ratio of subjects referred to committee to days of sitting was 1.09. In 1621, it was 1.18.

18. There is no evidence of royal electioneering in the debates, but Lando, the Venetian ambassador, in his "Relation of England" refers to it thus: "When his Majesty, compelled by force of circumstances, finally brought himself to summon a parliament, although he tried to limit the liberty of the commoners in choosing their representatives, and succeeded in some towns and countries, he could not manage it as a general rule, the relations of the favourite and even his own councillors being rejected" (C.S.P. Ven., 1621–23, 438). For evidence of Lord Zouch's electioneering in Kent, see C.S.P. Dom., 1619–23, 212, 213.

19. C.J., I, *passim*.

20. Despite this general tendency to conciliate, there is not lacking evidence of rashness and abandon in debate:

Mallory, March 9, 1620/1 (Notestein, Relf, and Simpson, eds., *Commons Debates, 1621*, V, 282: "That his mouth is open and his hart perfit. Hee feared not those that sit in thrones and chayres."

Alford, April 20, 1621 (*ibid.*, V, 119): "It's dangerous to give over business upon the motion of the kinge."

Sir William Herbert, May 20, 1621 (*ibid.*, III, 353): "I am sorry that we have so slender a requittall of the liberalyte of this Parliament as now by this sodden recess."

Alford (*ibid.*): "We must not carry them home rattles; lett us part fayrely with the Lords. They speak of matters of State. We all sawe how forward the King was at the beginning, but I have seene a greate quaileing since Easter."

Giles, May 28, 1621 (*ibid.*, III, 329): "My uncle Giles. That there never was so greate a grievance as the King's message for our dissolution . . ."

Alford, Nov. 23, 1621 (*ibid.*, III, 434–35): "We are no fitt Parliament yet to enter into anything, we are pinioned yet; lett's be at liberty till we enter into debate. Proclamations restrayne us from Bohemia speaking, etc. And are not matters of religion and church matters of state. Shall we be barred from speaking of theise. The kingdom in this cessation is so suncke, I pray God this age may renewe it."

21. C.S.P. Dom., 1619–23, 333, Jan. 4, 1621/2.

22. C.J., I, 579. Bill for the uniting of two parishes was committed on first reading.

23. The schedules for committee meetings, readings, and preparing bills are to be found in C.J., I, 507, 596, 641, 532, 511.

24. Notestein, Relf, and Simpson, eds., *Commons Debates, 1621*, IV, 211–12, Pym diary, April 6, 1621. In the record of committee work during a recess, the entry for the day contains a list of 16 petitions—the only entry for that day. Sir Edwin Sandys alluded in debate to the fact that there were at that time almost 80 petitions of grievances in the hands of the house. (C.J., I, 550, March 12, 1620/1).

25. The ratio of committees to days of sitting in 1604 was 1.2; in 1621, it was 1.67.

26. The search reveals 333 names in 1621, as opposed to 331 in the first session of the parliament of 1604.

27. The following chart shows the distribution of members according to the number of committees on which they served.

No. of Com- mittees:	Under 10	10–20	21–30	31–50	51–75	Over 75
1621	256 (77%)	35 (10%)	20 (6%)	15 (4.5%)	7 (2%)	0
1609–10	219 (68%)	54 (16%)	17 (5%)	26 (8%)	6 (1.8%)	3 (.9%)

28. See C.J., I, 544, 547, 595, 612, 613, 629, 630, 650, 659, 666, 668.

29. C.J., I, 514.

30. Notestein, Relf, and Simpson, eds., *Commons Debates, 1621*, II, 126, "X" journal, Feb. 23, 1620/1.

31. *Ibid.*, IV, 144, Pym diary, March 10, 1620/1.

32. *Ibid.*, V, 452, Wentworth diary, Feb. 13, 1620/1: "There was a dislike that there should be so many things referred to Committees of the whole House, the number breeding confusion and slow dispatch, and therefore in Edward the 6th's time, and till within twenty years there were not above eight or ten named of a Committee, which Use was not crept in by Custom, but upon good consideration, and therefore it was desired for expediting of business that so many things should not be referred to the Grand-Committee."

33. *Ibid.*, III, 251, Barrington diary, May 14, 1621.

34. *Ibid.*, III, 279, Barrington diary.

35. *Ibid.*, VI, 84, Holland diary, March 24, 1620/1.

36. *Ibid.*, IV, 237, Pym diary, April 19, 1621:

"It was moved that Sir Robert Phillips, who sate in the Chaire for receiving Peticions before the Recess, might by Order of the Howse receive that place againe, which during the recess was held by Sir Edward Sackvile.

"Against which was opposed: (1) That the makeing of such an Order was unproper for the Howse, it belonginge to the libertye of a Committee to call whome they will to the Chayre. (2) That such an order would make him that showld be so nominated to bee of the Quorum. Soe that if he should be either absent or come late the Committee could not proceede."

37. *Ibid.*, II, 24, "X" journal, Feb. 5: "After dinner the Committee being assembled, they called upon Sir Edward Coke to take the Chair at the Committee which, when with some seeming unwillingness he had accepted, Sir Carew Raleigh said that it was never seen that a Privy Councillor was called to the Chair. But answer was made that being all members of one House there was no difference and therefore the House might set up anyone whom they pleased."

38. The *Calendars of State Papers Domestic* have been thoroughly canvassed from 1603 to 1641 for this information.

39. Note the case of Sir Edwin Sandys, who continued independent after receiving a land grant in 1614, or that of Sir Francis Barrington or of Sir Peter Hayman or even of John Pym, all of whom were in some fashion tied to the crown before their defection. All together, I have found references to 16 such members who turned against the king in spite of some apparent indebtedness. There must have been many more.

40. Witness Sir John Grantham, Hackwell, Hayman again, Sir Thomas Rowe, and above all Sir Thomas Wentworth. There are naturally fewer of these who, having once "snuffed the tainted gale," came back to the acceptance of royal favors. I have counted but 7. The parliament of 1626 contained many more.

41. The important officeholders in 1621 were Sir Julius Caesar, Sir George Calvert, Sir Henry Carey, Sir Edward Coke, Sir Thomas Edmondes, Sir Fulke Greville, Sir Robert Naunton, Sir Richard Weston, all these of the privy council, and William Becher, Sir Thomas Coventry, Sir Lionel Cranfield, Sir Thomas Crewe, Sir Thomas Fleming, Sir Robert Heath, Sir Robert Hitcham, Sir James Ley, Sir Edward Montague, Sir Edward Moseley, Sir Walter Pye, Sergeant Thomas Richardson, and Sir John Walter.

42. It is well known, of course, that the office of sheriff declined

greatly in importance during Tudor times and that Charles I used it in 1626 and 1628 as a means of eliminating certain political enemies from the house. The reduced power and dignity of the office is well stated in a complaint of George Viscount Chaworth to the king, Nov., 1638: "It is 'cumd' to me that your Majesty has pricked me your vicecomes Notting-hamiae, which title, until the frequency of parliaments tied the nobility to attend on them, did fall on men of the best quality, and had that course continued the best subject should not hold it a disparagement. But the case is so changed as the choice of me to this can (in common opinion) be no other than a mark of your displeasure, and a shadowing, if not defacing, of your regal act in my creation, of which your ancestors have been so tender" (C.S.P. Dom., 1638–39, 135).

43. It is very significant, I think, that many sheriffs, lieutenants, and captains of castles and a few commanders of troops were taken, as the tension waxed strong after 1635, from this group of unimportant office-holders who had sat in the parliament of 1621. Though the office of sheriff had ceased to be an honor, it was a very vital office as the issue began to grow bitter between Charles and his people. I have noted 56 administrative offices of this sort held by men of the parliament of 1621 in the interval between then and 1641, most of them between 1635 and 1641.

44. Coke's case is very peculiar. He was a member of the privy council in 1621, but fell into disfavor after the parliament. Ever since his so-called "fall" he had been, and was to remain, one of the most independent characters in English public life. Although his speech was usually moderate, Coke could on occasion strike insolently at the mighty. "Sir Edward Coke. Ha, Mr. Attorney doe you talke with them afore hand? So doe not we. We came to talke with the Lords. As for you, Mr. Attorney, you may be as well against them as we" (Notestein, Relf, and Simpson, eds., *Commons Debates, 1621*, III, 86, Barrington diary, April 26, 1621).

45. But Digges, in 1626, showed a spirit not to be expected of him, when he participated in the attack upon Buckingham, to his cost.

46. A speech of Solicitor Coventry, Dec. 15, 1621, illustrates well the moderate view that could at least be affected, even at a time of acrimonious debate, by an important courtier. "That the liberty of parliament is the inheritance of the subject, but to go that way by which we should effect it, to pass by the phrase of his [the king's] letter, not to meddle with the prerogative of the king. To make a protestation of our liberties and to go to the king again, although I am sorry that we should not go on. That the pardon will be worth three subsidies, I dare make it known to any"

(Notestein, Relf, and Simpson, eds., *Commons Debates, 1621*, II, 526).

47. Christopher Nevill (*ibid.*, VI, 46, Holland diary, March 9, 1620/1).

48. Alford, Sir George Manners, Sir Henry Withrington, Sir Nathaniel Riche (*ibid.*, II, 201–2, "X" journal, March 9, 1620/1). See also *ibid.*, IV, 390, Pym diary, May 30, 1621: "And the Speaker offred to Restrayne by calling for the Keyes, for which he was reproved by Sir Samuel Sands: That he was our Speaker and not our Gaoler, and like a wise man showld rather labour to moderate mens passions then to imitate them."

49. The speaker was taken to task by Noye (*ibid.*, IV, 196, Pym diary, March 26, 1621).

50. The exceptions were Lowe, Riche, Horsey, Barrington, Edmondes, Greville, and Heath.

51. Naunton, Sackville, Giles, Perrott, and Wentworth.

52. Moore, Crewe, Montague, Coventry, Barrington, Edmondes, Cranfield, Greville, Heath.

53. Riche, Strode.

54. Poole, Lowe, Phelips.

55. Coke, Noye, Alford, Hackwell, Sandys, Horsey, Digges, Glanville, Rowe.

56. On Feb. 22, Sir Edward Coke acted as chairman of the committee of the whole and reported from it (Notestein, Relf, and Simpson, eds., *Commons Debates, 1621*, II, 116, 118, "X" journal). Again, on May 8, Noye was recorded as chairman of the committee of the whole and also reported (*ibid.*, III, 201–2, Barrington diary). On Feb. 18, Sir Edward Sackville reported from a select committee of which we know he was chairman (C.J., I, 554, 560).

57. An attempt has been made to elucidate this matter from the lists of speakers at committee, contained in the Book of Committees (Notestein, Relf, and Simpson, eds., *Commons Debates, 1621*, VI, 249–80). Nothing can be proved, however. The records of frequent speakers are few, and the committees included in the lists are not, as a rule, the same ones whose reports are included in the journal.

58. One reason for this good feeling was the gesture on the part of the government in the direction of the recusancy laws, in accordance with the request of the parliament of 1621 (C.S.P. Dom., 1619–23, 378).

59. C.S.P. Dom., 1623–25, 156, Chamberlain to Carleton, Jan. 31, 1623/4.

60. C.S.P. Dom., 1623–25, 162, William Pelham to Sir Edward Conway, Feb. 12, 1623/4.

61. C.S.P. Dom., 1623–25, 148, Naunton to Buckingham, Jan. 14, 1623/4.

62. C.S.P. Dom., 1623–25, 150, Chamberlain to Carleton, Jan. 17, 1623/4.

63. C.S.P. Dom., 1623–25, 192, 198, 200.

64. C.S.P. Dom., 1623–25, 200, 201.

65. Sir Richard Young to Lord Zouch, March 18, 1623/4. He refers to the house as "violent for free elections" (C.S.P. Dom., 1623–25, 192).

66. There are two journal accounts of this parliament. The first (C.J., I, 670–715) is the clerk's account. It begins and ends with the first and last days of the session, but is incomplete, containing only 51 out of the 79 days, and only 8 of the 21 afternoon sittings. The second account, written by the clerk's son (see note on p. 686, C.J., I) begins four days after the beginning of the meetings and covers the rest of the session (C.J., I, 716–98). The second account, being by a less experienced hand, contains many vagaries of spelling and has many omissions. Occasionally it contains speeches not found in the clerk's account. The two accounts, taken together, show very well how incomplete all early journals must have been and to what an extent the clerk's effort was a "catch-as-catch-can" affair, since two people, taking notes at the same time, got results which differed somewhat every day. In compiling the data for this parliament, I have pieced the two accounts together.

67. *History of England*, V, 235.

68. C.J., I, 749, March 24 (P.M.).

69. In 1621 there had been but 175 men who had served in the preceding parliament and only 205 who had served in any of the parliaments of James. These figures necessarily depend upon data so dubious that they are admittedly far from accurate. The tendency they reveal, however, can hardly be questioned.

70. C.J., I, 683.

71. The committee of the whole was much used in 1621, but even more frequently in 1624. See C.J., I, 688, 702, 703, 704, 709, 754, 758, 761, 789. From casual references to the act of going into committee of the whole, and from mention of the change from committee to house without first mentioning the change into committee, it seems clear that only a few out of many cases are reported in the journal. We know, moreover, that on designated days, as a matter of routine procedure, the house met as a committee of the whole on certain specified matters. See C.J., I, 672.

72. This was done for the first time to any considerable extent in 1621, but the increase of the practice is noticeable in the journal for 1624.

73. Seventy-nine days and 21 afternoons, as opposed to 101 days and 19 afternoons in 1621.

74. Eighty-three devoted to public bills, 59 to private messages, and so on, a total of 193 as compared with 169 in 1621.

75. No attempt has been made to record committee members other than those called by name in the journal, since it is quite impossible to tell which ones attended committee meetings, or even to estimate.

76. Robert Heath and Sir John Saville were the only others serving on more than 50.

77. Forty percent of the committees in 1621 contained such vague membership, and 47 percent in 1624.

78. There are numerous references to Mr. Speaker's going "out of his chair." See C.J., I, 688, 702, 705, 709, 754, 755, 758, 761. Even more interesting is the occasional casual observation that the speaker went into his chair again, seeming to indicate that, on many unrecorded occasions, the house may have "fallen to a committee." See C.J., I, 703, 704. Moreover, there were regularly scheduled committees of the whole house, as that for grievances every Monday and Friday at 2 P.M., for courts of justice every Wednesday, and for trade every Thursday (C.J., I, 672).

79. Often the record fails to note the disposition made of a bill at the time of the report. In 71 cases noted in which this was recorded, 54 bills were either engrossed or given their third reading without any debate, while 17 were further debated or recommitted.

80. In 1621 the number of members for whom no information could be secured other than that they were disciplined or defied the government was 21. In 1624 it was 25.

81. No claim is made for the accuracy of these figures. All that can be said for the estimates of patronage in connection with all the parliaments treated is that they were arrived at by the same type of research and calculation. Although their accuracy in an absolute sense may be small, they possess a certain importance as relative commentaries.

82. Naunton and Coke were still in the house in 1624, but no longer of the council. The privy council members in 1624 were Sir George Calvert, Sir Edward Conway, Sir Thomas Edmondes, Sir John Suckling, and Sir Richard Weston.

83. Sir Henry Carye, Sir Francis Cottington, Sir Thomas Crewe, Thomas Gewen, Robert Heath, Sergeant Hitcham, Sir Robert Maunsell, Sir Humphrey May, Sir Henry Mildmay, Sir Robert Naunton, Sir James Perrott, Sir Walter Pye, Sir Benjamin Rudyard, Sir Oliver St. John, Sir Thomas Trevor, Sir William Uvedall, Sir John Walter.

84. The large number of parliament men of 1624 who had served in 1621 is important in this connection.

85. C.S.P. Dom., 1623–25, 217, Sir Henry Goodere to Carleton: "Sir Edw. Coke took up the point of bribery, which, after his old habit, he took pleasure in aggravating. Sir Edwin Sandys accused him of breaking off the last Parliament, causing the benevolence that ensued, and the imposition on French wines, which, from tenderness to the prerogative, was called oppression, waiving the word imposition."

86. C.S.P. Dom., 1640, 153.

87. C.S.P. Dom., 1619–23, 333; C.S.P. Dom., 1629–31, 83.

88. C.S.P. Dom., 1619–23, 267; C.S.P. Dom., 1623–25, 150.

89. Poole, Coke, Alford, Noye, Pym, Palmes, Barrington, Digges, Glanville, Hayman, Phelips, Perrott, Sandys.

90. Heath, Saville, Moore, Finch, Pye.

91. Riche, Estcourt, Stradling, Hobby.

92. The Venetian ambassador, Contarini, in his "Relation of England," made a queer analysis of James's statecraft. It is at variance with my view of the relations with parliament, but bears out the foregoing interpretation of James's intentions in this regard. "They [parliament] believed in him [James] no more [after he turned pacifist] and if he had lived he ran the risk of having revolts, although his art and caution were so great that everyone was deceived, and he attained his ends with more prudence and artifice than any other prince in the world" (C.S.P. Ven., 1625–26, 599).

93. Berkley, Sir George Moore, Sir Thomas Smith, and Whitlocke.

94. Alford, Brooke, Crewe, Digges, Nevill, Perrott, Sir Samuel Sandys, and Wentworth.

95. Alford spoke 140 times and served on 51 committees; Digges spoke 83 times and served on 35 committees; Perrott spoke 65 times, and Wentworth 63; Crewe spoke 55 times and served on 55 committees.

96. Glanville spoke 55 times and served on 33 committees; Rowe served on 32 committees; Poole spoke 78 times and served on 70 committees.

97. Sir Francis Goodwyn, Thomas Mallett, Hugh Middleton, John Whitson.

98. Sir Henry Anderson, Sir Thomas Grantham, Greville, Horsey, and Strode.

99. He spoke 224 times in this parliament and served on 75 committees.

CHAPTER V: THE REVOLUTIONISTS APPEAR

1. It sat for 19 days and 3 afternoons and produced 7 public acts, 2 private, and a protestation of loyalty to Charles.

2. Gardiner, *History of England*, V, 337.

3. Birch, *The Court and Times of Charles the First*, I, 18.

4. C.S.P. Ven., 1625–26, 63, Ambassador Pesaro to the Doge and Senate, May 30, 1625: "The people were so fearful of suffering a disadvantage that in the elections they rejected all those who served efficiently in previous parliaments but with the title of royalists, wishing to maintain the parliament as moderator between the king and the public. Tricks have happened in these elections, and now they are expecting the opening of the Estates the Lower House will arrange its own house and deal with irregularities."

5. Sir John Coke, Sir Thomas Coventry, Sir Thomas Edmondes, Sir Humphrey May, Sir Robert Naunton, Sir John Suckling, Sir Richard Weston. There were but 5 members of the council in the parliament of 1624.

6. Sir Henry Carye, Sir Edward Coke, Sir Francis Cottington, Sir Thomas Crewe, Sir Henry Fane, Robert Heath, Sir Robert Hitcham, Sir Thomas Lake, Sir Robert Maunsell, Sir Albert Morton, Sir Walter Pye, Sir Oliver St. John, Sir John Trevor, Sir William Uvedall. There had been 17 members in this category in 1624.

7. There were 136 so noted in 1624.

8. Nineteen in 1625 and 21 in 1624.

9. C.J., I, 800, June 22, 1625: "Sir Ben. Rudyard:—The late Distastes between the late King and Parliament the chief cause of all the Miseries of the Kingdom: The First Turn whereof given by the now King, then Prince; wherein more Benefit to the Subject, than in any Parliament these many 100 years; and his Subjects expressed their Duty to the King. What may we then now expect from him, being King, and having Power? His good natural Disposition, his Freedom from Vice, his Travels abroad, his Breeding in Parliament . . ."

10. C.S.P. Ven., 1625–26, 35, Ambassador Pesaro to the Doge and Senate, May 9, 1625: "The parliament is expected to be brief; to offer congratulations to the king; to confirm the announcement of his succession; to carry out the coronation; to demand the observance of the laws in general; to grant free subsidies to his Majesty; postponing the more important discussions to another time, possibly the autumn. The confidence in the king's religion removes the pretext for guarantees on that score."

11. C.J., I, 801, June 22, 1625: "Mr. Solicitor:—That his Majesty had taken care of our Grievances preferred the last Parliament, and at any Day, when this House will assign, Satisfaction shall be given therein to the House."

12. C.J., I, 806, July 8, 1625: "Sir Jo. Cooke reporteth a Command-

ment from his Majesty.—That the King understandeth of our Grant of Two Subsidies; which the King most graciously accepteth, as an Argument of his Subjects Love to him: Accepteth the Manner of it, that not moved by any Officers of State: Is very well pleased with our pressing of the Accounts of the last Subsidies.—"

13. C.J., I, 813, Aug. 10, 1625. In a message delivered to the house by Weston, the king urged the house to give more. He said that if they would give more money now he would call them together in the winter for general legislation "for the Commonwealth."

14. C.S.P. Ven., 1625–26, 142, Ambassador Pesaro to the Doge and Senate, Aug. 21, 1625: "But the Lower House is incensed, and convinced that the duke means to tire them out by moving them from place to place.

"After the members had discussed these statements they seemed disposed to give every assistance; but they asked for the execution of the laws, that the money should be well administered, not as in the past, and that the government should not be in the hands of one man alone. In short, all their animosity was directed against the Papists and the duke against whom they spoke and harangued both directly and indirectly under the pretext of the necessity of bringing order into the state and council."

15. Sources for the data in this paragraph are found in the journal, as follows: C.J., I, 800, 802, 803, 807, 809, 810, 811, 812, 813, 814.

16. The "subsidy" was a tax on land and movables, and the "fifteen" or fifteenth one on movables. A subsidy and two fifteens would have yielded little more than £100,000, a very small sum in the face of Charles's needs.

17. Edward Alford, Sir Henry Anderson, Christopher Brooke, Henry Bulstrode, Sir Edward Coke, Sir Dudley Digges, Sir Edward Giles, John Glanville, Sir Francis Goodwin, Sir Thomas Grantham, John Hare, Thomas Mallett, John Maynard, Sir Hugh Middleton, Sir Henry Poole, Sir Edwin Sandys, Sir William Strode, Sir Thomas Wentworth, and John Whitson.

18. Sir John Eliot, first great martyr to the cause, died in 1632.

19. Coke's name appears in the returns, but the king cautioned the house not to let him sit, as he was sheriff of Buckingham. He did not sit (C.J., I, 817).

For Phelips' disqualification, see the letter of Sir Benjamin Rudyard to Sir Francis Nethersole, Nov. 23, 1625 (C.S.P. Dom., 1625–26, 156). Rudyard wrote that Phelips and six others had been thus disqualified. Gardiner mentions only the six I have listed, but adds that Sir William Fleetwood, aimed at in this maneuver, was chosen neither a sheriff nor a member of parliament (Gardiner, *History of England*, VI, 34). There was some inexact information current about this matter, as indicated by a letter of the Rev.

Joseph Mead to Sir Martin Stuteville, Nov. 26, 1625 (Birch, *The Court and Times of Charles the First*, I, 63): "Many of the sticklers in the last parliament are made sheriffs—Sir Edwin Sandys, Sir Robert Phillips, Mr. Alured, and others. Yea Sir Edward Coke himself, as they talk; to whom it is a piece of dishonour, to the rest none at all." The reference to Sandys is clearly a mistake, for he was in the house in 1626. In the foregoing citation, it is likely that Alured is an erroneous copying of Alford. For a contemporary reference to the exclusion of Coke, Phelips, and Sir Francis Seymour, see the letter of Chamberlain to Carleton, Jan. 19, 1625/6 (Birch, *The Court and Times of Charles the First*, I, 72–73.

This peculiar use of the office of sheriff for disciplinary purposes was not new. James had used it. Chamberlain mentions the practice in a letter to Carleton, dated Nov. 16, 1622: "Great strife about the elections of the Sheriffs; those whose names are returned often escape, and others are chosen unexpectedly, such as have been too forward in parliament, or too backward in the benevolences . . ." (C.S.P. Dom., 1619–23, 461).

20. C.S.P. Dom., 1625–26, 226, 237.

21. C.S.P. Dom., 1625–26, 218, 221.

22. Both were returned from other constituencies.

23. "For the meeting of this parliament the duke's dependents are bestirring themselves by enquiry and other means to secure a strong party, but it is not thought that it will be strong enough. The king in the letters of summons orders that sheriffs engaged on his service shall be excluded as representatives, but the commons claim that they are not bound by these orders, contrary to their privileges, and wish to elect Cuch [Coke] in particular" (C.S.P. Ven., 1625–26, 311).

24. There had been 35 statutes in 1624, and 9 in the irregular parliament of 1625.

25. There were 99 with third readings in the parliament of 1624, which must be considered the last normal parliament before this one.

26. As opposed to 152 second readings in 1624.

27. There were 169 first readings in 1624.

28. The ratio for 1624 was 1.78.

29. There were six recorded divisions of over 300. One was as large as 396 (April 24, 1626).

30. The total number of reports was 122.

31. The clerk's omission of record of debates is very conspicuous in 1626. Much more attention was given to the work of committees.

32. C.J., I, 817.

33. C.S.P. Ven., 1625–26, 535. There is no indication that Turner was imprisoned. The house refused to censure either of these members.

34. The increased number of such cases and the increased number of members who secured permission to depart were remarkable. The former must have been a fortuitous condition, but the latter was probably the outgrowth of timidity, as members saw the house taking a position which day by day became more dangerous.

35. C.S.P. Dom., 1625–26, 288.

36. C.J., I, 836.

37. Letter of Sir Martin Stuteville to Rev. Joseph Mead (Birch, *The Court and Times of Charles the First*, I, 82).

38. These charges are spread upon the journal for April 24 (C.J., I, 849).

39. C.J., I, 850 *et seq.*

40. C.J., I, 860, 862; Birch, *The Court and Times of Charles the First*, I, 101, Sir Simonds D'Ewes to Sir Martin Stuteville, May 11, 1626.

41. C.J., I, 863.

42. C.J., I, 867; C.S.P. Dom., 1625–26, 348.

43. C.S.P. Ven., 1625–26, 452.

44. C.S.P. Dom., 1625–26, 355.

45. C.S.P. Ven., 1625–26, 512, Contarini to the Doge and Senate, Aug. 21, 1626: "I may say that this kingdom is divided into two. The king, Buckingham and a few individuals, who being near at hand sun themselves in the rays of royal favour; the other party consisting of all the rest of the country. The most experienced think that those two extremes cannot last long without the destruction of one or the other, and they discuss the subject perhaps too freely as one which can have no other benefit.

"The king has greatly lost popularity, in such wise that the hatred increases against the duke, who since the last dissolution of Parliament, having availed himself of violent means to maintain his supremacy, is necessarily compelled to persevere in this course, without the least deviation."

46. Only 178 speeches, in addition to committee reports, are recorded.

47. Ratio of men serving to committees: 1626, 2.15; 1624, 1.8.

48. A comparison follows covering the distribution of members according to the number of committees on which they served.

No. of Committees:	Under 10	10–20	21–30	31–50	51–75	Over 75
1621	256 (77%)	35 (10%)	20 (6%)	15 (4.5%)	7 (2%)	0
1624	252 (72%)	56 (16%)	21 (6%)	18 (5%)	2 (.6%)	2 (.6%)
1626	213 (71.2%)	45 (15%)	22 (7.3%)	15 (5%)	3 (1%)	1 (.3%)

49. In comparing the 1626 parliament with its predecessors, I have usually chosen the parliament of 1624 instead of that of 1625 because the latter was too brief and irregular to be considered normal. In 1624 there were 304 old parliament men, 249 of whom had served in 1621.

50. In 1621 there were 135 men who had already established such connections, and in 1624 there were 136. In 1626, in spite of the fact that the total number of beneficiaries was smaller, those who had already received some favor numbered 151.

51. There were but 9 such men in the parliament of 1624.

52. The following table will show this similarity:

	1626	1624
Members of the privy council in the house	7	5
Other important courtiers	24	28
Men of medium political stature	112	123
Total recalcitrants (at any time)	52	30

The privy council members were: Sir Dudley Carleton, Sir John Coke, Sir Thomas Edmondes, Sir Humphrey May, Sir Robert Naunton, Sir John Suckling, Sir Richard Weston.

The other important courtiers were: Sir Henry Carye, Sir Edward Conway, Thomas Coventry, Sir Thomas Fanshaw, Heneage Finche, Sir Robert Hitcham, Sir Robert Maunsell, Sir William Mounson, Sir James Perrott, Sir Walter Pye, Sir Richard Shelton, Sir William Uvedall (these men had attained distinction before 1626); Peter Ball, John Banks, Sir Henry Fane, Sir John Finche, Sir Edward Herbert, Sir William Herbert, Sir Thomas Jermyn, Sir Edward Littleton, Sir Roger Northe, William Noye, Sir John Saville, Sir Christopher Wandesford (these 12 men were to become important supporters of the crown later). Littleton's politics after the 1630's were vacillating, and Noye went over to the court in 1631.

53. Sir Dudley Carleton, Sir John Coke, Sir Richard Weston.

54. Sir Dudley Digges, John Pym, John Selden.

55. The 119 reports were made by 39 men.

56. Edward Bisse, Sir Nicholas Saunders, Edward Whitby.

57. Sir Dudley Digges, Sir John Eliot, John Glanville, Sir Edward Herbert, Sir Henry Poole, John Pym, Sir Christopher Wandesford.

58. Sir John Finche, Richard Spencer.

59. John Darke, Sir Thomas Grantham, Peter Hayman, Sir George Moore, Sir Nathaniel Riche, Richard Spencer, Sir John Stradling, Sir Alexander Temple.

60. Sir Francis Barrington, William Coryton, Sir Dudley Digges, Sir Walter Earle, Sir Thomas Hobby, William Noye, Sir Henry Poole, John Pym, John Rolle, John Selden.

61. Sir Nicholas Saunders.

62. Sir Henry Anderson, Christopher Brooke, Sir Dudley Digges, Sir Miles Fleetwood, John Glanville, Sir Francis Goodwin, Sir Thomas Grantham, John Hare, Sir Robert Harley, Sir Thomas Hobby, Thomas Mallett, William Noye, Peter Peak, Sir Henry Poole, Sir Nathaniel Riche, Sir Edwin Sandys, Sir John Saville, Sir William Spencer, Sir William Strode, Sir William Walter, Sir Thomas Wentworth, John Whitson.

63. Clement Coke, Sir Lewis Dive, Sir John Eliot, Edward Herbert, John Pym, John Selden, Christopher Shereland, Samuel Turner, Christopher Wandesford.

64. C.J., I, 873, 895.

65. C.J., I, 884.

66. C.J., I, 874, 883.

67. C.J., I, 874 (Richard Greene and William Purefey for Coventry), 875 (Sir Charles Howard for Gatton), 877 (Anthony Stapeley for Lewys in Sussex), 893 (Sir Anthony Irby for Boston).

68. The complete list of these cases follows, with references to the journal: Cornwall (873, 895), Coventry (874), Newport Medina (874, 883), Gatton (875), Exeter (875), Colchester (876), Lewys in Sussex (877), York City (879), Bridport (881–82), Yorkshire (884), Taunton (886), Boston (893), Michell (902), Warwick (907), Flint (921).

69. They ran to May 31, and one case arose in the new session, Jan. 29, 1629/30.

70. C.J., I, 875 (Gatton), 876 (Colchester), 881–82 (Bridport), 893 (Boston), 907 (Warwick).

71. C.J., I, 886.

72. C.S.P. Dom., 1627–28, 568, 540, 541, 542.

73. C.S.P. Dom., 1627–28, 566.

74. C.S.P. Dom., 1627–28, 556.

75. C.S.P. Dom., 1627–28, 562.

76. C.S.P. Dom., 1627–28, 562. Faulke Reed reported to Conway that the answer of the people of Evesham was "faint" and that they would have to talk with their recorder, Mr. Crasswell. Yarmouth answered that they would choose one of their own country, and Newport that they would not choose Conway's son, as requested. (See C.S.P. Dom., 1627–28, 568, letter of Sir John Oglander to Conway, Feb. 17, 1628/9.)

77. C.S.P. Dom., 1627–28, 537; C.S.P. Dom., 1628–29, 7.

78. C.S.P. Dom., 1628–29, 5, 9.

79. C.S.P. Dom., 1628–29, 6.

80. C.S.P. Ven., 1626–28, 605, letter of Feb. 29, 1628/9.

81. As in the letter of Henry Holt, Feb. 6, 1628/9. The writer gave him carte blanche with regard to places (C.S.P. Dom., 1627–28, 548).

82. C.S.P. Dom., 1628–29, 13: "The generality of voices among the commons bred such a distraction that the writers could have no power over them so that they were not able to give the Duke and themselves content."

83. C.S.P. Dom., 1627–28, 592.

84. C.S.P. Ven., 1626–28, 595, Contarini to the Doge and Senate, Feb. 17, 1628/9: "Today at the election of a member of parliament for Essex, some of the villagers were excluded; so they rose and enforced the election of another member. The first named supported the duke; the other those who last year refused to pay the subsidies."

C.S.P. Ven., 1626–28, 605, same to same, Feb. 29, 1628/9: "The Duke stays in London, negotiating and working with all his might, so that the members returned for the Lower House may be on his side. But following the example of Essex, it is understood that many other counties mean to return members, who, as they say, suffered for the country and its liberties by going to prison rather than pay the late subsidies, which were illegal."

C.S.P. Ven., 1628–29, 10, same to same, March 9, 1628/9: "With respect to the outcome of this parliament, there is more doubt than hope, as not only in the more distant provinces, but even in the city of London, that is to say, under the eye of the Court, they have returned members who refused to pay the late subsidies."

85. C.S.P. Dom., 1627–28, 537.

86. C.S.P. Ven., 1626–28, 584.

87. C.S.P. Dom., 1628–29, 410, Dec. 19, 1628: "They are about to rectify some things both in religion and government, to sweeten things to the Parliament, but most men doubt that they are not sincerely intended, and so will give little satisfaction. The parliamentary men have an eye on Carlisle, and are afraid that he will 'rogue' with the Lord Treasurer, who though, as the writer thinks, an honest man and good patriot, has much ado to overcome those clouds of suspicion concerning religion that have hung over him all the while."

88. References covering the various episodes mentioned in this paragraph are found in C.J., I, 918a, 900a, 881a, 891a, 897a.

89. See C.J., I, 897b (370 on May 14), 901b (220 on May 20, P.M.), 907a (298 on May 30), 911b (380 on June 11).

90. C.J., I, 909b.

91. C.J., I, 897b.

92. Clement Coke, Sir Edward Coke, Coryton, Digges, Pym, Riche, Shelden.

93. C.J., I, 873a.
94. C.J., I, 873 (first session):
Committee of the whole on religion. Every Monday at 2 P.M. in the house.
Committee of the whole on courts of justice. Every Thursday in the house.
Committee of the whole on grievances. Every Wednesday and Friday at 2 P.M. in the house.
Committee of the whole on trade. Every Thursday at 2 P.M. in the house.

C.J., I, 920a (second session):
Committee of the whole on religion. Every Monday and Saturday P.M. in the house.
Committee of the whole on courts of justice. Every Tuesday in the house.
Committee of the whole on grievances. Every Wednesday and Friday P.M. in the house.
Committee of the whole on trade. Every Thursday P.M.

Minor changes are recorded (C.J., I, 927a):
Grievances. Wednesday and Thursday.
Trade. Friday, beginning Feb. 6.

95. Men who are known to have had some connection with the crown:
1621, 294 (135 established before 1621, and 159 after)
1624, 280 (136 established before 1624, and 144 after)
1626, 270 (151 established before 1626, and 119 after)
1628, 252 (146 established before 1628, and 106 after)

96. Men known to have been opposition at some time:
1624, 25
1626, 47
1628, 67

97. Hackwell, 15 (13 from committee of privilege); Sir Edward Coke, 13 (6 from grievances, 1 from subsidy, 1 from message to king); Earle, 10 (5 from liberty of the subject, 2 from grievances, 1 from the remonstrance); Pym, 11 (9 from religion); Littleton, 6 (all from liberty of the subject).

98. Clement Coke, Sir Edward Coke, Coryton, Digges, Pym, Riche, Selden.

99. Alford, Sir Francis Barrington, Sir Thomas Barrington, Earle, Eliot,

Fleetwood, Goodwin, Hackwell, Hayman, Hobby, Littleton, Martin, Noye, Phelips, Pye, Rolle, Rudyard, Waller, Whitaker.

100. Pye, Waller, and Whitaker seem to have been neutral.

101. Edward Alford, Sir Nathaniel Barnardiston, Sir Francis Barrington, Henry Belassis, Sir Richard Buller, William Coryton, Sir Walter Earle, Sir Miles Fleetwood, John Glanville, Sir Thomas Grantham, Harbottle Grimston, John Hampden, Sir Robert Harley, Edward Herbert, William Herbert, Edward Littleton, Sir Oliver Luke, William Mallory, Sir John Maynard, Sir Guy Palmes, John Pym, John Rolle, Sir Beauchamp St. John, Sir Oliver St. John (now Baron, who sat in the house of lords), John Selden, Sir Francis Seymour, Nathaniel Stephens, William Strode, Nicholas Trefusis, Christopher Wray, Sir John Wray.

102. Sir Nathaniel Barnardiston, Sir Walter Earle, Harbottle Grimston, Sir Robert Harley, Sir Walter Longe, Sir Oliver Luke, Sir John Maynard, John Pym, John Rolle, Sir Beauchamp St. John, Sir Oliver St. John, John Selden, Nathaniel Stephens, William Strode, Christopher Wray, Sir John Wray.

103. Sir Henry Berkley, John Delbridge, Sir Richard Grenville, Robert Grevill, Sir Miles Hobart, Denzil Holles, Sir Robert Howard, Sir John Jennings, Sir William Lytton, Lewis Morgan, John Saunders, Benjamin Valentine, Sir Francis Wenman.

104. Berkley, Holles, Howard, Jennings, Lytton, Valentine, Wenman.

105. Though both were called in 1640, there was a great change in personnel. Only 258 members of the Short Parliament were returned to the Long Parliament.

106. Sir Thomas Barrington, Sir William Brereton, Matthew Craddock, John Crewe, Oliver Cromwell, Henry Darley, Sir Ferdinand Fairfax, William Frankland, Sir Ralph Hopton (Hopton went over to the king, however, in 1642), Sir John Hotham, Sir John Ramsden, Robert Lord Rich, Sir Benjamin Rudyard, Nathaniel Tompkins, Christopher Yelverton.

107. The Covenant, whose religious declarations were *prima facie* evidence of the religious, and hence by this time of the political, persuasion of its signers, bears 228 signatures. Seventy-six were those of men who had sat in the house of 1628.

108. Sir Edward Ascough, Richard Barwise, Edward Bisse, Sir Ambrose Brown, John Brown, William Cage, William Cawley, Sir Thomas Cheke, Miles Corbett, Richard Cresheld, John Curzon, Sir Thomas Dacres, Francis Drake, Thomas Eden, James Fiennes, Sir John Franklyn, Francis Godolphin, Robert Goodwin, Giles Greene, John Harris, Thomas Hatcher, Sir John Hippesley, Thomas Hoyle, Sir Edward Hungerford, Sir Anthony

Irby, Sir Thomas Jarvaise, Robert Jenner, Richard Knightley, Sir Francis Knollys, Thomas Lane, Sir Henry Mildmay (a former courtier, who had followed the king until Sept., 1641), Poynings More, Sir Dudley Northe, Sir Roger Northe, Michael Oldsworth, Sir Richard Onslowe, Henry Pelham, Sir Francis Popham, William Purefoy, John Pyne, Francis Rous, Anthony Stapley, Edward Thomas, Sir John Trevor, Sir Thomas Walsingham, Sir Thomas Wenman, Lawrence Whitaker, William Whitaker, Richard Whithead, John Wylde.

APPENDIX A

PATRONAGE

IN THE PARLIAMENT OF 1604

C.J.   *The Journals of the House of Commons*
C.S.P. Dom.   *Calendars of State Papers Domestic*, 1603–10

Acland, Sir John. Recusancy commissioner in Devon, 1606 (Yonge, p. 6).

Antrobus. Lent money to Bacon (Spedding, IV, 40).

Aston, Sir Roger. Grant of estate, 1604 (C.S.P. Dom., 89); keeper of Cowling Park (*ibid.*, 57); grant of 2 manors (*ibid.*, 68); gentleman of the bedchamber, 1604 (*ibid.*, 65); patent for the green wax, 1604 (*ibid.*, 158); master of the great wardrobe (*ibid.*, 386); glass patent, 1606 (*ibid.*, 333); James's former barber (Weldon, p. 2).

Bacon, Sir Francis. King's learned counsel (Bowyer, p. 116); patent (C.S.P. Dom., 144); solicitor general (C.J., I, 352); "muttered" for speaker, 1604 (C.J., I, 141).

Bacon, Nathaniel. Grant of estate, 1604 (C.S.P. Dom., 123).

Barrington, Sir Francis. Deputy lieutenant of Essex, 1603 (C.S.P. Dom., 33).

Beeston, Sir Hugh. Controller of records and fines in 3 counties (C.S.P. Dom., 175).

Bellingham. The lord admiral's secretary (Birch, I, 124).

Bennett, Sir John. On some commission for royal business (Spedding, IV, 131); chancellor to the queen and judge of prerogative court of Canterbury (*ibid.*, IV, 53); master in chancery, 1608 (Haydn).

Bowes, Sir Jerome. Patent for Venice glass, 1607 (C.S.P. Dom., 373).

Bowyer, Robert. Doorkeeper of the exchequer, keeper of the council chamber of the court of Star Chamber, 1604 (C.S.P. Dom., 124, 198); clerk of the upper house (Official List, 447).

Bowyer, Sir William. Command of soldiers, 1605 (C.S.P. Dom., 257); captain of Berwick, 1607 (*ibid.*, 345).

Bromley, Sir Edward. Baron of the exchequer, 1610 (C.S.P. Dom., 586).

Bromley, Sir Henry. Queen's attorney (C.J., I, *passim*); grant of estate, 1604 (C.S.P. Dom., 147); sheriff of Worcester, 1606 (*ibid.*, 283).

Brown, Sir Richard. Clerk of the green cloth (C.S.P. Dom., 72).

Caesar, Sir Julius. Chancellor of the exchequer and member of the privy council (C.J., I, *passim* and *Acts of the Privy Council, passim*).

Capell, Sir Gamaliel. Deputy lieutenant of Essex, 1603 (C.S.P. Dom., 33); sheriff of Essex (C.J., I, 353).

Carew, Sir George. Master in chancery (C.J., I, 157a).

Carew, Sir George. Vice chamberlain to the queen (C.J., I, 153b *et passim*); Baron Carew of Clopton, 1605, and called to upper house (C.S.P. Dom., 214); ambassador to France (C.J., I, 315–16).

Carleton, Dudley. Controller of the household of the earl of Northumberland, 1605 (C.S.P. Dom., 222).

Carye, Sir Henry. Master of the jewels, 1603 (C.S.P. Dom., 15).

Cecil, Sir Edward. Favorite of Cranborne; reversion of Jersey, 1611 (Birch, I, 142).

Chaloner, Sir Thomas. In charge of the person and household of Prince Henry, 1603 (C.S.P. Dom., 30; Spedding, IV, 23); grant of land, 1604 (C.S.P. Dom., 142, 169).

Clinton, Lord. Called to upper house (Official List, 444).

Conway, Sir Edward. Lieutenant governor of The Brill in Holland (C.S.P. Dom., 302).

Cope, Sir Walter. Lent money to Bacon (Spedding, IV, 89); chamberlain of exchequer, 1608 (C.S.P. Dom., 436); grant of recusants' land, 1608 (*ibid.*, 403).

Corbett, J. One of the clerks of the privy council (Official List, 445).

Cornwallis, Sir Charles. Ambassador to Spain (C.J., I, 315–16).

Cornwallis, Sir William. Money grant, 1607 (C.S.P. Dom., 352).

Crofts, Sir Herbert. Steward of Leominster, 1606 (C.S.P. Dom., 307, 401).

Crompton, Sir Thomas. Advocate general in ecclesiastical causes, 1603 (C. S. P. Dom., 14); master in chancery, 1608 (Haydn).

Cromwell, Sir Oliver. Gentleman of the privy chamber (C.S.P. Dom., 365).

Dallyson, Sir Roger. Stewardship of a manor, 1604 (C.S.P. Dom., 106); impost on currants, 1604 (*ibid.*, 161); master of munitions and ordnance, 1606 (*ibid.*, 323, 478).

Denny, Sir Edward. Called to upper house (Official List, 443).

Denton, Sir Thomas. Receiver and surveyor of Tutbury, 1604 (C.S.P. Dom., 179).

Doderidge, Sir John. Solicitor general, 1604 (C.S.P. Dom., 162); grant of lands, 1606 (*ibid.*, 317); king's sergeant (C.J., I, *passim*).

Drury, Sir Robert. Game warden in Suffolk, 1607 (C.S.P. Dom., 387).

Dunne, Sir Daniel. Judge of high court of admiralty (Haydn).

Edmondes, Sir Thomas. Clerk of the privy council, 1603 (C.S.P. Dom., 59); secretary and keeper of the signet to the council of the North, 1603 (*ibid.*, 63); clerk of the crown in chancery, 1604 (*ibid.*, 105); ambassador to the archduke, 1606 (C.J., I, 315–16).

Fane, Sir Francis. Land grant, 1608 (C.S.P. Dom., 408).

Fanshaw, Thomas. Auditor of the exchequer, 1604 (C.S.P. Dom., 146); auditor of the northern parts of the duchy of Lancaster (Official List, 444; Bowyer, p. 114).

Ferne, Sir John. King's secretary and keeper of the signet in the North, 1609 (C.S.P. Dom., 532).

Fleetwood, Sir William. Receiver general of the court of wards, 1604 (Hist. MSS Com. Report, X, 2, 3 [1885], p. 364).

Fleming, Sir Thomas. Solicitor general to 1604 (Official List, 445); chief baron of the exchequer, 1604 (C.S.P. Dom., 162).

Fortescue, Sir Francis. Sheriff, 1608 (Birch, I, 82).

Fortescue, Sir John. Chancellor of the duchy, privy councilor (Official List, 442).

Francis, Edward. Paymaster of the gentlemen pensioners, 1603 (C.S.P. Dom., 13).

Gargrave, Sir Richard. Grant of estate, 1604 (C.S.P. Dom., 123).

Gawdie, Sir Bassingbourne. Received schedule of work to be done in parliament of 1604 (Hist. MSS Com. Report, X, 2, 3 [1885], p. 92).

Gee, Sir William. King's secretary and keeper of the signet in the North, 1609 (C.S.P. Dom., 532).

Goodyear, Sir Henry. Grant of an estate, 1605 (C.S.P. Dom., 221).

Hare, John. Clerk of the court of wards (C.S.P. Dom., 7, 152).

Harpur, Sir John. Collector of the aid in Derbyshire, 1609 (C.S.P. Dom., 520); grant of forfeited lands, 1608 (*ibid.*, 419).

Harvey, Sir George. Lieutenant of the Tower (Official List, 442).

Harvey, Sir William. Remembrancer of the first fruits, 1603 (C.S.P. Dom., 25).

Hastings, Sir Francis. "Muttered" for speaker, 1604 (C.J., I, 141); gets respite of debts from the crown, 1609 (C.S.P. Dom., 561).

Hawkins, Sir Richard. Vice admiral of Devon, 1608 (C.S.P. Dom., 457).

Hedley. Money surety for Bacon (Spedding, IV, 40).

Hele, Sir Warwick. Recusancy commissioner in Devon, 1606 (Yonge, p. 6).

Herbert, Sir John. Second secretary of state, member of privy council (Official List, 444).

Herbert, Sir Philip. Patent for cloth import, 1603 (Birch, II, 26); steward of Woodstock, etc., 1604 (C.S.P. Dom., 152); Baron Herbert and earl of Montgomery, 1605 (*ibid.*, 214).

Hesketh, Sir Thomas. Attorney of the wards (Official List, 444); small grant of mills, 1604 (C.S.P. Dom., 87).

Hickes, Sir Michael. Personal friend of Bacon (Spedding, IV, 217); lent money to Bacon (*ibid.*, IV, 40); court meeting held at his house (*ibid.*, IV, 131); receiver general of Middlesex, 1603 (C.S.P. Dom., 9), and of Essex, 1603 (*Egerton Papers*, p. 374); grant of estate, 1604 (C.S.P. Dom., 125).

Hitcham, Sir Robert. Queen's attorney, 1603 (C.S.P. Dom., 48); money grant from king, 1609 (*ibid.*, 557).

Hobart, Sir Henry. Attorney of the wards (C.S.P. Dom., 239); attorney general (C.J., I, 315–16).

Hobby, Sir Edward. Patent for wool (C.S.P. Dom., 368); "muttered" for speaker, 1604 (C.J., I, 141).

Holcroft, Sir Thomas. In charge of appointing subsidy collectors in Chester, 1608 (C.S.P. Dom., 443).

Hollis, Sir John. Received Savoyard ambassador, 1603 (Goodman, II, 88); *Camden Miscellany*, X, 117, journal of Sir Roger Wilbraham); "lorded at 10,000," 1616 (C.S.P. Dom., 1611–18, 384).

Horsey, Sir Jerome. Receivership of king's lands in 10 counties, 1604 C.S.P. Dom., 121).

Howard, Lord. Called to upper house (Official List, 584).

Hungerford, Sir John. Grant of recusants' goods, 1610 (C.S.P. Dom., 580).

Jeffreys, Sir John. Attorney of 5 counties, 1608 (C.S.P. Dom., 444).

Jermin, Sir Thomas. Reversion of Jersey, 1603 (Birch, I, 26).

Johnson, Sir Robert. Commissioner of king's forests, 1609 (C.S.P. Dom., 537); officer of the ordnance (Bowyer, p. 132).

Kighley, Sir Philip. Teller of the exchequer, receivership of the first fruits of the clergy, 1604 (C.S.P. Dom., 75, 599).

Killigrew, Sir William. Profit of sealing writs in king's bench, etc., 1603 (C.S.P. Dom., 95); chamberlain of the exchequer, 1606 (Birch, I, 46–47; C.S.P. Dom., 436).

Knevytt, Sir Thomas. Grant of estate, 1603 (C.S.P. Dom., 27); warden of the mint, 1604 (*ibid.*, 160); grant of forfeited lands, 1609 (*ibid.*, 528).

Lake, Sir Thomas. Secretary to the king (see Weldon, p. 17, for unfavorable description).

Lawson, Sir Wilfred. Commissioner of the Border, 1605 (C.S.P. Dom., 193, 316).

Leveson, Sir John. Receivership of certain rents, 1604 (C.S.P. Dom., 81); honorary office at coronation (*ibid.*, 24).

Leveson, Sir Richard. Directed to attend Lord Grey with 50 horse, 1603 (C.S.P. Dom., 48); gentleman of the privy chamber (C.J., I, 197a).

Lewkenor, Sir Lewis. Arrangements for receiving Spanish ambassador, 1603 (C.S.P. Dom., 35), and Florentine ambassador, 1609 (*ibid.*, 543); grant of forfeit goods, 1609 (*ibid.*, 535).

Ley (See, Leigh), Sir James. Attorney of the court of wards, 1608 (C.S.P. Dom., 468); later chief justice of king's bench (Official List, 447).

Lovelace, Sir Richard. Sheriff of Berks, 1608 (Birch, I, 82).

Maunsell, Sir Robert. Treasurer of the navy, 1604 (C.S.P. Dom., 98).

May, Humphrey. Groom of the privy chamber (C.S.P. Dom., 86); remembrancer of Ireland and clerk of the signet (Birch, I, 141); clerk of the council of Star Chamber, 1609 (C.S.P. Dom., 384, 530).

Middleton, Sir Robert. Receivership of 2 counties, 1604 (C.S.P. Dom., 114).

Mollineux, Sir Richard. Lent money to Bacon (Spedding, IV, 40); receiver of Lancs, 1607 (C.S.P. Dom., 364).

Montague, Sir Henry. Recorder of London (C.J., I, *passim*); on some commission for royal business (Spedding, IV, 131); learned counsel (Bowyer, p. 116; C.S.P. Dom., 369); "muttered" for speaker, 1604 (C.J., I, 141).

Mounson, Sir Thomas. Grant of tenements in the Tower, 1609 (C.S.P. Dom., 512); grant of recusants' goods (*ibid.*, 386).

Musgrave, Sir Richard. Commissioner of the Border, 1603 (C.S.P. Dom., 24); master of the ordnance in the North, 1608 (C.S.P. Dom., 405).

Mutton, Peter. Protonotary and clerk of the crown in 2 Welsh counties, 1605 (C.S.P. Dom., 231).

Neville, Sir Henry. "Muttered" for speaker, 1604 (C.J., I, 141); lent money to Bacon (Spedding, IV, 89); keeper of the game at Windsor, 1605 (C.S.P. Dom., 275); incurred Salisbury's displeasure, but reconciled in 1609 (*ibid.*, 486).

Parker, Sir John. Keeper of Falmouth Castle, 1607 (C.S.P. Dom., 353).

Parry, Sir Thomas. Master of the court of wards, 1607 (C.S.P. Dom., 353); chancellor of the duchy and member of the privy council (Official List, 444; C.J., I, 435).

Percival, Sir Richard. Auditor of the court of wards, 1607 (C.S.P. Dom., 383).

Percy, Allen. Brought the Venetian ambassador to court, 1603 (Birch, I, 24); pension, 1608 (C.S.P. Dom., 420).

Perkins, Sir Christopher. Later became master of requests (Goodman, I, 333).

Peyton, Sir John. Captain of Jersey, 1603 (C.S.P. Dom., 26; Birch, I, 26); lieutenant of the Tower, 1603 (C.S.P. Dom., 4, 26).

Phelips, Sir Edward (speaker of the house). King's sergeant, 1603 (C.S.P. Dom., 9); justice of common pleas, Lancs, 1604 (*ibid.*, 133).

Raleigh, Sir Carey. Ranger of the forest, etc., Gillingham, 1603 (C.S.P. Dom., 48); lieutenant of the Isle of Portland, 1608 (*ibid.*, 432).

Ridgeway, Sir Thomas. Treasurer at wars in Ireland, 1607 (Official List, 443; C.J., I, 315–16).

Rivers, Sir George. Grant of a borough, 1606 (C.S.P. Dom., 338).

St. John, Sir Oliver. Master of the ordnance in Ireland, 1606 (C.J., I, 315–16).

St. John, Oliver. Pension, 1604 (C.S.P. Dom., 143).

Saville, Sir John. Free gift from king, 1607 (C.S.P. Dom., 364).

Selby, Sir William. Commissioner of the Border, 1605 (C.S.P. Dom., 193, 196, 201); pension, 1605 (*ibid.*, 186).

Skinner, Sir Vincent. Officer of the receipt of the exchequer (C.S.P. Dom., 15; Spedding, IV, 6).

Skipwith, Sir William. A high sheriff.

Slingsby, Sir William. Patent for founding of sea coal, 1610 (C.S.P. Dom., 625).

Smith, Sir Thomas. Secretary and keeper of the signet to the council of the North, 1603 (C.S.P. Dom., 63); receivership of 3 counties, 1604 (*ibid.*, 93, 112); clerk of the privy council, 1608 (*ibid.*, 432).

Snigg, Sir George. Baron of the coif of the exchequer, 1604 (C.S.P. Dom., 125, 156).

Somers, Sir George. Admiral for Virginia (Official List, 443).

Somerset, Sir Thomas. Clerk of the treasury in common pleas (C.S.P. Dom., 71); keeper of the records (*ibid.*); clerk of the Arches in common pleas, 1605 (*ibid.*, 231); money gift, 1607 (*ibid.*, 380).

Strode, Sir William. Recusancy commissioner in Devon, 1606 (Yonge, p. 6).

Swynnerton, Sir John. Lent money to Bacon (Spedding, IV, 40); rent for French wines, 1608 (C.S.P. Dom., 459).

Tanfield, Lawrence. Justice of king's bench, 1606 (Birch, I, 46–47).

Tate, Francis. Justice in 3 Welsh counties, 1604 (C.S.P. Dom., 80).

Trevor, Sir John. Keeper of Oatlands, 1603 (C.S.P. Dom., 52); steward and receiver of Windsor Castle, 1603 (*ibid.*, 13); keeper of a castle near Chatham, 1603 (*ibid.*, 22); surveyor of the navy, 1606 (*ibid.*, 286); farmer of impositions of sea coals, 1610 (*ibid.*, 631).

Twynhoe, William. Patent of smalt, 1606 (C.S.P. Dom., 323; Bowyer, p. 132).

Vavasour, Sir Thomas. Knight marshal, 1603 (C.S.P. Dom., 48, 184); composition for butlerage of the port of London, 1604 (*ibid.*, 66); profit from discovery of titles, 1607 (*ibid.*, 376).

Waad, Sir William. Lieutenant of the Tower, 1603 (C.S.P. Dom., 234, 435).

Waller, Sir Thomas. Lieutenant of Dover Castle, 1607 (C.S.P. Dom., 345).

Walsingham, Sir Thomas. Receiver of certain rents, 1604 (C.S.P. Dom., 81); keeper of the queen's wardrobe, 1608 (*ibid.*, 420).

Washington, Lawrence. Registrarship, etc., of books in chancery, 1604 (C.S.P. Dom., 96).

Wilbraham, Sir Roger. Keeper of the records in the Tower—surrendered for pension, 1603 (C.S.P. Dom., 15); commissioner to regulate Tower boundary, 1606 (*Egerton Papers*, p. 405); master of requests (Bowyer, p. 200).

Winch, Humphrey. Chief baron of exchequer in Ireland, 1606 C.J., I, 315–16).

Wright, Richard. Clerk of the king's jewels, 1609 (C.S.P. Dom., 558).

Wroth, Sir Robert. Keeper of Woodford Walk, 1606 (C.S.P. Dom., 285).

Yonge, Walter. Later sheriff of Devon, 1628 (Yonge, p. x).

APPENDIX B

MEMBERSHIP

OF THE PARLIAMENT OF 1614

WITH NOTES ON PATRONAGE, EXPERIENCE, AND ROYAL DISPLEASURE

Adams, Lawrence
*Alford, Edward
Amhurst, Richard
Anderson, Sir Henry. Sheriff of Northumberland, 1616 (C.S.P. Dom., 1611–18, 360, 389).
Ashley, Francis
Ashley, Sir John
Ashton, William. Grant of recusancy fines of £62, 1611 (C.S.P. Dom., 1611–18, 100).
*Askwith, Robert
Awdley, Sir Marvin. Lieutenant of Llanymthivery Castle, 1614 (C.S.P. Dom., 1611–18, 249); grant of estate in Dorset, 1617 (*ibid.*, 451).
*Backhouse, Sam
*Bacon, Sir Francis. Attorney general, 1614 (C.S.P. Dom., 1611–18, 231); privy council, 1616 (*ibid.*, 373); lord keeper, 1617 (*ibid.*, 448); Lord Verulam, 1618 (*ibid.*, 553).
Baildon, Sir Francis
Bamfield, Sir William. Captain of Sandsfoot Castle, 1612 (C.S.P. Dom., 1611–18, 130).

* Asterisk indicates that member had served in a previous parliament.

Banester, Henry
*Barker, Robert (sergeant)
*Barkley, Richard
*Barnham, Sir Francis
Barrett, Sir Edward. Grant of a grange in Shropshire and Stafford,
    1617 (C.S.P. Dom., 1611–18, 434).
Bartie, Sir Peregrine
Bash, Edward
Baskerville, Sir Humphrey
Battman, Robert
Bawtrey, Leonard
Baynton, Edward
Beale, Francis
Beddingford, Sir Henry
Beecher, William. Reversion of auditor of court of wards, 1614
    (C.S.P. Dom., 1611–18, 240).
*Beeston, Sir Hugh. Comptroller of records and fines in 3 shires
    (C.S.P. Dom., 1603–10, 175).
Belassis, Sir Thomas
*Bennett, Sir John. In diplomatic service, 1617 (C.S.P. Dom.,
    1611–18, xcii, 452, 458).
*Berkley, Sir Maurice. Chamberlain suggested that he had sufficient
    influence at court to extricate himself from a law suit, 1615
    (C.S.P. Dom., 1611–18, 276).
*Bigge, Thomas
Billison, Sir Thomas
*Binge, Henry
Binge, Thomas
Binge, William. Captain of Deale Castle, 1618 (C.S.P. Dom.,
    1611–18, 614).
Bingley, John. Evidently some clerkship in chancery or the ex-
    chequer, 1614 (C. S. P. Dom., 1611–18, 238, 248).
*Borlase (Burlacy), Sir William
Bourchier, Sir John. Government man for council of York, 1611
    (C.S.P. Dom., 1611–18, 40); monopoly of alum, 1611 (*ibid.*,

* Asterisk indicates that member had served in a previous parliament.

81); "merchant royal," 1613 (*ibid.*, 197); monopoly of copper, 1614 (*ibid.*, 250).

*Bowes, Talbott
*Bowyer, Sir Edmund
Bowyer, Thomas
Braken, Francis
Brereton, Sir William
*Brett, Sir Robert. Lieutenant of Dover Castle, 1613 (C.S.P. Dom., 1611–18, 199); deputy warden of the Cinque Ports, 1614 (*ibid.*, 243).
Bretton, Henry
Bromfield, Arthur
*Brooke, Christopher. Reversion of secretary and keeper of the signet in the North, 1612 (C.S.P. Dom., 1611–18, 125).
Brooke, Sir John. Annuity of £200 for life (C.S.P. Dom., 1611–18, 33).
Browne, George
Browne, John
Browne, Sir William. Pursuivant of court of wards and liveries, 1615 (C.S.P. Dom., 1611–18, 283).
Bulstrode, Henry
Burgess, Richard
Burgess, Thomas
Butler, George
Button, James
Button, Sir William. Reversion of forfeited property, 1611 (C.S.P. Dom., 1611–18, 43); overseer of little customs, Port of London, 1618 (*ibid.*, 528).
Caesar, Sir Charles
*Caesar, Sir Julius. Chancellor of the exchequer (C.S.P. Dom., 1611–18, 174); master of the rolls, 1614 (*ibid.*, 256); privy councilor (C.S.P. Dom., 1611–18, *passim*).
Cage
Carew, Ralph
*Carye, Sir Henry. Master of the jewel house, 1603 (C.S.P. Dom.,

* Asterisk indicates that member had served in a previous parliament.

1603–10, 15), 1617 (C.S.P. Dom., 1611–18, 504); comptroller, 1618 (*ibid.*, 598).

*Carie, Sir Edward. Reversion of teller's place in exchequer, 1611 (C.S.P. Dom., 1611–18, 94); master of jewels (*ibid.*, 594).

Carie, Philip. Grant of manor in Kent, 1611 (C.S.P. Dom., 1611–18, 94); keeper of Marybone Park, 1615 (*Ibid.*, 275).

Cavendish, Sir William. Master of the game, etc., 1614 (C.S.P. Dom., 1611–18, 249).

*Cecil, Richard

Charnock, Roger

*Cheeke, Sir Thomas

Cheeke, Thomas, Jr.

Chettle, Thomas

Chetwinde, Sir Walter

Chibborne, Charles. Sergeant, 1616 (C.S.P. Dom., 1611–18, 371).

Chicheley, Sir Thomas. Evidently an "Undertaker" (C.J., I, 485).

Chudley, George

Chute, Sir Walter. Cutter of the king's meat, 1614 (C.J., I, 434); imprisoned after parliament (C.S.P. Dom., 1611–18, 237).

Clare, Ralph

Clerke, James

Clerke, Matthew

Clifford, Henry, Lord. Extensive correspondence with Salisbury, 1611 (C.S.P. Dom., 1611–18, 1, 2, 4, 12, 25, 43, 51, 60, 80); lord lieutenant of Cumberland, 1618 (*ibid.*, 537); in disfavor, 1617, and committed suicide, 1618 (*ibid.*, 505, 584).

*Clifton, Sir Jervaise

Colbey, Hunt

Conningsby, Sir Ralph

*Conningsby, Thomas

Connock, Richard, Auditor for Prince Henry (C.S.P. Dom., 1611–18, 160); 1000 marks free gift, 1617 (*ibid.*, 440).

Conyers, William

Cooke, Clement

Cooke, Sir Richard. Some office in Ireland, 1614 (C.S.P. Dom., 1611–18, 262).

* Asterisk indicates that member had served in a previous parliament.

*Cooke, Sir William. Grant of fines and amercements in Gloucestershire, 1611 (C.S.P. Dom., 1611–18, 25).

*Cope, Sir Anthony. Contractor with disposal of chantry lands (C.S.P. Dom., 1611–18, 63).

*Cope, Sir Walter. Public registrar for general commerce, 1611 (C.S.P. Dom., 1611–18, 14); master of court of wards (*ibid.*, 157).

*Cope, Sir William. Office of keeping the armory for life, 1615 (C.S.P. Dom., 1611–18, 276).

*Cornwallis, Sir William. Grant of £500 forefeited property, 1611 (C.S.P. Dom., 1611–18, 43); another recusancy forfeit (*ibid.*, 52); £2000 free gift, 1612 (*ibid.*, 159).

Cotton, George

Courtman

*Covert, Sir Walter

*Cowcher, John

Coxe, Edward. Yeoman of the wardrobe in Wales, 1617 (C.S.P. Dom., 1611–18, 424).

Crane, Francis. Reversion of clerk of parliament, 1611 (C.S.P. Dom., 1611–18, 75).

Cranfield, Sir Lionel. Lieutenant of Dover Castle, 1613 (C.S.P. Dom., 1611–18, 190); master of requests, 1616 (*ibid.*, 406, 514); £100 pension, 1617 (*ibid.*, 448); reversion of master of rolls, 1618 (*ibid.*, 540); keeper of the great wardrobe, 1618 (*ibid.*, 570).

*Crewe, Randolph (Randall). Government nominee for speaker.

*Crewe, Thomas. Notes confiscated, 1614 (Birch, I, 322).

Croftes, William

*Crofts, Sir Herbert. Steward of Leominster, 1606 (C.S.P. Dom., 1603–10, 307, 401); king's displeasure, 1614 (C.S.P. Dom., 1611–18, 233, 469); turned papist, 1617 (*ibid.*, 489).

Crompton, Henry

Crompton, John

*Crompton, Thomas. Protonotary of court of common pleas (C.S.P. Dom., 1611–18, 234).

*Cromwell, Sir Oliver. Ranger and game keeper, etc., 1614 (C.S.P.

* Asterisk indicates that member had served in a previous parliament.

Dom., 1611–18, 251); grant of forfeited lands, 1617 (*ibid.*, 506).

Crooke, Henry. Clerk of the pipe, 1617 (C.S.P. Dom., 1611–18, 486, 507).

*Crooke, Sir John. Probably a justice, 1618 (C.S.P. Dom., 1611–18, 541).

*Culpepper, Thomas

*Cuttes, Sir John

Dackombe, John. Promised master of requests, 1613 (C.S.P. Dom., 1611–18, 206); chancellor of the duchy, 1616 (*ibid.*, 372).

Dade, Henry

*Dallison, Sir Roger. Lieutenant of the ordnance, 1612 (C.S.P. Dom., 1611–18, 137).

Danvers, Charles

*Danvers, Sir John. Warden of the forests in Wilts, 1611 (C.S.P. Dom., 1611–18, 68).

*Davies, Matthew

Delbridge (Dellaverge), John

*Denton, Sir Thomas. Receiver and surveyor of Tutbury, 1604 (C.S.P. Dom., 1603–10, 179).

Devereux, Sir Walter

*Digges, Sir Dudley. King's displeasure, 1614 (Birch, I, 324); ambassador to Muscovy, 1618 (C.S.P. Dom., 1611–18, 537).

*Digges, Richard

*Dormer, Sir John. Grant of recusants' lands, 1611 (C.S.P. Dom., 1611–18, 84).

Doubleday, Edmund. Warden of the mint, 1611 (C.S.P. Dom., 1611–18, 23).

Drake, John

*Drury, Sir Robert. Game warden in Suffolk, 1607 (C.S.P. Dom., 1603–10, 387).

*Duncombe, Edward. License to recover concealed moneys, 1618 (C.S.P. Dom., 1611–18, 590).

*Dunne, Sir Daniel. Judge in the Arches, till 1617 (C.S.P. Dom., 1611–18, 483).

* Asterisk indicates that member had served in a previous parliament.

Dunne, John. Given the doctorate by king's order, 1615 (C.S.P. Dom., 1611–18, 282); judge of admiralty (*ibid.*, 515).

Earle, Walter

*Egerton, Sir John. Son of Lord Chancellor Ellesmere.

Elliott, John

Eyton, John

Fairfax, Sir Ferdinand

*Fane (Vane), Sir Francis. Grant of grange in Shropshire and Stafford, 1617 (C.S.P. Dom., 1611–18, 434); grant, 1618 (*ibid.*, 408).

*Fane (Fanne, Vane), Sir George

Fane (Fanne), Sir Henry

Fanshaw, Thomas

Fanshaw, William

Ferne, Sir Thomas

Fielding, Basil

Finch, Henry. Sergeant at law, 1616 (C.S.P. Dom., 1611–18, 373).

Finch, Sir Theophilus

Fleetwood, Sir Miles. Receiver of the court of wards, 1618 (C.S.P. Dom., 1611–18, 558).

Fleming, Philip

*Fleming, Sir Thomas. Chief justice of common pleas, 1611 (C.S.P. Dom., 1611–18, 108).

*Francis, Sir Edward

*Freak, John

*Fuller, Nicholas. London chose him as a patriot, 1614 (C.S.P. Dom., 1611–18, 225).

Gardiner, Sir Robert

Gauntlett, Roger

Gawdie, Framlingham

*Gawdie, Philip

*Germyn, Sir Thomas

Gerrard, Gilbert. Clerk of the duchy, 1616, 1617 (C.S.P. Dom., 1611–18, 389, 419, 467).

* Asterisk indicates that member had served in a previous parliament.

Gibbs, Thomas

Giles, Sir Edward (incorrectly called Robert in the *Calendars*). Confined to London after parliament (Birch, I, 324).

Glanville, Francis

Glanville, John

Glemham, Sir Henry

*Godfrey, Thomas

*Goodwin, Sir Francis

Goslyn, John

Gourney, Thomas

Gowan, Walter

*Grantham, Sir Thomas

*Graye, Sir Henry

Gregory, Sir William

*Gresham, Sir Thomas

Griffith, Nicholas

Grimes, Sir Thomas

Grimstone, Sir Harbottle

Gwynn, Rice

*Hackwell, William. Notes confiscated, 1614 (Birch, I, 322); made queen's solicitor, 1618 (C.S.P. Dom., 1611–18, 515).

*Hales, Sir Edward

Hallswell, Sir Cuthbert

Hallswell, Robert

Hardweare, George

*Harris, John. Patent to discover titles, 1616 (C.S.P. Dom., 1611–18, 385).

Hasselrigge, Sir Thomas

Hastings, George

*Hatton, Sir Christopher. Officer of Waltham Forest, 1614 (C.S.P. Dom., 1611–18, 243); remembrancer in the exchequer, 1616 (*ibid.*, 355); chancellor of the exchequer, 1617 (*ibid.*, 381); seneschal of a manor in Berks, 1617 (*ibid.*, 430).

Hatton, Robert. Bought handsome property income of the crown, 1616 (C.S.P. Dom., 1611–18, 386).

Heale, Sampson

* Asterisk indicates that member had served in a previous parliament.

*Heale, Sir Warwick. Recusancy commissioner in Devon, 1606 (Yonge, p. 6).

Hendon, Edward

Herbert, Arnold. Pension of £100, 1611 (C.S.P. Dom., 1611–18, 62).

*Herbert, Sir William. Keeper in Windsor Forest, 1611 (C.S.P. Dom., 1611–18, 94).

Herne, Sir Thomas

Hickford, William

Hickman, Walter

*Hitcham, Sir Robert. Queen's attorney, 1603 (C.S.P. Dom., 1603–10, 48); money grant from king, 1609 (*ibid.*, 557); sergeant at law, 1617 (C.S.P. Dom., 1611–18, 423).

Hitchcock, Thomas

*Hobby, Sir Edward. Patent for wool (C.S.P. Dom., 1603–10, 368).

*Hobby, Sir Thomas P.

Hodson, Christopher

*Hollis, Sir John. Fined and imprisoned for words on the Overbury trial, 1616 (C.S.P. Dom., 1611–18, 344).

Hopkins, Sampson

*Horsey, Sir Jerome. Receiver of king's land in 10 counties, 1604 (C.S.P. Dom., 1603–10, 121).

Horsley, George

*Hoskins, John. Imprisoned after parliament (C.S.P. Dom., 1611–18, 237).

Houghton, Sir Gilbert. Patent to recover fines, 1615 (C.S.P. Dom., 1611–18, 299).

Howard, Sir Charles. Pension of £300, 1611 (C.S.P. Dom., 1611–18, 94); ranger of Bigshot, 1614 (*ibid.*, 243); keeper of park, 1614 (*ibid.*, 288).

Howard, Sir Edward. Keeper of privy lodgings and wardrobe at Hampton Court, 1611 (C.S.P. Dom., 1611–18, 128); lighthouse monopoly, 1615 (*ibid.*, 299); monopoly of fines, 1617 (*ibid.*, 450); park keeper, 1618 (*ibid.*, 598).

Howard, Sir George

Howard, Henry

* Asterisk indicates that member had served in a previous parliament.

*Howard, Sir Thomas. Keeper of Newelm, 1610 (C.S.P. Dom., 1603–10, 584).

Hughes

*Hungerford, Edward

*Hyde, Nicholas

Ingram, Sir Arthur. Secretary and keeper of the signet in the North, 1612 (C.S.P. Dom., 1611–18, 125); alum monopoly, 1613 (*ibid.*, 188); monopoly of Irish customs, 1613 (*ibid.*, 195); cofferer of king's household, 1615 (*ibid.*, 276), but removed same year (*ibid.*, 282); grant of land, 1617 (*ibid.*, 488).

*Ireby, Anthony

Ireland, Thomas

James, Thomas

Jaye, John

*Jeffrey, John. Attorney in 5 counties, 1608 (C.S.P. Dom., 1603–10, 444).

Jennison, William

*Johnson, Sir Robert. Officer of ordnance (Bowyer, p. 132); commissioner of king's forest, 1609 (C.S.P. Dom., 1603–10, 537); alum monopoly, 1614 (C.S.P. Dom., 1611–18, 256).

*Jones, William. Sergeant, 1617 (C.S.P. Dom., 1611–18, 469); lord chief justice, 1618 (*ibid.*, 515).

Kent, William

Killigrew, Sir Joseph

Killigrew, Sir Robert. Captain of Pendennis Castle, 1614 (C.S.P. Dom., 1611–18, 242); pension of £100, 1614 (*ibid.*, 248); captain of Falmouth, 1618 (*ibid.*, 589).

*Killigrew, Sir William. Some sort of clerkship, 1611 (C.S.P. Dom., 1611–18, 80); protonotary of chancery for life, 1618 (*ibid.*, 589).

*Kirton, James

Kneviton, Sir Gilbert

*Knollys, Sir Robert

Lacon, Rowland

Lake, Sir Oliver

* Asterisk indicates that member had served in a previous parliament.

*Lake, Sir Thomas. Secretary of state (C.S.P. Dom., 1611–18, 443 *et passim*); sworn of privy council, 1614 (*ibid.*, 228).

Lasher, James

Launceston, Sir Anthony

Lawley, Edward

*Lawson, Sir William

Lea, Henry

*Lea, Sir James. Clerk of the council, 1611 (C.S.P. Dom., 1611–18, 50); attorney of court of wards, 1618 (*ibid.*, 519).

Lea, Matthew

*Leech, Edward

Leeds, Sir John. Imprisoned for talk about Overbury case, 1616 (C.S.P. Dom., 1611–18, 344).

*Leigh, Sir Francis

*Leigh, John. Lieutenant of Isle of Wight, 1614 (C.S.P. Dom., 1611–18, 243); patent to discover titles, 1615 (*ibid.*, 293).

Leonard, Sampson

LeStrange, Sir Hammond

*Lewkenor, Sir Edward

Littleton, Edward

Lloyd, Elisha

*Lovelace, Sir Richard. Sheriff of Berks, 1608 (Birch, I, 82).

Lovelace, Sir William

Lowe, Richard

*Lowe, Sir Thomas. Chosen by London as a patriot, 1614 (C.S.P. Dom., 1611–18, 225).

*Lucy, Sir Thomas. Wardship of rich widow, 1613 (C.S.P. Dom., 1611–18, 193).

*Ludlow, Sir Edmund

Ludlow, Henry

Machen, Thomas

Mallett, Thomas

*Mallory, William

*Maney, Sir Anthony

*Manners, Sir George

* Asterisk indicates that member had served in a previous parliament.

*Mansfield, Sir Robert
*Manwood, Sir Peter
 Marshall, George
 Martin, Thomas
*Maunsell, Sir Robert. Imprisoned, 1613, for disobedience in matter
    of navy reform (C.S.P. Dom., 1611–18, 186); £10,000 gift,
    1616 (*ibid.*, 406); treasurer of the navy, 1618 (*ibid.*, 537).
*Maunsell, Sir Thomas
*May, Sir Humphrey. Clerk of council of Star Chamber, 1609
    (C.S.P. Dom., 1603–10, 384, 530); surveyor of court of wards,
    1618 (*ibid.*, 514); chancellor of the duchy, 1618 (*ibid.*, 525).
*Maynard, Sir William
 Merrick, Rowland
 Mervin
*Middleton, Sir Hugh
 Middleton, John
*Middleton, Robert. Receiver of 2 counties, 1604 (C.S.P. Dom.,
    1603–10, 114).
 Mitchell, Barnard
 Mohun, Sir Reginald
*Mollineux, Sir Richard, Jr. Receiver of Lancs, 1607 (C.S.P. Dom.,
    1603–10, 364); receiver general of the duchy, 1616 (C.S.P.
    Dom., 1611–18, 383).
 Mompesson, Giles
*Montague, Sir Edward. Lord chief justice, 1616 (C.S.P. Dom.,
    1611–18, 405).
*Montague Sir Henry. Sergeant; recorder of London (C.J., I, *pas-
    sim*); defeated in London, 1614, as known courtier (C.S.P.
    Dom., 1611–18, 225); lord chief justice of king's bench, 1616
    (*ibid.*, 405).
 Montague, Sidney. Master of requests in ordinary, 1618 (C.S.P.
    Dom., 1611–18, 314).
 Montague, Sir Walter. Deputy in the Forest of Dean, 1615 (C.S.P.
    Dom., 1611–18, 296).
*Moore, Francis
*Moore, Sir George. Chancellor of the Order of the Garter, 1611

* Asterisk indicates that member had served in a previous parliament.

(C.S.P. Dom., 1611–18, 56); lieutenant of the Tower, 1616 (*ibid.*, 377, 428).

*Moore, Sir Robert. Surveyor in London and Westminster, 1613 (C.S.P. Dom., 1611–18, 205, 217).

Morgan, Meredith. Granted manors in Shropshire, Lincoln, and Essex, 1613 (C.S.P. Dom., 1611–18, 190).

Morgan, Thomas. Monopoly on wool export, 1618 (C.S.P. Dom., 1611–18, 590).

Morley, Edward

Moseley, Edward. Attorney of the duchy, 1613 (C.S.P. Dom., 1611–18, 202, 298).

*Munson, Sir Thomas. Keeper of armory, Greenwich, 1611 (C.S.P. Dom., 1611–18, 15, 40); keeper of naval stores, 1612 (*ibid.*, 153); steward of the duchy, 1618 (*ibid.*, 606).

*Naunton, Robert. Master of requests, 1616 (C.S.P. Dom., 1611–18, 376); surveyor of court of wards, 1616 (*ibid.*, 401); secretary of state, 1618 (*ibid.*, 512).

*Needham, Robert

Nevill, Christopher. Imprisoned after parliament, 1614 (C.S.P. Dom., 1611–18, 237).

*Nevill, Sir Henry. Aspired to secretaryship, 1614, but failed (C.S.P. Dom., 1611–18, 35, 215, 295).

Newman, George. Judge in the Arches, 1617 (C.S.P. Dom., 1611–18, 488).

Newport, Richard

Norton, Sir Thomas. Guide and surveyor of ways, 1616 (C.S.P. Dom., 1611–18, 417).

Noyes, Peter

*Owen, Sir Roger. Notes confiscated, 1614 (Birch, I, 322).

*Oxborough, Thomas

Palmer, Roger. Cupbearer to prince (C.S.P. Dom., 1611–18, 248); pension of £100 a year, 1614 (*ibid.*).

Palmes, Sir Guy

Parry, Sir James

*Parry, Sir Thomas. Chancellor of the duchy (C.S.P. Dom., 1611–18, 344).

* Asterisk indicates that member had served in a previous parliament.

Pawlett, John. Sheriff in Wilts, 1617 (C.S.P. Dom., 1611–18, 344).

*Pawlett, Sir Richard

Payne, Sir Robert

Penruddock, Sir Thomas

Perrient, Thomas

*Perrott, Sir James. Confined to London after parliament (Birch, I, 324).

Peyton, Sir Samuel

*Phelips, Sir Robert. Reversion of petty bag in chancery, 1613 (C.S.P. Dom., 1611–18, 206); "factious" in parliament (Birch, I, 326).

Pierse, John

Pitt, William. Grant of manor in Kent, 1611 (C.S.P. Dom., 1611–18, 94).

*Poole, Sir Henry

Poole, Sir Nevill

*Popham, Sir Francis

Price, James

Price, Sir Richard

Price, William

*Prowse, John

Raleigh, Gilbert. Reversion of lieutenant of the Isle and captain of the Castle of Portland, 1611 (C.S.P. Dom., 1611–18, 69).

Rashley, Jonathan

Ratcliffe, Sir John.

Ravenscroft, Robert

Ravenscroft, William

Reynell, Sir George. Marshal of king's bench, 1618 (C.S.P. Dom., 1611–18, 550).

*Reynolds, Sir Carey. Lieutenant of the Isle and captain of the Castle of Portland, 1611 (C.S.P. Dom., 1611–18, 69).

Rich, Sir Robert

Riche, Sir Henry. Captain of the guard, 1617 (C.S.P. Dom., 1611–18, 494).

* Asterisk indicates that member had served in a previous parliament.

Riche, Nathaniel, Bought valuable money rent from crown, 1616 (C.S.P. Dom., 1611–18, 386).

Richardson

*Rivers, Sir George

Rives, John. Overseer of king's alum works, 1615 (C.S.P. Dom., 1611–18, 294).

*Rolle, William

Rowe, Sir Thomas. Ambassador to the Great Mogul, 1614 (C.S.P. Dom., 1611–18, 260).

Roye, John

Russell, Thomas

St. Albin, John

St. Albin, Thomas

St. John, Alexander

*St. John, Sir Oliver. Master of ordnance in Ireland, 1606 (C.J., I, 315–16); Irish privy council (C.J., I, Ireland, 11).

St. John, Rowland

*Sammes, Sir John. Recommended by Sussex for deputy lieutenant of Middlesex, 1612 (C.S.P. Dom., 1611–18, 135).

*Sandys, Sir Edwin. Grant of land in Kent, March, 1614 (C.S.P. Dom., 1611–18, 226); notes confiscated, 1614 (Birch, I, 322).

*Sandys, Sir Miles

*Sandys, Sir Samuel. Notes confiscated, 1614 (Birch, I, 322).

Sandys, Sir William

Savage, Edward

*Saville, Sir George. Created baronet, 1611 (C.S.P. Dom., 1611–18, 53).

*Saville, Sir Henry

*Saville, Sir John. Free gift from king, 1607 (C.S.P. Dom., 1603–10, 364).

Scott, Edmund

*Scott, Sir John

*Scudamore, Sir James. Steward of various places in Wales, 1612 (C.S.P. Dom., 1611–18, 115).

Searle, John

* Asterisk indicates that member had served in a previous parliament.

Selby, Sir John
*Seymour, Sir Edward
Sheffield, William
Shelley, Thomas
Sherwill, Thomas
*Shirley, Sir Thomas. Patent for old debts, 1613 (C.S.P. Dom., 1611–18, 195).
*Sidney, Sir Robert (Viscount Lisle). Annuity of £1000 for life, 1616 (C.S.P. Dom., 1611–18, 370).
Singe, Richard
Slingsby, Sir Henry
Smith, Edward
Smith, Sir Nicholas
Smith, Sir Richard
*Smith, Sir Thomas. Clerk of the privy council, 1608 (C.S.P. Dom., 1611–18, 432).
Snelling, Robert
Southworth, Thomas
Spencer, William
Spiller, Henry. Recusancy fine commissioner, 1615 (C.S.P. Dom., 1611–18, 281).
Spray, Nicholas
Stables, Richard
Stewart, Sir Simeon. "Insurance" monopoly, 1617 (C.S.P. Dom., 1611–18, 496).
*Stoughton, George
Strange, Robert
Strangeways, Sir John
*Strode, Sir William. Recusancy commissioner in Devon, 1606 (Yonge, p. 6).
Sucklyn, John. Receiver of fines, 1611 (C.S.P. Dom., 1611–18, 9).
Symeon, Sir George
Tate, Sir William. Pension officer in war department, 1616 (C.S.P. Dom., 1611–18, 419).
*Terringham, Anthony
Thelwell, Simon

* Asterisk indicates that member had served in a previous parliament.

Thinne, Charles
Thomas
Thorpe, George
Tichborne, Sir Richard
Tichborne, Sir Walter
Tomkins, Nathaniel
*Tooker, Giles
Toothby, Richard
Towes, William
Townsend, Sir Henry. Associate justice in Chester, 1611 (C.S.P. Dom., 1611–18, 45).
*Townsend, John
Trevour, Sir John. Surveyor of king's ships, 1611 (C.S.P. Dom., 1611–18, 30); surveyor of Windsor, 1611 (*ibid.*, 58).
*Trevour, Thomas
Trott, John
Tufton, Richard
Turner, Arthur
*Twissenden, Sir William
Uvedall, Sir William. Reversion of treasurer of chamber, 1615 (C.S.P. Dom., 1611–18, 294), received it, 1618 (*ibid.*, 513).
Vaughan, Sir Charles
*Vavasour, Sir Thomas. Knight marshal, 1612 (C.S.P. Dom., 1611–18, 159, 281).
Venables, Richard
Verney, Greville
*Verney, Sir Richard
Wallop, Sir Henry. Sheriff of Hants, 1602, and Shropshire, 1605 (D.N.B.); member of council of the Marches, 1617 (*ibid.*).
*Walsingham, Sir Thomas
Walter, Sir William
Warr, Thomas
Warsley, Sir Richard
Watson, Thomas. Reversion of teller's place in exchequer, 1618 (C.S.P. Dom., 1611–18, 94).
Weare, Humphrey

* Asterisk indicates that member had served in a previous parliament.

Wentworth, Sir Thomas. Imprisoned after parliament, 1614 (C.S.P. Dom., 1611–18, 237).

*Weston, Sir Richard. Recommended by Sussex for deputy lieutenant of Middlesex, 1612 (C.S.P. Dom., 1611–18, 135).

Wetherid, John

Wharton, Sir Thomas

Whitby, William

White, Sir Richard

*Whitlocke, James. Imprisoned, 1613, for speaking against the marshal's court (C.S.P. Dom., 1611–18, 186)

Whitson, John

*Wilbraham, Sir Roger. Clerk of council, 1611 (C.S.P. Dom., 1611–18, 50); reversion of constable of Chester Castle, 1614 (*ibid.*, 226); later master of requests (*ibid.*, 390).

Wilcock, Robert

Wilmott, Charles. Governor of Connaught, 1616 (C.S.P. Dom., 1611–18, 360).

Williamson, Sir Richard

*Willoughby, Sir Percival

Willoughby, Sir Walter

Wind, Sir Robert

Wingfield, William

Winwood, Sir Ralph. Principal secretary of state, 1614 (C.S.P. Dom., 1611–18, 228).

Wogan, John

Wolverston, Robert

Woode, John

*Woodhouse, Sir William

*Woodrington (Withrington), Sir Henry

Woodward, Thomas

Wooton, Sir Henry. Spoken of for secretary, 1612 (C.S.P. Dom., 1611–18, 137); sent on mission to Cleves, 1614 (*ibid.*, 246); ambassador to Venice, 1617 (*ibid.*, 425).

Wray, Sir John

*Wymark, Edward

Wynne, Richard

* Asterisk indicates that member had served in a previous parliament.

Yarwood, Richard
*Yaxley, Sir Robert
*Yelverton, Henry. Solicitor general (C.J., I, *passim*); attorney general, 1617 (C.S.P. Dom., 1611–18, 440).

* Asterisk indicates that member had served in a previous parliament.

BIBLIOGRAPHY

THE conclusions of this study have been drawn mainly from an intensive analysis of the day-by-day records of the house and from the piecing together of bits of information concerning the activities of members, both inside and outside the house. Where contemporary writings and correspondence other than the extensive collections of the *Calendars of State Papers* have touched upon the work of parliament in general or upon the activities of particular members, they have been used. Many works besides those included under "Primary Sources" have been canvassed without result. For example, the materials in the reports of the Historical Manuscripts Commission were found to have little bearing, and although many of them have been viewed, they are scarcely cited. The study has, of necessity, been written largely out of the various journals, official and otherwise, and out of the materials of the *Calendars*.

PRIMARY SOURCES

Acts of the Privy Council. Edited by J. R. Dasent. London, H.M. Stationery Office: 1558–70, 1571–75, 1575–77, 1586–87, 1588, 1597, 1601–4. This material has been put to several uses. It has facilitated the identification of members of the house who were also privy councilors, by means of dated records of attendance at meetings of the council interspersed throughout the reports. In several cases the council indiscreetly left on record the instructions to sheriffs, which illuminate in a very interesting way the matter of election practices.

Birch, Thomas. *The Court and Times of James the First.* 2 vols. London, 1848. This is a miscellany of seventeenth-century correspondence, of which by far the most extensive and valuable is that of John Chamberlain and Sir Dudley Carleton. While Carleton was away from England on a diplomatic mission to Venice, Chamberlain undertook to keep him informed of doings in London. Although the information is of a general nature, it includes considerable news of parliament, from the point of view of a gossipy outsider, and a number of allusions to members. Some of the material of the *Court and Times* correspondence is duplicated in the selection for the *Calendars of State Papers Domestic.*

—— *The Court and Times of Charles the First.* 2 vols. London, 1848. Vol. I.

Bowyer, Robert. *Parliamentary Diary, 1606–1607.* Edited by D. H. Willson. London, Oxford University Press, 1932. This account by a member of parliament is much fuller in the matter of debate than the journals for the corresponding period. It gives more insight into the working of committees and reports in greater detail the speeches of members. It is not as complete as the official account in the minutiae of the day's work and in the lists of committee appointments.

Calendars of State Papers Domestic (cited as C.S.P. Dom.). The volumes from 1603 through 1640 have been canvassed. In these *Calendars* there are two types of useful information: (1) memoranda and orders for payment of pensions, granting of petitions, transfer of title to property, etc., which give indication of the connection of members and matters of patronage; (2) correspondence containing comment upon the work of parliament as a whole and upon the conduct of individual members. It need hardly be remarked that the *Calendars* are not, in the strict sense, a "source," since many of the entries are abridgments. In the citations, passages in quotes indicate the exact wording of the *Calendars*, not necessarily the words of the *Papers.*

Calendars of State Papers Venetian (cited as C.S.P. Ven.). The volumes cover 1613 through 1628. Curiously, the dispatches of the Venetian ambassador to the Doge and Senate are among the most valuable contemporary commentaries on parliament. In particular, the over-all view of the relations of the king and parliament are presented with a lack of reserve seldom found in English writings.

Camden Miscellany. Vol. X. Edited by H. S. Scott. London, 1902. The journal of Sir Roger Wilbraham has been cited in Appendix A.

D'Ewes, Sir Simonds, ed. *The Journals of All the Parliaments during the Reign of Queen Elizabeth, both of the House of Lords and House of Commons.* London, 1682. The exact date at which this compilation was completed is unknown, probably at some time in the fourth decade of the seventeenth century. Sir Simonds had access to those parts of the official journals which have since been lost. Hence his account for the period 1580–1601 is invaluable. The D'Ewes work, however, is based upon other sources, as well as upon the journals, for it is in many places fuller than what remains of the journals. Nevertheless, it is so marred by omissions that no exact tabulations can be made from it. D'Ewes is the principal source for the internal analysis of Elizabethan parliaments which constitutes the introductory portion of this book.

Egerton Papers, The. Edited by J. Payne Collier. Camden Society, Vol. XII, London, 1840.

Journals of the House of Commons, The (cited as C.J.). Vol. I. Reprinted by Order of the House of Commons, 1803. This volume covers the period 1547–March, 1628/9. It is the main source for internal study of the English house during the Jacobean period and the reign of Charles I. Because of its erratic nature in the part covering the reign of Elizabeth and especially because of the gap in the record from 1580 to the end of the reign, it has been less used than D'Ewes and Townshend for the parliaments of Elizabeth. It is upon the journals that the various counts and tabulations for the parliaments after 1604 are based. The journal account is by no means full and is obviously subject to deletions and omissions, particularly in the records of the Addled Parliament and the parliament of 1625. The account in the journal consists of two different kinds of writings, the finished and rewritten record and the "scribble book" or rough draft of the clerk's original notes. In certain sessions of parliaments the "scribble book" alone appears (sessions of 1605–6 and 1609–10 and parliament of 1614). For the session of 1603–4 and the parliament of 1624, both accounts appear. Otherwise the journal account is the clerk's finished or "fair" copy.

Loseley Manuscripts. Edited by St. George K. Hyland. London and New York, 1920. There are several interesting references here to the corrupt electioneering practices of the privy council.

Nichols, John. *The Progresses, Processions, and Magnificent Festivities of King James the First, His Royal Consort, Family, and Court.* 3 vols. London, 1828.

Notestein, Wallace, Frances Helen Relf, and Hartley Simpson, eds. *Commons Debates, 1621.* 7 vols. New Haven, Yale University Press, 1935. This large and meticulously edited collection of parliamentary diaries for 1621 throws much light on personalities and committee work of the parliament of that year. Many indiscreet or pointed speeches omitted by the clerk are found here and are very helpful in identifying the sentiments of members. The Barrington, Belassis, Holland, Pym, and Wentworth diaries and the anonymous "X" journal have been cited.

Parliamentary Accounts and Papers. London, Vol. XVII, 1878. This volume contains a series of lists of returns for the house of commons from 1213 to 1874. It is based upon the returns preserved in the Public Record Office, supplemented, where the returns are lacking, by reference to the writs and to the Crown Office lists. There are no returns for the parliaments of 1571 and 1614, but for the latter year there is included a list of returns, unofficial, found in the Duke of Manchester Papers. None of the lists are complete. They are of some help in determining the connections of members, for in a number of cases titles are included in the notice of the return. They are invaluable, of course, in discovering the proportion of new members in the various parliaments.

Parliamentary Debates in 1610. Edited by Samuel R. Gardiner. Camden Society, No. 81, London, 1861. These are the notes of an unknown member. The *Debates* correspond very exactly in form to Bowyer's *Diary* for the earlier session. For a study such as this, the *Debates* and Bowyer must be used as material supplementary to the main works (D'Ewes and the journals), since they are not systematically written.

Statutes at Large, The (England). Edited by John Cay. London, 1758. Vol. II covers the period 24 Henry VIII to the end of Charles II.

Townshend, Heywood. *Historical Collections.* London, 1680. Townshend was a member of parliament in 1597 and 1601. His account of those parliaments, based upon his own notes, and of the parliaments of 1588–89 and 1592–93, based upon the notes of someone else, duplicates somewhat the material of D'Ewes, but digresses sufficiently at points to make a careful independent reading necessary. It is a much less important source than D'Ewes.

Weldon, Sir Anthony. *The Court and Character of King James.* London, 1650. Weldon was hostile to the court and especially to the Scottish favorites. He reflects, I think, the popular antipathy, outside parliament, to Salisbury and Lake.

Whitlocke, Sir James. *Liber Famelicus.* Edited by J. Bruce. Camden Society, No. 70, London, 1858. There are a few references to Whitlocke's connection with the opposition group and to his activity against the impositions.

Yonge, Walter. *Diary.* Edited by George Roberts. Camden Society, Vol. XLI, London, 1848. This diary covers the years 1604–28. References to it are few and bear upon the activities of members.

SECONDARY SOURCES

Burnet, Gilbert. *History of the Reformation of the Church of England.* Revised by E. Nares. London, 1850. A brief allusion to violent and corrupt elections under Elizabeth has been found in this work.

Dictionary of National Biography. Constant use has been made of this work, in particular for checking on the later careers of men active in parliament in the 1620's.

Gardiner, Samuel R. *History of England, 1603–1642.* 10 vols. London, Longmans, Green, 1901. Use has been made of this famous history in writing the narrative background of the study. It is not concerned with the mechanical aspect of the house or indeed with the general approach that this study has taken. Gardiner refers mainly to the general aspects of parliament, but also throws light on the matter of personnel.

Goodman, Godfrey. *Court of James I.* Edited by John S. Brewer. London, 1839. Vols. I and II. Several personal references bearing on partisan activity have been taken from Goodman.

Haydn, Joseph. *Book of Dignitaries.* London, 1894. The titles of sergeant, attorney general, solicitor general, etc., may be conveniently run down in this valuable compendium of English officers of state.

Kennett, White. *Complete History of England.* London, 1706. Vol. II. A hint as to the personnel of the privy council in 1603 is taken from this old book.

Porritt, Edward and Annie G. *The Unreformed House of Commons.* 2 vols. Cambridge, Putnam, 1909. The first volume of this painstaking and exhaustive book deals with the parliaments of England and Wales. Procedure, elections, the partisan speaker, committees—all these are discussed. In a few cases, comparative references to Porritt have been made, but the research in general has been independent of this source.

Smith, Sir Thomas. *The Commonwealth of England.* London, 1621. Sir Thomas' work is, of course, too antiquated to be of use to the modern scholar, from a technical standpoint, but I have found it a very interesting contemporary reference to the speaker of the house.

Spedding, James. *Letters and the Life of Francis Bacon.* 7 vols. London, 1861–74. From the correspondence in this collection one extremely important allusion to the factions in the parliament of 1604 has been found. A number of references to the connections of Bacon and of members of the house are also contained therein. It is, of course, the standard life of Bacon, but does not bear directly upon his parliamentary career.

Turner, E. R. *The Privy Council of England in the Seventeenth and Eighteenth Centuries, 1603–1784.* 2 vols. London and New York, Johns Hopkins University Press, 1921. This authoritative work on the privy council is of only incidental use in this study. It furnished some information on the personnel of the council in the house and several references to the activity of opposition members and is also of some help in determining the members of the opposition in the Addled Parliament.

Usher, Roland G. *The Institutional History of the House of Commons,*

1547–1641. St. Louis, Washington University, **1924**. Washington University Studies. The extensive analysis of the house during this period involves an elaborate tabulation of statistics. My conclusions do not entirely agree with those of Professor Usher regarding the change in control of the house in the reign of Elizabeth. In a few cases, use has been made, as indicated, of figures from this work.

Willson, David H. *The Privy Councillors in the House of Commons, 1604–1629.* Minneapolis, University of Minnesota Press, **1940**. This is a thorough and masterly analysis of a phase of parliamentary activity to which my study has paid frequent but not sustained attention. Few actual references have been made to it, however, since its sources and mine naturally overlap continually, and the original sources, which I had canvassed before reading this book, were cited.

INDEX

THE CHOOSING PEOPLE

By the same author :

IDEOLOGICAL CHANGE IN ISRAEL